A LITTLE MORE LOVE

A LITTLE MORE LOVE

The Life and Legacy of Olivia Newton-John

Matthew Hild

BLOOMSBURY ACADEMIC
NEW YORK • LONDON • OXFORD • NEW DELHI • SYDNEY

BLOOMSBURY ACADEMIC
Bloomsbury Publishing Inc, 1359 Broadway, New York, NY 10018, USA
Bloomsbury Publishing Plc, 50 Bedford Square, London, WC1B 3DP, UK
Bloomsbury Publishing Ireland, 29 Earlsfort Terrace, Dublin 2, D02 AY28, Ireland

BLOOMSBURY, BLOOMSBURY ACADEMIC and the Diana logo are trademarks of
Bloomsbury Publishing Plc

First published in the United States of America 2026

For legal purposes the Acknowledgments on pp. 242–243 constitute
an extension of this copyright page.

Cover design: Sally Rinehart
Cover image © Pictorial Press / Alamy Stock Photo

A catalog record for this book is available from the Library of Congress.

ISBN: HB: 979-8-216-36802-1
          ePDF: 979-8-216-35232-7
          eBook: 979-8-216-35231-0

Typeset by Integra Software Services Pvt. Ltd.
Printed and bound in the United States of America

For product safety related questions contact productsafety@bloomsbury.com.

To find out more about our authors and books visit www.bloomsbury.com
and sign up for our newsletters.

This book is dedicated to the memory of Tara Palmer-Tomkinson, who during her all-too-short lifetime supported numerous cancer (and, particularly, breast cancer) charities, the Brain Tumour Charity, the British Heart Foundation, the Nordoff and Robbins music therapy charity, Speur-Ghlan (Blue Sky Autism Project), and Tommy's Charity (for research into miscarriage, stillbirth, and premature birth).

CONTENTS

INTRODUCTION

"When people used to say to me, 'What is she like?'" recalls Australian journalist Neil McMahon of his friend Olivia Newton-John, "I'd always say, 'She is exactly like you'd think she would be like, but better.' She just really was, you know, the human being that the world believed her to be… they always say that about heroes, but with her it was true."

And yet, McMahon adds,

I always thought she got a bit of a bum rap by being labeled "nice." It was a bit of a shallow word to describe her. She was so much more than nice… if you're looking for the English word, I guess "nice" is the word. But she was so much more than that. There was a real depth and substance and roundness and genuineness to her, that you sort of walked away thinking, *wow*! And everyone felt it, it didn't matter who you were.

McMahon also recalls that Olivia "had the most extraordinary laugh… she just loved to laugh. Wonderful sense of humor, and just very warm, engaged, and interested in the world around her, really."

The "bum rap" label that she often received was, in fact, more damning than "nice." Even though she had, to some degree at least, shed her almost impossibly wholesome girl-next-door image with her transformation from the virginal "Sandy #1" to the vixen "Sandy #2" in *Grease*, and with subsequent hits such as "Physical," her obituary in the London *Daily Mail* nevertheless mentioned the "'Miss Goody Two-Shoes' reputation" that she never entirely escaped. Olivia had smartly made light of this label, however, in her television special *Olivia Newton-John: Hollywood Nights* (1980), when she quipped, "There's a rumor going around that I'm 'Miss Goody Two-Shoes' from Australia. Well, that's a laugh. I'm really 'Miss Goody Two-Shoes from England!'"

For all her sincere kindness and sweetness, however, to call Olivia Newton-John "Miss Goody Two-Shoes" was a superficial and, as McMahon suggests, shallow reading of her personality and character. As Chris Christian, a singer, songwriter, and record producer who befriended Olivia when he participated in the making of her album *Don't Stop Believin'* in 1976, puts it, "She really did go through some bad things in life… but she handled that gracefully." Greg Mathieson, an accomplished pianist/keyboardist who began working with Olivia shortly after that album was made, says that she was "less naive" than people thought. "She knew what she wanted," he reflects.

[She] wasn't intimidated by men, she could hold her own. She wasn't that meek little thing that she was in that movie [*Grease*]. She wasn't that. She had her head on straight, and knew who she was, but wasn't judgmental of anybody. That's why when she died, I felt so bad, because she was one of the *good* ones… and I've been around so many other ones, you know, that… [weren't like her].

To the public at large, Olivia was (and remains) best known for her career as one of the most popular singers in the world during the 1970s and the first half of the 1980s, during which time she had number one hits in Australia, Italy, the United States, Canada, Ireland, the United Kingdom, Belgium, Germany, the Netherlands, New Zealand, Norway, Spain, Sweden, Switzerland, Zimbabwe, Austria, and Denmark. Her starring role in *Grease* (1978), which gave a big boost to her recording career at a time when her popularity had been slipping, would introduce her to new generations of fans for decades to come. Her single "Physical" (1981), which *Billboard* ranked as the biggest hit of the 1980s, became the anthem of the decade's fitness craze, partly due to a clever video that Olivia conceived because she feared backlash against the song's suggestive lyrics.

Yet, as remarkable as her career as a pop icon was, Olivia Newton-John proved to be far more than an entertainer. Just a very abridged list of her honors besides Grammy Awards, gold and platinum records, and her posthumous induction into the Women Songwriters Hall of Fame makes that abundantly clear: the first Goodwill Ambassador to the United Nations Environment Programme in 1990; the Rainforest Alliance's Arts & Nature Green Globe Award in 1998; the Red Cross Humanitarian Award for her work with breast cancer foundations, children's charities, and environmental advocacy in 1999; Companion of the Order of Australia (2019); Dame Commander of the Order of the British Empire (DBE) in 2020; and Japan's Order of the Rising Sun in 2021. Even these don't convey all that she did as an advocate for the rights of animals and marine life. Nor do they indicate what the American writer Alison Stine suggested about Olivia's deep, broad sense of humanity in an obituary for her, in which she called attention to Olivia's considerable "[cultural] impact, particularly as a queer icon before it was cool, and a gay ally beginning at a time well before it was popular, accepted or even safe to do so."

"Her music," notes her former backup singer Dennis Tufano, "was the foundation of everything that she did." Like her friend Elton John, she used her wealth and the power of her fame to build a legacy that extended far beyond her music. Chong Lim, who worked with Olivia for many years as music director onstage and producer in the recording studio, marvels at her contributions as both a performer and a person. "An artist like Olivia," he reflects, "comes along once in a lifetime." But her kindness and compassion made an even bigger impact on him. "She was a remarkable person, you know? One of a kind," he muses. "She had the power, so she utilized her power in the best possible manner. She used her fame for good… for pure, unadulterated good."

Olivia Newton-John expressed her outlook on life in many of the songs that she wrote and recorded after her commercial heyday had passed, such as "Grace and Gratitude," which she wrote with her friend and longtime collaborator Amy Sky and recorded in 2006. Just after Olivia's passing, her niece Tottie Goldsmith recounted a conversation that she'd had with Olivia a few years earlier, while Olivia was being treated at the cancer center that she had founded in Australia. "She was really skinny and really unwell, and I said to her, 'Are you afraid of dying?' She said 'Plonker,' which was my nickname, she said, 'I'm not, I'm not afraid. I've done more in my life than I could have ever imagined.' She honestly never imagined her life would be how it was."

1 IT'S ALWAYS AUSTRALIA FOR ME

"When I was a young girl, I was so crazy about animals that I wanted to do something associated with them, and I thought of being a vet. But then again, I figured I had to go to medical school and science wasn't a good subject for me, so I dropped the idea pretty soon and thought maybe I could be a vet's assistant," Olivia Newton-John told an interviewer in 1983. "And then I thought of a mounted policewoman, because I figured I could ride horses and be paid for it—what a job! But they didn't have them then, so I was kind of before my time. Suddenly, this singing career came along, and I had to make that decision."

That science "wasn't a good subject" for the young Olivia Newton-John was ironic given her lineage. Her mother's father, Max Born, earned a doctorate at the University of Göttingen in Germany in 1907 for his dissertation on the stability of elastic wires and tapes, and in 1954 he won the Nobel Prize in Physics for his "statistical formulation of the behavior of subatomic particles." Born was friends with Albert Einstein for over four decades. His great-grandson Emerson Newton-John told journalist Michele Manelis that "Einstein would come to the house and play violin with Max, who would accompany him on piano." Like Einstein, Born was a German Jew who fled the Third Reich; whereas Einstein settled in the United States, Born emigrated to England. Olivia never met her illustrious grandfather, who died in 1970. She would express regret about that in her later years, calling it "one of the sad things of my life" and saying that she wished she had listened to her mother when she used to tell her, "You need to come meet your grandfather because he's getting old."

Olivia's father, Brinley Newton-John, who was born in Cardiff, Wales, on March 5, 1914, earned bachelor's and master's degrees at the University of Cambridge before World War II. When the war broke out in 1939, he joined the Royal Air Force, but his linguistic skills (in multiple languages including German) earned him a position with the Enigma code-breaking team at Bletchley Park in Buckinghamshire, England. Like Max Born, Brinley Newton-John had musical as well as academic inclinations: while attending high school in Cardiff, he played violin and sang in the school choir. He had aspired to become an opera singer, and Olivia recalled that he had a "beautiful singing voice."

Max Born and his wife, Hedwig Ehrenberg, had three children: daughters Irene (Olivia's mother), born in 1914, and Gritli, born in 1915, and one son, Gustav Victor Rudolf, born in 1921. Gustav Born became a renowned professor of pharmacology at King's College, London, and research professor at the William Harvey Research Institute, Barts, and the London School of Medicine and Dentistry. Irene, who pronounced her name "Iraina," married Brinley Newton-John, who called himself "Brin," in 1937. Their first child, Hugh Francis, was born in Buckinghamshire on July 3, 1939. Hugh was followed by two daughters, Rona (born on February 1, 1941) and Olivia (born on September 26, 1948), both of whom were born in Cambridge. Hugh became a physician, specializing in infectious diseases, and during the 1970s and 1980s he worked at the Fairfield Infectious Diseases Hospital in Melbourne, Australia.

Like most men who served in World War II, Brinley Newton-John returned to civilian life shortly after the war ended. In the BBC Wales documentary *Coming Home: Olivia Newton-John* (2008), the British historian Stephen Mallinson told a clearly proud Olivia, "I think your dad absolutely was a hero. When he went to Bletchley Park, he was a flying officer. When he left Bletchley Park at the end of the war, he was a Wing Commander, which is a meteoric rise and demonstrates that great talent your father had for the job that he did." In 1946, he returned to the academic world, accepting an appointment as the headmaster of the Cambridgeshire County High School for Boys.

By this point, Brin and Irene's marriage had become rocky. A handsome, charismatic man, Brin engaged in at least one indiscretion during the war, which Irene found out about when the woman came to her front door and told her. In her later years, Olivia would say that she thought she was born out of an attempt by her parents to save their marriage; she was, as she wrote in her autobiography, "the makeup baby."

Of Brin and Irene's three children, Hugh would follow the academic path, like not only his father and maternal grandfather but also his maternal grandmother, who was a mathematician. (Irene, too, would contribute to the world of academics by translating the correspondence between her father and Einstein for the English-language book *The Born-Einstein Letters*, published by Macmillan in 1971.) Rona and Olivia, even as children, showed signs that they would instead pursue careers in entertainment, as Brin might have done had he had more confidence in his ability as an opera singer. "At only about a year old," Irene would recall of Olivia, "I noticed that she could sing a note correctly after me, which is quite unusual, I think, and she started to learn folk songs and songs she heard on the radio at a very early age and used to entertain us with them." One of Olivia's strongest memories of her early childhood in Cambridge would be of her father singing in a strong, loud voice in church, a source of pride for her as well as embarrassment, since she didn't like being noticed.

Even her name was a source of embarrassment for Olivia at that young age. "I *hated* my name: *Olivia Newton-John*," she said emphatically in an interview for Lifetime's *Intimate Portrait* documentary in 1998. "Can you imagine? Triple-barrel name with an unusual name for a first name. I wanted to be like Claire Smith or Margaret Brown or, you know, anything but what I was," she laughed. "Now I'm really thrilled that I have a name that is different, but I think it's just a normal thing for a child to want to fit in and be like everybody else."

In 1954, prior to Olivia's sixth birthday, Brin Newton-John accepted a prestigious appointment as master of Ormond College at the University of Melbourne in Australia. The family boarded the RMS *Strathaird*, a liner that was launched in 1931 and accommodated over one thousand passengers, and arrived in Australia after just over one month. "I don't remember much about the trip except that I lost Fluffy, my favorite toy," Olivia told the American rock music journalist Timothy White in 1978. "I was very upset; I guess somebody nicked it, some nasty little girl. It didn't really look like anything. It was just a fluffy thing with two eyes, a nose and a mouth, a little animal comforter of some sort, so I called it Fluffy."

Olivia also developed a strong affinity for real animals at a young age. "I remember as a little girl I could tell you the name of the dog next door, but I couldn't tell you the names of the kids," she told an interviewer in 1983. "The dog was my best friend. I love animals. They give so much to you and demand so little. And you can trust them." Her love of animals extended to nature in general. "Mum always loved people and nature—two traits I inherited from her." After Olivia became a star and moved to California in 1975, she usually had what she referred to as a "zoo" of dogs, cats, and horses. At one point she had a psychologist/scientist, Dr. Raja Parasuraman, living in a house that she owned but wasn't occupying just so that he could take care of some of her dogs. Dr. Parasuraman had just completed his doctorate in England in 1976 and accepted a postdoctoral fellowship at UCLA. "His girlfriend at the time knew some friends of Olivia's," recalls his daughter, Shanta Parasuraman. "She had so many dogs and there are laws in California that you can only keep so many dogs in one house, so he dog sat for her in one of her houses in Malibu." In 1980 Olivia went to court to fight the Malibu ordinance that allowed no more than three dogs per household, and she was granted permission to have eight.

Both of Olivia's parents doted on her. Emerson Newton-John, Rona's son, said that as close as his mother and Olivia were, all the way until Rona's passing in 2013, the preferential treatment that Olivia, the baby of the family, received was not easy for his mother. "Irene," Emerson told Michele Manelis, "was just more interested in Olivia, even at the end of her life." As a result, he said, "as much as Rona and Olivia loved each other, had a close relationship and would have done anything for each other, there was resentment, definitely, and on a lot of levels."

Hugh and Rona were both in their late teens by the time Brin's infidelities finally ended his marriage to Irene (the first of his three marriages) in 1958. For Olivia, just about to turn ten, her parents' divorce was a bitter pill to swallow. Not only would she no longer be living under the same roof as her father, but the administration at Ormond College forced him to resign now that he was a divorced man. He immediately found a new academic position, becoming an associate professor of German and head of the department of arts at the University of Newcastle. But Newcastle is over one thousand kilometers, or six hundred miles, from Melbourne. Thereafter Olivia, much to her dismay, only saw her father once or twice a year, although she would have extended Christmas visits with him and his second wife and, eventually, her half-siblings Toby and Sarah. Forty years later, Olivia still looked pained as she recalled in an interview, "My father was the one that told me [about the divorce], and I still remember that day. I was *devastated*."

The divorce, Olivia later reflected, made it difficult for her to concentrate in school. After school, she spent a lot of time alone. "I remember one of my teachers taking me to the zoo and then taking me home. I think they were checking to see where I lived. I was a latchkey kid because mum had to go to work," she told an interviewer decades later. "Coming from the academic sort of family background I have, with my grandfather having won the Nobel Prize, my parents hoped that I would at least go on to university," she said. Hugh had already done that, but Rona "left school at the legal age of fifteen to become an actress."

By the time Olivia reached that age, she had started down the career path that would lead her to international superstardom. "What happened was my mother gave me an acoustic guitar when I was thirteen, which led me to Ian and working in coffee lounges on weekends only. Meanwhile, I had been singing with three other girls in a group called the Sol Four; we did traditional jazz." "Ian" was Ian Turpie, a native of Melbourne who was five years Olivia's senior and had already starred in stage musicals and an Australian National Theatre production of *Macbeth*. He "was as cute as can be," recalled Rona, who introduced him to Olivia. When Olivia was fifteen, Ian became her first boyfriend. He took her on her "very first date… at a drive-in," Olivia remembered. "I'd never been to one before and my mother did not approve at all. Of course, I didn't see any of the movie."

John Capek, who would cowrite a pair of songs with Olivia during the late 1980s, first encountered her around this time. Capek was born in Prague in 1947 and came with his parents (both of whom were Nazi concentration camp survivors) to Australia when he was three years old. "I grew up in Melbourne, same city she

[Olivia] grew up in. And she went to high school with a bunch of friends of mine," he recalls. "It was University High in Melbourne." Capek's father, a concert pianist and mechanical engineer, taught his son to play the piano by the time he was three. When he and Olivia were teenagers, there were a lot of jazz clubs in Melbourne. "There was one particular one," according to Capek, "called the Campus Jazz Club, where they had a basement where they had kind of folk music. I was hired as a piano player down there." The Sol Four were among the acts that sang there. "We used to swap sets," and he would watch them perform.

Olivia later described the Sol Four as having worn "denim jeans and Hessian jackets and black turtlenecks and the long, beatnik hair." "We were pretty bad," she told an interviewer for the US trade publication *Radio and Records* in 1975. "But it was just for fun. Two of the girls sang completely off-key and we got booed off the stage most of the time!"

The Sol Four didn't last long, although getting booed was not the reason why. "My mother put an end to that," Olivia told an interviewer in 1998, "because she thought it was taking too much of my time." Irene had not given up on academic ambitions for Olivia, even though she was supportive and foresightful enough to send her to a vocal coach in Melbourne. (Olivia only went once, though, disliking how the coach tried to get her to sing more forcefully.)

It was Rona, however, who then stepped in to help Olivia keep singing for audiences. Rona's own plans for a career as an actor or model had by then taken a backseat to her growing family. In 1961 she had married Brian Goldsmith, who owned a coffee shop in Melbourne at the time and eventually became known, according to his obituary in the *Sydney Morning Herald*, as "the man who virtually invented the nightclub in Melbourne and whose name became a byword for glamour and fun over four decades." Brian and Rona had three children (Fiona, Brett, and Caroline [Tottie]) by the end of 1962. After the Sol Four was no more, Rona started to take Olivia to Brian's coffee shop on the weekends, when a folksinger named Hans Gorg would sing and play guitar. In her memoir, Olivia recalled sitting at the edge of the stage and singing harmonies while Gorg performed. Eventually he invited her onstage to sing with him.

Before long, Olivia was performing beyond just her brother-in-law's coffee shop. John Capek remembers that "she played all these clubs [in Melbourne] with this older hippy guy [Gorg] who played guitar, and she stood there and sang." Capek and his friends were quite struck by her. "She sang, she looked and sang, like an angel. We were kind of captivated by how she presented [herself], even then. It was almost obvious that she'd become a superstar.… She was remarkable. She was quite special."

Olivia made her television debut, at Rona's suggestion, in 1963 on *The Kevin Dennis Auditions*. Kevin Dennis was a Melbourne-based businessman and car dealer who conceived of this televised talent show as a way of promoting his business. Like the later US television program *The Gong Show*, Dennis's show made use of gongs, but whereas the gong was used to cut performances short and humiliate contestants on the American show, it was used to signify approval of performances on the Australian show. "They had a panel of judges, and they'd stop you if they didn't think you were any good," Olivia recalled fifteen years later. "Or at the end, they'd give you one, two or three gongs. I sang something like 'Lemon Tree,' and I got three gongs." About four decades after saying that, however, she wrote in her memoir that she sang the 1930s standard "Summertime" on the show, while Ian Turpie accompanied her on guitar. Apparently the latter is correct, although no footage of the appearance survives.

During the winter of 1964, Olivia made what she considered "my initial professional appearance… on a TV show called *Sunnyside Up*, which is like Lawrence Welk. I sang 'Melodie d'Amour,'" an English-language version of an old French song that the American group the Ames Brothers had popularized in 1957. Shortly thereafter, once again urged on by Rona, she entered a talent contest on the television show *Sing Sing Sing*, hosted by Johnny O'Keefe. O'Keefe was a rock-and-roll singer; as Olivia noted in her memoir, he "was known as the Elvis Presley of Australia." (Aside from both being flamboyant performers, there was also a tragic similarity between the two men: O'Keefe was born on January 19, 1935, eleven days after Presley, and lived only about a year longer than Elvis, passing away on October 6, 1978.) *Sing Sing Sing* was a top showcase for up-and-coming Australian talent. The show had just featured (in January 1964) Olivia's future friends, the Bee Gees, who were little known at the time. In a sure sign of a different era, Olivia, accompanied by Ian Turpie, auditioned for O'Keefe in his hotel room at South Melbourne's prestigious Southern Cross Hotel for her shot at being on his show. She sang "Summertime" with Turpie on guitar.

Olivia passed the audition, and five weeks later, on April 19, 1964, she appeared on the show. She sang "Anyone Who Had a Heart," a Burt Bacharach–Hal David composition that had recently been a top ten hit in Australia, the United States, and several other countries for Dionne Warwick, and "Everything's Coming Up Roses," which Ethel Merman had introduced in the Broadway musical *Gypsy* five years earlier. She emerged triumphant as the winner among the female contestants, while Derek Lee, a twenty-year-old from Wollongong, a coastal city south of Sydney, was chosen as the winner among the males. "Everything's coming up roses," reported the *Sydney Sun-Herald*, "for 15-year-old Melbourne schoolgirl Olivia-Newton John…. Both [winners] get £150 cash, and a return sea trip to England."

Olivia, however, "didn't want to actually take it [the trip] at the time," noted the Australian pop/rock journalist and historian Glenn A. Baker. A Sydney newspaper headline about her summarized part of her quandary: "School or Stardom?" She had not been enjoying school. "I'd always get in mix-ups with these groups of bitchy girls who liked to tease me," she said in an interview in 1978. When asked why they teased her, she replied, "Well, it was for being on TV all the time. I just didn't know anyone at school who was growing up quite the way I was." But she knew that her education was important to her parents. "My mom was just concerned that I wouldn't do my last year of high school, that I wouldn't matriculate." In another interview she said, "My parents wanted me to go to university."

Another factor also influenced Olivia's decision about whether to take the trip to the country of her birth. More television opportunities opened up for her in Australia after she won the *Sing Sing Sing* contest. She made additional appearances on *Sunnyside Up* and on a new show called *Teen Scene*, hosted by the young singer Johnny Chester, who toured Australia and New Zealand that year on a bill with the Beatles. As the time approached for Olivia to return to University High for her final year, she was offered a position on a children's program, *The Tarax Happy Show*. "So, I went to see one of my favorite teachers," she recalled in 1998,

and asked him what he thought. And he said, "Well, I can just say that if you're going to be thinking about singing and trying to finish this last year of school, which is the hardest year, you're not going to make it. So I recommend that you follow your heart and what you want to do." And I followed his advice, and I left school.

"My mother," Olivia recalled with a laugh, "was not happy." But as Irene later admitted, by then it was clear that Olivia "was more or less destined to get into the entertainment business, and so I couldn't see much purpose in her staying in school longer." In fact, soon Irene became her manager.

Olivia stayed in Australia as still more opportunities came her way in 1965. *The Tarax Happy Show* only lasted two months, but a better role came her way on the variety show *Time for Terry*, hosted by Terry O'Neill, an English comedian and jazz musician. Olivia sang and performed in sketches on the show, which also starred her boyfriend, Ian Turpie. Olivia soon began appearing on another series called *The Go!! Show*, which was similar to the 1964–1966 US rock-and-roll variety show *Shindig!*. Turpie was the host, and Olivia was a regular on the weekly series, typically singing a couple of songs per episode.

Singing teen-oriented pop and rock-and-roll songs on television every week boosted Olivia's profile and popularity in Australia considerably. She certainly caught the notice of her fellow migrant from England, Barry Gibb, who was two years older and lived in Sydney at the time. "This was the most *incredible* looking girl," Gibb recalled in 1998. "Still is. She made your heart beat. I suspect that every young guy, anyone around my age at that time, had a thing about Olivia Newton-John." Barry would later tell New Zealand writer Tim Roxborogh that he had first met Olivia in Melbourne in 1966. One year later, Olivia would find herself face-to-face with the Bee Gees on Carnaby Street in London.

The Go!! Show introduced Olivia to two people who would not only play important roles in her career but would also become two of her closest friends. Pat Carroll was another regular singer on the show, and John Farrar, whom Pat married in 1970, played lead guitar in a band called the Strangers, who were the show's regular backing band. Pat would remember that when one episode called for Olivia to sing "The Loco-Motion," the classic pop song written by Gerry Goffin and Carole King in 1962, "she was so scared of television… [that] she didn't move. So, the producer asked me to take her aside and teach her to dance a little bit because I was an ex-dancer… and we became friends that way."

By the end of 1965, however, Olivia had to choose between continuing to perform on television in Australia or going to England. "The trip that I'd won from the talent contest was overdue—I had to take it soon or lose out," she would recall. "My mother said, 'You're going to have to take this trip.' I said, 'I don't want to go.' She insisted that it would broaden my, er, horizons."

Irene may have had other motives as well. Olivia, seventeen, and Ian Turpie, twenty-two, had been dating for two years at this point. They had completed a film in which they were co-stars—Olivia's film debut—called *Funny Things Happen Down Under*, a Christmas comedy/musical in which she sang "Christmas Time Down Under." Irene was apparently concerned that the couple were getting too close, and she didn't want Olivia getting married at such a young age. "As soon as the romance started getting really serious, she whisked Olivia off to London, leaving a broken-hearted Ian behind," a "family friend" of Ian's told an Australian *Woman's Day* journalist decades later. Olivia wasn't happy either, but she admitted in her memoir that Ian, being five years her senior, was ready for a spouse and family, which she at the time was not. Turpie would later say, "I don't think her mother approved of me personally or of her daughter having boyfriends generally."

Olivia's mother also wanted her to enroll in London's Royal Academy of Dramatic Arts. Olivia refused, but she did seem to feel some guilt about disappointing her parents, particularly her father, by not completing her education. In 1978, she told journalist Timothy White about a nightmare that repeatedly marred her sleep: "I'm sitting in this classroom, about to take my final exam, and I don't know the subject I'm writing about. I'm completely unprepared for it. It's dreadful."

Olivia longed to return to Ian and Australia, but Irene thwarted her attempts to sail back for more than three months. That length of time was significant, for, as Olivia and Ian both would later publicly state, they had made an agreement when she left for London: neither would date anyone else provided they were not apart for more than three months. Olivia asked him to come to London, but he didn't want to leave Australia, where he had lived (and would live) for his entire life. "She'd phone me every month with reports of how she was going, and of her big hopes of landing a recording contract," Turpie told journalist Jim Murphy in 1981. But by the time she finally returned to Melbourne, she had been "away for more than three months." It had been more like ten months, and by then, Turpie had met and begun dating a model named Jan Hamilton. "I was busy trying to keep them apart" once Olivia returned, he said. "Olivia and I nearly took up where we'd left off, and I have to admit that I was doing a bit of juggling between Olivia and Jan for a short while." But Olivia's return was only temporary. By the spring of 1967, she returned to England, leaving Ian behind again.

"They got together behind my back some time later, and it was all Jan's doing," Turpie recalled. "She was inquisitive about Olivia." The two women "had a long talk… about the times I'd broken dates with Olivia because I was supposed to be recording, and broken dates with Jan because of 'rehearsals.' They compared notes and knew exactly what had been going on."

Ian and Jan married in 1968, had three children, and remained married until Ian's death from esophageal cancer at the age of sixty-eight on March 11, 2012. Olivia and Jan became "firm friends," as Ian put it, after their long talk, and Olivia remained friendly with Ian, too. In his feature on Turpie in the *Australian Women's Weekly* in 1981, Jim Murphy wrote that "he [Turpie] reckons that he and Jan are the first people she calls after her family" upon her visits to Australia. When the Australian version of the television show *This Is Your Life* did an episode on Ian in 1998, Olivia taped a short greeting in which she said, "You were my first love. I still love you and Jan." Turpie was visibly moved. In an interview that year for another Australian TV program, Olivia said of him, "He taught me a lot about music and performing—amongst other things that we won't talk about!" Laughingly, she added, "Thank God my daughter isn't watching!" After Ian's passing, the Australian publication *Woman's Day* reported that "a broken-hearted Olivia fought back tears at the bedside of Ian Turpie in his final days."

Once Olivia and her mother set sail for England on January 28, 1966 (where Rona had already settled after leaving her philandering husband, Brian Goldsmith, bringing with her a married partner of her own), Olivia would never again be more than a visitor to or, later, a part-time resident of Australia. But even though she ultimately spent more of her life in California, her connection with Australia always remained very strong. John Capek, who wrote the homage "It's Always Australia for Me" with her in 1988, reflects, "I think because she went to school there and had her formative years there, she always thought of herself as Australian. I mean, she always spoke with an Australian accent."

In the words of Johnny Chester, who appeared on television with Olivia on his show *Teen Scene* in 1964 and as a guest on *The Go!! Show* the following year, "She never forgot those that helped her get started." Chester was delighted when, "in the early '70s, after her many successes and when I was working in radio at 3UZ in Melbourne, Olivia, who was touring Australia at the time, just wandered up to the station, unannounced and unaccompanied, just to say hello." "She was very special," he adds.

She didn't forget Johnny O'Keefe and the role that he played in launching her career, either. O'Keefe visited her in London at least once years later, in 1972, and thirty years after that, long after his passing, Olivia recorded a duet with him thanks to the wonders of recording technology. For her duets album titled *(2)*, which was recorded and released in 2002, the analog master tape of O'Keefe's 1961 single "I'm Counting on You" was digitally transferred and remastered, allowing Olivia to overdub her own vocals to create a recording on which they sang together at points and also each took solos. The recording appeared again on Olivia's *Just the Two of Us: The Duets Collection (Vol. 2)*, released in 2023. Since O'Keefe, for all his considerable success in Australia, never made the record charts in the United States or the United Kingdom, Olivia introduced him, decades after his passing, to many listeners who had never heard his voice or of him.

Glenn A. Baker, who served as the Australian editor of *Billboard* for more than twenty years, postulated a theory just after Olivia's passing. "Part of the reason," he suggested, "why she was so successful, is that she stuck to Australians. She had them as writers and producers, and as friends and mentors, all the way through her career…. I think she trusted being around Australians." "They were," he wrote, "her secret ingredient."

But like the Bee Gees, Olivia had to return to England to advance her career—although, unlike Barry, Robin, and Maurice Gibb, who went back in 1967, Olivia didn't see it that way in 1966. "I didn't want to go, and I was mad at her [Irene]," she said in 2019. "She dragged me, kicking and screaming. Now I'm so grateful, because she had the wisdom to see a future. If I'd stayed in Australia, I wouldn't have had the opportunities to do what I've done."

2 TOOMORROW

" I walked the streets of London with Olivia, just telling her how incredible she was gonna be," Don Kirshner recalled several years after the fact. "Talent is the key to her success but there's a powerful magnetic quality about her, something that immediately gets under your skin and you can't shake it." An American music impresario who helped launch the careers of stars such as Bobby Darin, Carole King, and Neil Diamond, among many others, Kirshner had an uncanny knack for spotting future pop legends and helping them achieve that status. In the case of Olivia Newton-John, he managed to do only one of those things. For all the star potential that Kirshner and others saw in her, it would take five years for her to reach that status after her move to London in early 1966.

Upon their arrival in London, Irene and Olivia found a small apartment to rent in the city's Hampstead section on Perrin's Court, two blocks from a subway or tube station, for £9 a week, which Olivia said seemed like a lot of money at that time. Olivia was not impressed with her new surroundings, finding everything, as she recounted in her memoir, "so old and dirty." Mother and daughter's first few months there, as later described by Olivia, sound almost farcical in her efforts to get back to Australia (and Ian Turpie) and Irene's repeated measures to stop her. Olivia would book a ticket on a ship, and Irene would call the booking agent and cancel it. This happened repeatedly during their first two months in London. Olivia went to a lawyer to see if she could pursue what would today be called "emancipation" from her mother, but she was told that wouldn't be feasible. She would have to wait until she turned eighteen, and that was still months away (September 26).

Nor did Olivia's professional efforts in London get off to a great start. The first gigs she landed there were at what she described as a "terrible little dive called the Poor Millionaire's Club. I sang three or four songs to open for the main act, a folk singer. I used to sing everything, cabaret stuff, the Beatles, old tunes, blues, rock and roll, ballads, everything." She kept tapes of some of these performances, as well as some of her earlier performances in Australia. In her typical modest fashion, in 1975 she told an American journalist, "You'd kill yourself laughing if you heard my old tapes. I sound like Joan Baez, only louder."

The *Sing Sing Sing* prize included not only the trip to London but also the opportunity to record a single for Decca Records, a venerable and well-respected record label, albeit one that was infamous in the United Kingdom by this point for having turned down the chance to sign the Beatles in 1962, months before the Fab Four recorded and released "Love Me Do" for EMI's Parlophone label. (The US Decca Records label was not affiliated with the UK label during this period, but the US label was owned by MCA, for whom Olivia would record many of her records later.) Decca gave Olivia a song written by the American singer-songwriter Jackie DeShannon called "Till You Say You'll Be Mine." DeShannon had recorded and released the song as a B-side on a single in 1963 to little notice. Olivia's debut single seemed to be a low-budget production—she later said it "sounded like it was cut in someone's bathroom"—with what sounds like a crude attempt at creating a Phil Spector–like "Wall of Sound" backing. Olivia's voice does not sound very clearly recorded or mixed. The engineering, choice of song, and arrangement of the B-side "For Ever" (*sic*) suited her much better, and the folkish-countryish recording sounds like one she might have cut in the early 1970s.

A Decca press release with a photo of her that took up more than half the page said more about her appearance than about her voice or the record: "If Olivia's looks are a sample of what's to be found 'down under' then it's pretty certain we're about to lose the cream of British manhood… via Australia's assisted passage scheme!" Aside from this coquettish press release, however, Decca did little to promote the single. Released on May 13, 1966, it soon disappeared, and Decca did not offer Olivia the opportunity to make any additional recordings.

Just before Decca issued the single, a most welcome visitor turned up in London. Pat Carroll had just won a talent contest, too, being crowned the "most promising young Australian artist" in March 1966 by Melbourne radio station 3XY, and she, too, won a free trip to London. Unlike Olivia, Pat didn't take long to accept it. Her trip was by airplane rather than by ship, and when she arrived at the airport in London, Olivia met her there. Pat's prize also included accommodations, but when they turned out to be, in Pat's words, "horrendous," Olivia invited her to stay with her and Irene. Pat accepted, even though it meant sleeping on an air mattress on the floor.

At first, Pat performed as a solo act, and Olivia, who did not have any live gigs at the time, accompanied her and provided moral support. Both of them were finding that competition among female solo singers trying to make it in London was fierce. Athol Guy, a member of the Melbourne-based group the Seekers—the first Australian pop group to have a Top 5 hit in Australia, the United Kingdom, and the United States—suggested that the two of them form a duo. They decided it made sense, both musically and logistically, and so they became "Pat and Olivia," beginning in July.

Some of the duo's initial experiences onstage could be the stuff of a comedy. They would perform two shows a night at, in Olivia's words, "sleazy clubs around the country," although she found that "it was really fun. It was exciting." During their first performance, however, they kept getting tangled in or tripping over the cords attached to the microphones, which was something they hadn't dealt with while rehearsing. Shortly after that, their agent booked them in a strip club. Pat and Olivia didn't realize this until they were onstage singing and saw, as Pat recalled, that "there were just these little sleazy men just staring at us." "They're waiting for us to take our clothes off," Olivia realized, still looking and sounding startled as she told the story more than thirty years later. She laughed as she exclaimed, "I don't know what our agent was thinking!" Pat and Olivia got fired from that gig before the night was over.

The duo's gigs soon improved, primarily as an opening act. By late June, Philips Records had offered Pat and Olivia a recording contract, although they couldn't sign it because Olivia was still under contract with Decca, the lack of any further recordings notwithstanding. Olivia, by her own recollection, wasn't taking the duo as seriously as Pat was. "She was really focused, and I was like, 'Oh, this is fun,' and I was enjoying it, but I was more interested in getting back to my boyfriend in Australia. But that didn't actually work out because he was going to get married to someone else," she laughed. Pat agreed that Olivia, at that time, "never wanted to be a star. She really had no desire at all. I was the one that wanted it, and I was the one that pushed us."

Soon Pat and Olivia began to get better bookings, primarily as an opening act for established recording artists. They made their first British television appearance together around the end of August on the BBC's long-running *The Dick Emery Show*. They opened shows for the aforementioned Seekers, and late in the summer of 1966 they secured a spot on the bill for a week of concerts at Bournemouth headed by Cliff Richard and the Shadows.

If Johnny O'Keefe was Australia's homegrown answer to Elvis Presley, then Cliff was the same for England. Cliff would have far more international success than O'Keefe, although his US success was limited. Americans already had Elvis, plus, in Ricky Nelson, a performer who was much like Cliff: clean-cut, attractive, talented, but more wholesome in his appearance and stage manner than Elvis, with weekly exposure on his family's television sitcom. As such, Cliff only managed to crack the US Top 40 twice during the pre-Beatles era (once in 1959 and once in January 1964, one week before the Beatles entered the US Top 40 for the first time with "I Want to Hold Your Hand"). A superstar in England, with fifteen number one hits, he persevered and eventually racked up five Top 20 hits in the United

States from 1976 to 1981, including a duet with Olivia. The Shadows, while never successful in the American market, were stars in their own right in the United Kingdom as well as being Cliff's backing band. Meeting Cliff and the Shadows in Bournemouth would have significant consequences for Olivia, both professionally and personally.

Bruce Welch, a guitarist and vocalist in the Shadows, took an immediate liking to Olivia. More than fifty years later, he told a journalist he could still clearly remember the moment he met her. "She was absolutely stunning," he said. Cliff Richard later said that he, too, found her very attractive, and that "I don't know anybody that knew her that didn't actually fall in love with her at some point." But it was Welch, seven years Olivia's senior and married with a son, whom she would tentatively start seeing that fall, even though she didn't necessarily consider herself split from Ian Turpie yet.

While Olivia was a British citizen, Pat Carroll, a native of Australia, was not, and as such she was going to have to leave Great Britain by the end of 1966, at which time her visa would expire. Olivia, now eighteen, decided that she would go back to Australia with Pat in November. Soon the two of them were working—along with Ian Turpie—on *Time for Terry* again, and it was also at this time that Olivia and Ian figured out that their relationship was over, now that Ian had begun dating the woman he would marry. Pat and Olivia recorded a television special that would air in Australia in July 1967. After the new year, they performed in South Africa as an opening act for the English pop singer Matt Monro and then returned to Australia.

Pat and Olivia soon returned to England. "Two talented and attractive young Australians in search of a songwriter are appearing in cabaret in Bristol this week," the Bristol *Evening Post* reported on May 4, 1967. The article mentioned that while Pat had released singles in Australia (without any hits) and Olivia the one in England, "they hope to come up with that first record together shortly." It never happened though.

Olivia did, however, resume her relationship with Bruce Welch upon returning to England, now fully understanding that her romance with Ian Turpie had come to an end. At the end of the summer, Pat and Olivia again appeared on a bill headlined by the Shadows, this time at the famed Coventry Theatre and without Cliff Richard. By the end of February 1968, however, Pat and Olivia were back in Australia. Pat had been denied a work permit extension, and so Olivia "came home with Pat rather than break up the team," reported the Melbourne *Age*. Ironically, by the time they got back to Melbourne, Pat's mother had received a letter granting Pat an extension until August. "Fat lot of help it is now," Pat told a reporter. On April 5, the *Age* reported that Pat and Olivia had split their duo. By now, not only was Olivia involved with Bruce Welch, whose divorce was granted in a London court in late June, but Pat was seeing Strangers guitarist John Farrar.

Decades later, Pat laughingly said, "So that's *really* why we [Pat and Olivia] split up, because of boyfriends, I guess." Olivia returned to England in June, and in October, she and Bruce announced their engagement, although Bruce told the press that they would not marry until after Olivia's twenty-first birthday.

After Olivia returned to England, Peter Gormley, a London-based Australian native who managed Cliff Richard and the Shadows as well as the popular British-Australian singer Frank Ifield, among others, became her manager. One of the first things Gormley did for her was introduce her to Don Kirshner. "I'll never forget it," Kirshner said nearly a decade later.

> I walked into Peter Gormley's London office one day and there was this kewpie doll in knee socks. I knew she could be the darling of millions! And I loved her three names—unusual, it sticks with you, and the bit of her grandfather winning the Nobel thing—very marketable press stuff. Then, when I heard her sing, I knew with some double-tracking that we could get a great, sweet sound out of her.

Kirshner, too, found Olivia to be irresistibly charming. "Back in London," he recalled,

> she had this red terrier, and before I went to her place one night for dinner, I spent the day going to pet shops all over the city, looking for this certain kind of dog food she liked, to bring it as a gift. Funny way to spend an afternoon… but I finally found it! It's crazy, but that's the kind of effect she has on you.

Kirshner had by this point famously and bitterly parted ways with the Monkees, after overseeing the making of their phenomenally successful first two albums, and he had subsequently launched a television-based band that couldn't rebel against his control: the Archies, which consisted of session singers and musicians making records that would be mimed by comic book characters on television. Nevertheless, at the time that Gormley introduced him to Olivia, Kirshner was trying to manufacture another photogenic pop group, albeit with a different twist this time. As the US record industry trade magazine *Cash Box* (the leading competitor to *Billboard* for decades) reported in its February 8, 1969, issue, "Having had a hand in the creation of two hit groups for TV (the Monkees and the Archies), Don Kirshner is attempting to turn the same trick in feature films." Kirshner and film producer Harry Saltzman, coproducer of the first nine James Bond movies, had agreed to coproduce a musical film titled *Toomorrow*, which *Cash Box* reported would "hopefully" be "the first of a series featuring a group of the same name." The movie would be released by United Artists, the distributor of the Bond films, and the group's records would be issued by Kirshner's Calendar Records, which would be distributed via RCA Records.

After a "six-month worldwide talent hunt," Kirshner chose Olivia plus a twenty-two-year-old "rhythm and blues drummer" from Philadelphia named Karl Chambers, a twenty-five-year-old English pianist and organist named Vic Cooper, and a twenty-four-year-old singer and guitarist from the US state of Georgia named Ben Thomas. (The original drummer was Chris Slade, who later went on to fame with AC/DC, but he, perhaps wisely as it turned out, jumped ship before filming began.) Kirshner, ever the ambitious impresario, told the press that Toomorrow "can be the biggest thing in the history of the business." The chaotic nature of the filming did not bode well; delays were frequent. When Olivia flew with Rona to New York City—her first visit to the United States—for a meeting that would precede the start of filming, the producers told them that they needed to postpone the meeting for a week, so they sent the Newton-John sisters on an all-expenses-paid one-week vacation in Florida. Bruce Welch would accompany Olivia to New York on subsequent trips related to the film, even though the movie would be filmed at Pinewood Studios in the English village of Iver Heath, about eighteen miles west of central London.

Despite the involvement of Kirshner and Saltzman, the production of the film proved chaotic, beset with delays and financial difficulties. Olivia found the project frustrating at times. When she discovered that one scene called for her to be wearing nothing but her undergarments, she burst into tears and refused, later saying that it was at least a good lesson in standing up for herself. Overall, though, she said that making the movie, which she described as "a space fantasy musical," and recording the soundtrack album was "a great experience." In a documentary about Olivia some thirty years later, Kirshner said that he had dropped out of the production of the film while it was in progress because "creatively, I felt it was going in the wrong direction."

Bruce Welch felt the same way about the film and, especially, the soundtrack. "The film was a disgrace. It was reminiscent of so many of the low-budget pop pictures that were made during the early sixties, and the biggest let down of all was the music," Welch wrote in his memoir, *Rock 'n' Roll: I Gave You the Best Years of My Life*. "It was all so lightweight. There were no hit songs—the numbers were naive and instantly forgettable…. Instead of going for the best songwriters available, Kirshner had simply handed the job to some unknown writers he had signed to his publishing company and, of course, it couldn't possibly work." Welch had wanted to bring in established, hit-making songwriters to improve the soundtrack, but the producers nixed the idea because it would require more refilming than they were willing to do.

The film premiered at the London Pavilion cinema on August 27, 1970, but after a week it was gone. Some British soldiers saw it in military base theaters over the next couple of years, but no one saw it in America until it was shown, once, at the Egyptian Theatre in Los Angeles on July 8, 2000. (Olivia attended the screening with Rona and their friend Del Shores.) Eventually it would be released on DVD and now it can be streamed, but at the time "it flopped," Olivia admitted, "and it was very disappointing." The film's choreographer, Australian native Bob Ainslie, told a journalist in 1983 that "it was quite a putrid film. It's not something one would want to their credit." Olivia made a similar remark to journalist Debbie Kruger in 1994. When Kruger recalled that *Grease* had been widely referred to in the media as her feature film debut, Olivia replied, "Well, it [*Toomorrow*] wasn't something I wanted to rave about." Karl Chambers quit the group about two weeks before the film even came out.

RCA Victor released the *Toomorrow* soundtrack album in Great Britain, but it too sank without a trace, as did the accompanying single, "You're My Baby Now." The group nevertheless recorded a follow-up single, "I Could Never Live without Your Love," produced by Welch and released by Decca, but it flopped as well. The soundtrack wouldn't be released in the United States until 2011, despite Olivia becoming one of the best-selling recording artists in the States during the 1970s.

Soon Toomorrow—the film and the band alike—fulfilled the *New Musical Express* headline of September 12, 1970: "Toomorrow—It's More Like Yesterday." The failure of Toomorrow didn't damage Olivia's career, though. If anything, all the publicity surrounding the film put her unique "triple-barrel name" and her attractive face into newspapers and industry publications. Furthermore, Olivia still had a powerful manager, Peter Gormley, in her corner, and fiancé Bruce Welch, a talented musician, arranger, and producer as well. Both personally and professionally, Olivia received a boost in the summer of 1970 when John Farrar & Pat Carroll, who had married at the beginning of the year, moved to London. Farrar had gotten to know the Shadows when his group, the Strangers, had opened for them in Melbourne. As he told a British interviewer in early 1971, "About six months ago, I got a phone call from Bruce Welch of the Shadows, and he asked me if I'd like to come over and be part of a new group that Hank Marvin [also of the Shadows] and himself were forming." The group was Marvin, Welch & Farrar. All three of its members would play an important role in what was ahead for Olivia's career.

After Toomorrow came and went, Olivia got an opportunity to work with Cliff Richard. "He was looking for a girl to do a duet with him," Olivia told Barry Scott, the host of the American radio program *The Lost 45s*, nearly twenty years later. "We tried out together and our voices went [together] really well." She and Cliff recorded "Don't Move Away," written by the popular London songwriting team of Harold Spiro and Valerie Avon, which came out as the B-side of a Richard single at the beginning of 1971. By then she had also appeared on Cliff's 1970 BBC-TV Christmas Eve special. In January 1971, Cliff's BBC-TV series, *It's Cliff Richard,* began its second season. Hank Marvin was a regular during the thirteen-week season, and Marvin, Welch & Farrar performed on five of the episodes. Olivia made three appearances on the show that season, and after all thirteen episodes had been taped, she joined Cliff on his tour of Holland, Belgium, West Germany, and Switzerland. "[I] did his backups and everything," she told Scott.

At the same time, Peter Gormley and Bruce Welch were both encouraging Olivia to make a record of her own. Since Hank Marvin was occupied throughout the thirteen weeks of Cliff's show, as well as, Farrar later recalled, with Beatles protégé Cilla Black on her BBC-TV show, Welch and Farrar both had free time to work with Olivia. Gormley, still a well-known figure in the music business in Australia, secured a record deal for Olivia with Sydney-based Festival Records.

In early 1971, she entered the legendary Abbey Road Studios in London for her first solo session since she had recorded the lone single for Decca in 1966. This, of course, was where the Beatles had recorded from 1962 until 1970, and in her memoir Olivia wrote that "the Beatles were in the next studio with George Martin recording their new album" while she was recording what became her first album. But while she did meet each of the Beatles (and Yoko Ono, too), her memory must have been incorrect on this point. The group's last session, which John didn't show up for, had occurred on January 3, 1970, when Paul and Ringo joined George in completing his song "I Me Mine" for the *Let It Be* soundtrack album, a full year before Olivia's first sessions at Abbey Road. Olivia had first met Paul when she and Welch "went round to Paul's house one day," she recalled.

> He said, "I have just written this song," and he started playing "Lady Madonna." At the time, I didn't even realize what I was hearing. I was thrilled to meet Paul and all, but I had no sense of what was really going on at the time. When I look back, I know it's amazing that I was there when he wrote that song.

Gormley suggested that Olivia record "If Not for You," a recent Bob Dylan song which George Harrison had covered on his triple album *All Things Must Pass* (1970). John Farrar confirmed to writer Wesley Hyatt in 1999 which version Olivia was covering, although listening to the three recordings makes it pretty clear: "It was off a George Harrison album when we first found it. I guess it was a pretty hip tune at the time." Farrar, who coproduced the recording with Bruce Welch and played all the guitars on the track, even played slide guitar on it, which was featured on Harrison's version but not Dylan's. Longtime Shadows drummer Brian Bennett also played on the record and recalled finding "a medium groove that felt good for the song but not loud. I used a hard brush played at the bass where the brush meets the rubber grip. It's always about the song."

Olivia felt reluctant about recording "If Not for You." "I didn't think it was my type of song at all," she said, "and I had a little bit of trouble being convincing in putting it over. But everyone else was so enthusiastic that I came round to liking it eventually." One of her favorite memories of making the record involved, not surprisingly, one of her dogs. "There was a moment when my dog [an Irish setter named Geordie] actually grabbed the mic during a guitar solo in 'If Not for You,'" she wrote in an essay that accompanied the deluxe fiftieth-anniversary release of the *If Not for You* album.[1] "We left the sound on the album and it still makes me smile when I hear it." By then, she had totally changed her initial mixed feelings about the song, writing that she was "surprised and extremely grateful that my team knew what they were doing and picked a hit song to launch my career. An interesting aside, my husband John Easterling's favorite song is 'If Not for You.' There are no coincidences in life—for this to be his favorite song??? Of all the songs in the world. Wild!!" Once she learned this, she would dedicate the song to him at her concerts.

Festival Records released "If Not for You" in Australia, and Gormley arranged for the Pye International label to release it in the United Kingdom. The B-side was "The Biggest Clown," written by John Rostill, who had been the bass guitarist in the Shadows, and who would later write A-sides for Olivia. The single received favorable reviews from the British trade papers *New Musical Express* and *Record Mirror*. The latter referred to Olivia as "the girl from the ill-fated Toomorrow group" in its review, adding that "this [record] could make it because it's a lovely little song and the lovely little girl has a lovely little voice." The single did indeed "make it," reaching the Top 10, according to Craig Halstead's book *Olivia Newton-John: All the Top 40 Hits*, in the UK, Australia, New Zealand, Ireland, Norway, and Zimbabwe. When *Billboard* reviewed "If Not for You" in May 1971, it noted another international success for the single, while predicting similar success for its Stateside release: "The Bob Dylan material along with an exceptional performance by the artist, no. 1 in Italy, makes this a hot contender for programming and sales action here as well."

Billboard's prediction proved at least partially accurate. "If Not for You" reached No. 25 on the Hot 100 and No. 1 on the easy listening/adult contemporary chart, which measured airplay on radio stations that were in that format. The single was the first of twenty-nine Top 40 pop hits that Olivia would rack up over a period of twenty-five years, and the first of ten number one hits on the Easy Listening/ Adult Contemporary chart that she achieved from 1971 through 1980. In Canada, "If Not for You" reached No. 18 on the pop chart, and on the chart of Toronto's powerhouse "Hit Parade" radio station CHUM, it reached No. 3.

The North American release of the single marked the beginning of Olivia's long affiliation with MCA, a relationship that lasted through 1988, briefly resumed in the late 1990s, and was mutually beneficial but at times contentious, even after Olivia was no longer signed with the company. In 1971 the label MCA Records did not exist yet; an MCA Inc. subsidiary, Uni Records, released the single. MCA (which stood for, at least originally, Music Corporation of America) began as a Chicago-based music booking agency in 1924. The company eventually expanded into representing radio, film, and television stars and also began producing television programs during the early 1950s, by which time the company had moved to the Los Angeles area. By the late 1950s, MCA began making moves toward getting into the film industry, and in June 1962 the company purchased US Decca Records, then the nation's fourth-largest recording company. Decca Records owned nearly 90 percent of Universal Pictures, which, most in the entertainment industry believed, was the major reason why MCA bought Decca. Attorney General Robert F. Kennedy immediately announced antitrust suits against MCA, which consequently got out of the talent agency business but kept Decca and Universal.

The American Decca Records label and others that had been its subsidiaries, such as the Brunswick and Coral labels, carried on under MCA's ownership. MCA executives Berle Adams, who had cofounded Mercury Records in 1945, and Ned Tanen formed Uni Records as another MCA subsidiary label in 1966. Its name was short for Universal City, MCA's corporate headquarters. Adams was active in the record industry in both the United States and the United Kingdom. He had signed the Who to the Decca label for American releases, and he and his MCA colleague Brian Brolly signed the English composers Andrew Lloyd Webber and Tim Rice to record the score for the rock opera *Jesus Christ Superstar*. Uni's biggest artist signings would be Neil Diamond, Elton John, and Olivia Newton-John.

Uni Records proved successful but short-lived. Near the end of 1972, MCA consolidated all of its labels into the new MCA Records label. Mike Maitland served as the first president of MCA Records, and he held the post until 1979. He would be, in a professional sense, an asset to Olivia at some times and an adversary at others.

Uni had a small staff but a hardworking, skilled national promotion director, Russ Regan, and he gave "If Not for You" a big push. Decades later, he told writer Michael Sigman that he had encountered some resistance to this effort within the company. "I thought we had a hit," Regan recalled of Olivia's debut for the label. "They [his colleagues] thought I was crazy. They said, 'She'll never make it. She's too beautiful and too plastic.' I said, 'We're gonna bring plastic back.'" Within weeks, Regan was phoning Olivia, telling her that she had a hit and needed to come to America. When MCA Records absorbed Uni Records, he stayed on and continued to play an important role in Olivia's career.

Uni Records was satisfied enough with the sales of "If Not for You" to release Olivia's first album, of the same title, that fall. The album was loaded with additional cover versions, such as "Me and Bobby McGee" and "Help Me Make It through the Night," which were written or cowritten by Kris Kristofferson; the Bread hit "If"; Gordon Lightfoot's "If You Could Read My Mind"; and Tom Rush's

"No Regrets." Welch and Farrar came up with an arrangement of an American ballad from the nineteenth century, "Banks of the Ohio," which Joan Baez had recorded in 1961. The album had a light pop/easy listening, but also country, folk-tinged, vibe. American music critic Angie Rizzo wrote that the album "is definitely recommended for your record library…. She has a great little voice—young but with a lot of control and the backing on the disc is mostly gentle and nice—guitars, piano, drums and bass." Other labels released the album internationally, but it was not a hit anywhere except Australia, where it reached No. 14 on the national album chart. It sold modestly in the States, but well enough to reach No. 158 on the *Billboard* album chart.

The *New Musical Express*, which had mocked the failure of Toomorrow in 1970, reversed course in 1971: "Tomorrow looks bright for Olivia Newton-John."

3 IF YOU LOVE ME (LET ME KNOW)

" told everyone that I was going away for the weekend and not to bother calling me, but I forgot about the window cleaner," Bruce Welch said in an interview in 2004. "He found me on the Tuesday.... I had taken the pills on the Sunday." Welch attempted suicide after Olivia suddenly ended their relationship, with, he said, no warning and no explanation, in April 1972. A gossip columnist for the London *Daily Mirror* wrote, "I'm told Olivia, as much as she adored the ex-Shadows guitarist, didn't want to commit herself to marriage." Asked about the breakup two months later by journalist Anne Latreille, Olivia, "with heightened color," wrote Latreille, replying, "I don't want to say anything. Bruce still produces my records and we're still friends. But I simply won't talk about it." Several weeks before that interview, Welch discovered that Olivia had been having an affair, reportedly with the married French singer Sacha Distel, with whom she was co-starring in the revue *Paris to Piccadilly* in London's West End. He didn't tell the press, nor did he ever confirm the identity of Olivia's lover when the press picked up on it.

By then, Olivia's recording of "Banks of the Ohio" had become her second Top 10 hit in the United Kingdom and a No. 1 in Australia, and she had recorded and released another song from George Harrison's *All Things Must Pass*, this time one that he had written called "What Is Life." In much of the world, that song had been Harrison's follow-up hit to "My Sweet Lord," but not in the United Kingdom, where it had been on the B-side of that single. Olivia's cover of "What Is Life," which stayed faithful to the arrangement of the original, was released as a single in the United Kingdom and the United States. It gave her another British Top 20 hit, but like "Banks of the Ohio," it made little impact on American radio programmers and record buyers.

Between recording her second album, again at Abbey Road with Welch and Farrar producing (at least a couple of tracks had been recorded before Olivia broke up with Bruce), appearing as a regular performer on Cliff Richard's BBC-TV program, the live performances with Distel, and appearing in one of Cliff's TV specials, Olivia did not make it to the United States as soon as Russ Regan had hoped. The album, which would be titled *Olivia*, would be completed over the summer of 1972. Like her first album, it was heavy on cover versions, including George Harrison's "Behind That Locked Door" as well as "What Is Life," another Bread hit ("Everything I Own"), Don McLean's "Winterwood," and a Ricky Nelson rock-and-roll hit from 1959, "Just a Little Too Much." John Farrar contributed two songs as writer or cowriter, though, and Olivia wrote one herself titled "Changes."

The lyrics of "Changes" dealt with the end of a marriage and the impact it would have on a child, something that apparently still weighed on Olivia. By now, she and Rona and their mother were all living in St. Johns Wood in London, while Brin and her brother Hugh were still living in Australia. "I'd have to be very, very sure before I married," she told a reporter. "My parents' marriage broke up when I was a child and so have the marriages of many of my friends and relatives…. I'm wary of marriage." Writing "Changes," she said, came easily to her. "I've never written any music before, and I don't play the guitar, but one day I was fooling round with three chords I'd been taught and in ten minutes I'd written the thing."

The album (titled *Olivia Newton-John* in continental Europe) came out in August, and it flopped everywhere, even in Great Britain and Australia, as did its second single, "Just a Little Too Much." In the United States, Uni released "Just a Little Too Much," but after it failed to dent the Hot 100, the label declined to release the album. Late in the summer of 1972, Olivia finally made a trip back to the States to try to build on the success of "If Not for You."

One of the first things she did on this trip to America was see the King of Rock and Roll, Elvis Presley, "her idol," according to the London *Daily Mirror*, in concert in Las Vegas. (She would never meet him, though.) She met and got to work with another famous American singer, the King of Cool, Dean Martin. MCA had arranged for Olivia to be a guest on his long-running (1965–1974) NBC weekly TV show—not a shabby way to make her American television debut. In her memoir, Olivia fondly recalled Martin's kindness and professionalism, as well as the fact that the whiskey that viewers undoubtedly thought he was drinking was actually dark iced tea. Olivia sang the Bread song "If," which she had covered on her first album, and she and Dean duetted on a medley of "Just a Little Lovin' (Will Go a Long Way)," an Eddy Arnold song that Dean had recorded nearly a decade earlier, and "True Love," the Cole Porter song that Bing Crosby and Grace Kelly had a big hit with in 1956.

Olivia's episode of *The Dean Martin Show* aired on October 26, 1972, but she returned to England in September, in time for another international tour with Cliff Richard, this time covering Indonesia, Hong Kong, and Japan. Cliff bought her a wedding gown for her twenty-fourth birthday after she had admired it in a shop window in Tokyo. (He laughingly told a reporter, "But before you jump to conclusions let me say the gown was for Olivia to wear on stage and not in church.") After the tour ended, Olivia was back in the studio with Welch and Farrar to record her next single, a cover of John Denver's "Take Me Home, Country Roads." Denver's record had been a huge hit in the United States and Canada in 1971, but the song was still largely unknown in Great Britain at the time. Olivia's version hit the radio stations and record stores in November 1972, and after a slow start it peaked at No. 15 on the UK chart in February 1973. MCA Records subsequently released the single—Olivia's first to be released on that label—in the United States, but several million Americans already had the Denver original on either a single or an album. Olivia did some promotional legwork for the single when she visited Los Angeles in May 1973; MCA promo man Chuck Meyer took her to radio stations for on-air interviews and to the offices of *Cash Box* for a visit with its publisher, George Albert, and staff members. But her Denver cover only managed to reach No. 119 on *Billboard*'s "Bubbling Under the Hot 100" chart and made no showing at all in *Cash Box*.

Even though the executives at MCA Records couldn't have been too happy with the single's reception by radio stations and record buyers, the label's vice president of A&R (artists and repertoire), Artie Mogull, saw that it had gotten some airplay on country stations in the Southeast. He suggested to Peter Gormley that Olivia record "a more country-oriented pop record" for her next single. Gormley, Welch, and Farrar, Olivia would later say, all steered her in that direction. "I didn't know what country music was, to tell you the truth, until I came to America," she told journalist Debbie Kruger. But Gormley "loved that kind of music," and Olivia told *Rolling Stone* writer Ben Fong-Torres that Welch and Farrar thought her voice was well suited for it. Olivia said that she and Welch both became fans of the Eagles, who released their first album in 1972, and their "laid back" sound. Greg Mathieson, who played piano for Olivia on tours and records during the mid- to late 1970s, remembers that when the Eagles' album *Hotel California* (1976) came out, "she was listening to it non-stop." In an interview with *Record Mirror* in early 1973, Olivia cited a variety of female country and pop singers that she liked. "The songs I like are often done by someone like Rita Coolidge. And I adore the beautiful rich voice of Anne Murray, lovely, lovely sound," she said. "The Carpenters are also very good, some excellent guitar bits on their albums. I enjoy Barbra Streisand as well. I enjoy both ends of the scale." Olivia also mentioned Dusty Springfield as a favorite.

When Olivia returned to London from the trip to LA, she, Bruce Welch, and John Farrar went back to Abbey Road to continue recording her third album, which in England would be released with the title *Music Makes My Day*. Welch brought her a song that his former Shadows bandmate John Rostill (with whom Welch was still collaborating) had recently composed. "I first heard 'Let Me Be

There,'" Olivia recalled years later, "when Bruce Welch played it for me, and I knew, immediately, it was a catchy song. It was his idea of putting a bass voice on it in the chorus, which gave it a very different sound." Mike Sammes sang that bass voice, as he also had on Olivia's recording of "Banks of the Ohio." His vocal group, the Mike Sammes Singers, had sung background vocals on hit records for artists including Tom Jones, Englebert Humperdinck, and the Beatles (most notably, in the latter case, on "I Am the Walrus").

"Let Me Be There" first hit the market in the United Kingdom, not on Pye International but on Festival Records' (Olivia's Australian label) Interfusion subsidiary, on June 22, 1973. Whether the label switch had anything to do with the single's commercial reception in the United Kingdom is unclear, but the record flopped, reportedly selling a puzzlingly low total of about eight thousand copies. In the United States, MCA released the record in July. The label placed an ad in the October 20, 1973, issue of *Cash Box*: a black-and-white photo of Olivia wearing a dark, semi-long-sleeved shirt, white bell-bottoms, and sandals, with the caption "Olivia Newton-John lives in the country in England and sings for the country in America and is as pretty as her newest single."

In reality, as the London *Daily Mail* later reported, "Deeds show that on March 19, 1973, Newton-John, then aged just 24, spent £19,500 on [a] second-floor flat with its own small roof terrace just off West Hampstead's main thoroughfare West End Lane"—London, not "the country." Her mother lived there with her. Welch and Olivia tried to rekindle their romantic relationship that spring, but, according to Welch, they both decided it was hopeless after about two months. Some three decades later, Cliff Richard still seemed puzzled. "It seemed to me that their relationship could have worked," he said, "and even now I'm not quite sure why it didn't."

The American song publisher of "Let Me Be There," Al Gallico, a thirty-six-year veteran of the business by then, took it upon himself to help promote Olivia's single. "It had a country feeling," he recalled. "It's harder to get songs played on Top 40 stations because they have such a tight playlist. I thought there would be a better chance to get it played first on country music stations." The single made its first *Billboard* chart appearance on the country chart dated August 25, 1973, and it would peak at No. 7.

"Let Me Be There" entered the *Cash Box* Top 100 (the pop chart) at No. 99 the week after MCA ran the ad. It crawled up to 96 the next week, but it eventually reached No. 4. The record was three weeks slower to reach the *Billboard* Hot 100 (debuting on November 17), but it fared very well there, too, reaching No. 6. It also reached the Top 10 on the adult contemporary chart. Olivia, with the help of Welch, Farrar, and Rostill, had found the sound that would make her red hot—virtually everywhere except the United Kingdom—for the next two years.

Tragically, John Rostill wouldn't see this and other songs that he had written propel Olivia to stardom in America. On November 27, 1973, an English newspaper near his home reported that "Rostill was found dead in his workroom [recording studio] at his home in Radlett, Hertfordshire, yesterday, surrounded by electronic equipment." "A friend, Bruce Welch," the report added, "had forced the door after being unable to get a reply." (This was most ironic, since someone had saved Welch's life under somewhat similar circumstances the year before.) Initial reports suggested that Rostill's death had been the result of accidental electrocution. But the coroner's inquest revealed that he'd had a history of suicide attempts. "I knew of John's mental troubles," Welch stated. "I knew of a suicide attempt in 1967. He tried to take his life with drugs and gas poisoning." More recently, Rostill's marriage had been dissolving. "Divorce was on his mind a great deal," Welch said. "When we weren't working, he would talk a lot about it. He would talk about the divorce, of selling the house, of sharing the property, and he got very upset indeed." The coroner's verdict, reached about two weeks after Rostill died, stated that he had "killed himself with an overdose of drugs while in a depressed state of mind." He left behind not only his wife—they hadn't divorced yet—but also a one-year-old son. "Let Me Be There" reached the Top 10 on the Hot 100 about one month after the coroner issued his report. In her memoir, Olivia remembered Rostill as "incredibly talented."

She hadn't expected "Let Me Be There" to be a breakthrough hit in America though, especially given its failure in the United Kingdom. "I just couldn't believe it when it happened," she recalled in 1998. She also found the record's crossover success surprising. "I don't really know why it made it in country music, other than it had that flavor to it. It had a sort of rhythm guitar and a chorus and a verse, though we didn't record it strictly as a country song. We just recorded it as a pop song." Olivia had been paying close attention when "Let Me Be There" landed her in the American Top 10 for the first time. "Singles are important to me," she told a British journalist in 1973. "It's fun watching them going up and down the charts."

By 1973, though—actually ever since Beatles albums had started selling in the millions beginning with, in the United States, *Meet the Beatles!* (1964)—record companies were far more interested in selling albums than "45s," as singles were commonly referred to in those days. Singles tended to be pressed on low-quality vinyl, or even the cheaper, more-brittle, faster-wearing styrene, a plastic substance, and while a big hit single could be profitable for a record company (and, perhaps, a recording artist), major record companies primarily viewed singles as a way to advertise the albums from which they were taken. Therefore, MCA Records, which had yet to release an Olivia Newton-John album (1971's *If Not for You* had been released on the Uni label), issued one titled *Let Me Be There* in the United States on November 20, 1973, about as fast as possible once the single made the charts.

The album was, to an extent, a rehash of her first US album, with six of the same tracks, including "If Not for You." It also included one track from her second album, the one MCA had declined to release in the States, plus the singles "Just a Little Too Much," "Take Me Home, Country Roads," and, of course, "Let Me Be There." The album fared only modestly on the *Billboard* album chart, peaking at No. 54, but it reached No. 1 on the country album chart at the beginning of March 1974. During the same week that the album reached that pinnacle (March 2), the single "Let Me Be There" won the Grammy Award for Best Country Vocal Performance, Female. Even though Artie Mogull at MCA and Olivia's friends Helen Reddy and Jeff Wald (Helen's husband and manager) had all urged her to get over to America now that she'd had a smash hit there, Olivia did not attend the ceremony; she was home in England, preparing to represent Great Britain in the annual Eurovision Song Contest. "It is a terrific honor for her to do it," said her mother, who by then was living in Pentlands Close, Cambridge. "It is a very big thing, and she feels the responsibility of it."

The contest was held on April 6 in the Brighton Dome, a historic venue that opened in 1867 and still remains in use. Olivia sang "Long Live Love," which was written by Harold Spiro and Valerie Avon, the same team that wrote "Don't Move Away," the Cliff Richard B-side on which Olivia had sung over three years earlier. BBC-TV viewers had selected the song in the run-up to the contest, which, according to the London *Sun*, she was favored at the odds of 7–2 to win. She finished tied for fourth.

Interviewed just after the show, Olivia expressed her unhappiness, particularly with the song, which she declared "totally wrong" for the contest. "I would never have chosen it," she said. "I don't think it was a suitable song for me or the contest. I would have preferred a nice ballad." "I wasn't the only one who didn't particularly like our song," she added. "All of us [presumably including Peter Gormley as well as John Farrar, who produced her recording of the song] felt very frustrated, but we couldn't do anything about it. It was the viewers' choice, and we all had to accept that." The *Sun* reported that Olivia "was close to tears at the BBC reception after the contest" and that she "talked briefly to the Director General, Sir Charles Curran, and then left" without participating in a post-contest program on BBC Radio. "I'm going to America for four months at the end of this week," Olivia told reporter Brian Wesley. "I have got something to look forward to."

Three months later, however, during a one-week return to London for recording sessions at Abbey Road, Olivia said that the press had exaggerated her reaction to the loss. "It wouldn't have been fair to say before the contest that I wouldn't have chosen the song myself," she said. "So, after the contest was over, I thought it was fair enough to say 'no' when people asked if I would have chosen the song if I had had the choice. It was a straight answer, given with no bitterness. But it was misinterpreted, and the press had a go at me."

Olivia still wished nearly twenty years later that she had not had to sing "Long Live Love" in the contest and record it as a single. In spring 1992, she did an on-air interview for WNCI-FM in Columbus, Ohio, to promote her soon-to-be-released single "I Need Love" and album *Back to Basics: The Essential Collection 1971–1992*. One of the two disc jockeys asked her, "Do you look back on your twenty-year career, and are there any songs that you think, 'Oh my God, I don't believe I did that?' Or that you're real embarrassed when you hear it on the radio or [when] somebody brings it up?" He noted that she was smiling before he even finished asking her. "I'm not going to tell you 'cause you'll find it," she answered. "You'll dig it up!" He replied with a teasing "No!" and she said, "There's just one song that I didn't like." She explained how she had represented England in the Eurovision Song Contest, and how television viewers had voted for the song that she would have to sing for it. "Well, the one they chose was, of course, *of course*, was the one I *hated*," she said, even though she laughed as she said it. When he pressed her, in a good-natured way, to reveal the name of the song, she replied, still laughing, "I'm not telling you!" Then she named the song ("Long Live Love"), adding, "It's like an oompah, oompah…"

Of the three acts that finished ahead of Olivia in the 1974 Eurovision Song Contest, only one went on to a comparable level of success. A quartet from Sweden won the contest with a song that its two male members had written. The group was called ABBA, and the song was "Waterloo." "Our success means a big career for us," said one of the group's two female vocalists, Anni-Frid (Frida) Lyngstad, after the group's victory. "We've done a lot in Sweden, Austria and Holland but this is just the sort of boost we need to get well known in other places. We are all thrilled." "Waterloo" became ABBA's first hit in the United States, reaching No. 6 on the Hot 100, and the group's first big hit in the United Kingdom, where it reached No. 1. Four years later, ABBA would be featured on one of Olivia's US TV specials.

Even though Olivia clearly wasn't thrilled with "Long Live Love"—she had hoped its B-side, a lushly orchestrated ballad titled "Angel Eyes," would be the song she sang for Eurovision—it just missed reaching the British Top 10, in contrast to "Let Me Be There," which missed the British charts altogether. Nevertheless, her career was now at a turning point of sorts; until 1974, she had been a much bigger star in her native country than in the United States, but that situation began to reverse itself with the release of "Let Me Be There," and the trend would only accelerate with subsequent releases. MCA didn't release either "Long Live Love" or "Angel Eyes" in the United States, and neither sounded much like "Let Me Be There" or the single that MCA chose as the follow-up to that smash hit. That single, "If You Love Me (Let Me Know)," arrived at American radio stations and record retailers about a week before the Eurovision contest.

Another song written by John Rostill (but produced by John Farrar without Bruce Welch, who gradually stepped back from producing Olivia's records while still contributing as a guitarist), "If You Love Me (Let Me Know)" sounded so much like its predecessor that years later Farrar described it as "kind of 'Let Me Be There' again in a different key." *Record World*, a US competitor to *Billboard* and *Cash Box*, noted the similarity in its review, predicting "a similar kind of success saga" for the new release. "If You Love Me (Let Me Know)" actually did a bit better, reaching the Top 5 on the Hot 100 as well as *Billboard*'s adult contemporary and country singles charts.

Each of Olivia's first two major US hits found favor not only with record buyers and radio stations in a variety of formats, but they also appealed to some top American performers. Ike and Tina Turner covered "Let Me Be There" shortly after Olivia's record became a hit, and Tina recorded "If You Love Me (Let Me Know)" on her debut solo album, *Tina Turns the Country On!*, which came out in September 1974. Elvis Presley promptly added both songs to his concert set list. Tony Brown, who would sign Olivia to MCA Nashville Records in 1997 and produce some of her recordings for the label, recalls,

> When I played with Elvis for three years… when he would do covers, he would do either gospel songs, or he would do country songs. He would do "Let Me Be There" and "If You Love Me (Let Me Know)" *every night*, every night. And he only did "Return to Sender" one time in three years that I played with him!

"That speaks to Olivia, to me," Brown reflects. "That's what it speaks to, Olivia and those songs." Live performances of both songs would be released on Presley albums.

Peter Gormley came with Olivia when she left England for America a few days after the Eurovision Song Contest, as did John Farrar. A photo in the May 4, 1974, issue of *Billboard*, taken two to three weeks earlier, shows Olivia, Gormley, Farrar, and MCA Records president Mike Maitland holding Olivia's bevy of new American awards: a gold record (her first in the United States) commemorating one million copies sold of the single "Let Me Be There," her Grammy Award, and a plaque from the Academy of Country Music naming her the "Newcomer of the Year." Gormley didn't stay in America for long, though; he had a roster of clients in England, including Cliff Richard, who, despite still not having had even one Top 20 hit in the United States yet, had been Gormley's most lucrative client for years and was still an international superstar.

Olivia, however, brought someone else along from England in addition to Gormley and Farrar. In mid-1973, she met a young Englishman while she was vacationing with a girlfriend. His name was Lee Kramer. "I was 21 [three years younger than Olivia] and holidaying in Monte Carlo; I had a boat there and came down often from London for long weekends," he told journalist Timothy White five years later. "My cousin was a fiancé of one of Olivia's closest friends and they both came down with him for a day on my boat." (Kramer and his brother Mike had become millionaires by selling cowboy boots to retailers across Europe.)

> There wasn't a pier in Monte Carlo to pick them up, so we dropped anchor a half-mile off the beach and I swam in to greet them. As I was coming out of the water there was this beautiful, tanned, blonde-haired girl with the biggest eyes I had ever seen in my entire life! We just looked at each other and that was it, a real lightning flash. We had about two days in Monte Carlo and then she told me she was going back to England. I cancelled the rest of my holiday, finagled a seat next to her on the plane and we've been together, more or less, ever since. A classic romance on the French Rivera!

The "more or less" referred to a brief breakup in the early stage of their relationship, after which Olivia reconciled with Bruce Welch, but that didn't last and soon she was back with Lee.

When Olivia set off for her four-month visit to America in April 1974, "I saw I'd have to come too or lose her," Kramer said. Gormley spent most of that time in England. "Since I was with her all the time and I was the one who cared about her, I slowly took over [her management]," Kramer told White. He had no experience in the music business, though, and for a while he would often call Artie Mogull for advice—not necessarily an ideal situation, since part of a manager's job is to represent his artist's interests with the record label.

Olivia stayed for a time at the Sunset Marquis in West Hollywood. On her first day there, she met Glenn Frey, and after they chatted, he sent her a dozen red roses the next day with a note welcoming her to America. She had come to California without Lee, but he soon arrived and they rented a house together.

British rock journalist Nick Dent-Robinson got to know Olivia around this time. "I was working in Los Angeles… and living in a home on Topanga Beach, adjacent to Malibu. I remember meeting Olivia—or Livvy as she preferred to be called—on many occasions as she either strolled alone or rode her horse along the beach in the early morning, right outside my home," he wrote shortly after her passing.

> She was always happy to chat and initially seemed the epitome of sunny innocence—though I quickly appreciated there was rather more to her than that. She would talk enthusiastically about London where she had lived for over eight years, relating many amusing anecdotes—and she clearly missed many of the friends she had left behind. She was nostalgic about Australia too—and her family back there. At this point Olivia was by no means sure she wanted

to remain in America and on one occasion suggested she'd give it just another couple of years before returning to London or Australia, if she hadn't made a major breakthrough.

The entire year of 1974 would pass without Olivia setting foot in Australia.

Upon her arrival in California, Olivia had yet to play a full concert in the United States. She had appeared on a multi-artist bill at the Chester Fritz Auditorium in Grand Forks, North Dakota, in August 1973, where she performed only one song, "Let Me Be There," before a small audience. With a second smash hit and a Grammy Award on her résumé, it was time for her to set off on her first American tour. But even with mounting credentials and popularity, she still lacked one of the necessities for staging full concerts in America: a band. Among the musicians who had played on her records, only John Farrar was available to cross the Atlantic and tour with her, as lead guitarist and musical director.

Olivia had a concert scheduled for May 5, 1974, at the St. Paul Civic Center Theater in Minnesota. She and John went there a couple of weeks in advance to rehearse with local musicians that her agency had hired. The plan was to travel by bus to some smaller towns for shows and then return to St. Paul for the show there. But after an eight-hour rehearsal, it became clear to John and Olivia that these musicians couldn't come close to duplicating the sounds on her records (which, after all, featured some of the top musicians in England). Farrar called the local musicians' union and inquired about who else might be available.

An organ/keyboard player (and flutist) named Robyn Lee, who was the same age as Olivia and a graduate of the University of North Dakota, showed up with his friend and bandmate, guitarist Dale Strength. Lee, who despite Olivia's major success in the States over the past few months had never heard of her, played and was offered the job, but he didn't want to leave his band, a quintet with the stylized name thisOneness. But when Olivia noticed that Strength was wearing cowboy boots, she asked him, "Do you play country?"

The group was not a country band. "We were street rock kids," said the band's drummer, Bernie Pershey, "and our ears were exploding with new influences like Chick Corea, John McLaughlin, Larry Coryell, Freddie Hubbard, [and] Weather Report," all of whom were jazz or jazz fusion musicians. "We were too rocky for the jazz clubs and too jazzy for the rock clubs," according to pianist Gregg Inhofer. But Dale's father was Texas Bill Strength, a country music singer-songwriter and (later) inductee into the Country Music DJ Hall of Fame. He told her that he could play country music, and the rest of the band (Pershey, Inhofer, and bassist Doug Nelson) soon showed up. They listened to her records and, with some help from John Farrar, learned the songs in one night. They learned the backup vocal parts too. Robyn Lee would sing the bass parts that Mike Sammes had sung on the records. Olivia and Farrar offered thisOneness the job. Later that year, Olivia told the Associated Press (AP) music journalist Mary Campbell that "they [thisOneness] play everything; they can play country, and they can play jazz."

The band, after just one all-night rehearsal with Olivia and John, joined them on a Greyhound bus—without a working bathroom—bound for what, Lee recalled, they thought might well be their only show with her, her first full American concert at the Frost Arena at South Dakota State University in Brookings on April 24. But Olivia was thrilled with how well the concert went, and thisOneness would be her band for live performances in America for about a year and a half. It would be quite an experience for the band. "I'm from Leeds, North Dakota. If I played in front of 100 people, I was lucky," Lee told a journalist in 2023. "With Olivia, we played in front of 54,000 at the Houston Astrodome. We played at the Hollywood Bowl in LA, the Red Rocks Amphitheater in Denver, at Radio City Music Hall in New York." They also performed live with her on NBC-TV's popular weekly concert show, *The Midnight Special*, in February 1975.

For the first few weeks of her first American tour, Olivia stuck to the "heartland"—away from the coasts—and mostly played on college campuses. Before she and the band returned to St. Paul, they played at two more colleges, the University of Tennessee at Martin (UTM) and Quincy College in Illinois. Her next two concerts after St. Paul were also at colleges.

At least two newspapers reviewed Olivia's UTM concert: the Clarksville *Leaf-Chronicle* and the campus newspaper, the *Pacer*. The reviewer for the *Pacer*, Larry Rhodes, expressed a bit of skepticism at the beginning of his review, noting that "country female singers aren't rare. But they seldom come from England or speak with an Australian accent." Olivia's show won him over, though, for he wrote, "Nevertheless, her concert at UTM… proved that country is only one of many facets of this fine vocalist." *Leaf-Chronicle* critic Richard McFalls praised Olivia's "hauntingly beautiful renditions of 'Love Song' ('my favorite song of all time,' she said) and 'If,'" noting that they "mesmerized the crowd," which was "a wildly appreciative audience of over 1,000."

Both reviews noted that Olivia seemed inexperienced at putting on concerts, pointing out that she started the show with "Let Me Be There," which, with "If You Love Me (Let Me Know)" still climbing the charts, was her biggest hit at the time. Then when, to her apparent surprise, the audience called her out for an encore, she told them, "You are all fantastic! I'll have to repeat another song. Is 'Let Me Be There' alright?" By then, enthusiastic fans had "flocked to the front of the stage," and they demanded another encore (apparently another repeated song, although neither review notes which) after that. Olivia admitted to reporters after the show that this type of concert was different than what she was used to doing in nightclubs in England. "The atmosphere is a little different in colleges than in the clubs, and I like it better. College audiences seem to be more listening audiences."

Olivia seemed to be coming to the realization that the United States would offer her a better career than would Great Britain.

Having won a Grammy Award in a country category and the "newcomer" award from the Academy of Country Music, Olivia seemed to be aware of skepticism or even resentment from some country music purists. She told McFalls, "The Grammy Award, I believe, is for best performance on a country-western record. I don't think it has anything to do with where you were born as to how you perform on a song."

That brewing controversy, the question of whether an English/Australian singer deserved to be considered a bona fide country artist—as absurd as it seems with half a century of hindsight—was nevertheless a mounting one for Olivia. When MCA Records released her third American album, *If You Love Me Let Me Know*, on May 28, it soon became her second number one album on the *Billboard* country chart. Indicative of her crossover appeal, it also became her first number one album on the pop chart. Tony Brown, who was working with one of the original pop/country crossover stars (Elvis Presley) at this time, and later produced records for Olivia and Lionel Richie but also for a long list of country stars such as George Strait and Reba McEntire, says today that he "always considered her [Olivia] kind of like John Denver, a contemporary country artist in my opinion."

Olivia and Denver, who became friends, would soon both discover that some of the country traditionalists of the mid-1970s didn't take as broad-minded a view of them as Brown did. Longtime Nashville music journalist Francis "Red" O'Donnell, who in 2019 would be posthumously inducted into the Tennessee Journalism Hall of Fame, wrote an article about a luncheon that country music legend Owen Bradley, who was the head of MCA's Nashville division, held for Olivia on her first visit to the "Music City" in August 1974. O'Donnell noted her major success in the country field over the past nine months, the two million-selling singles, and the Grammy, but he also seemed a bit puzzled or piqued: "Frankly, I always considered her to be a pop singer."

4 ODE TO OLIVIA

"Olivia Newton-John, where do your loyalties lie?" wrote music journalist John Beattie. "Are you becoming a little ole country girl, or is it the pop field?" The article was dated July 6, 1974, but it didn't appear in the Nashville *Tennessean* or *Billboard* or *Cash Box*; instead, the question was posed in Great Britain's *Record Mirror*. Olivia had returned briefly to London in June to record some new tracks at Abbey Road for her third British album (and first to be released on the EMI label there), *Long Live Love*. This also meant that she was in England for the BBC-TV premiere of her own four-episode miniseries, *Moods of Love*, which she had taped earlier in the year.

"Well, in America," she told Beattie, "I'm in a fortunate position because I'm considered a country crossover act, which means that I'm accepted by both country and pop. It's fantastic…. I've got to keep going along as I am—not completely country and not all pop either."

Long Live Love included six of the ten songs that had already been released on the American *If You Love Me Let Me Know* album, plus six additional songs. Among the songs that appeared on both albums were a cover version of the Beach Boys' "God Only Knows" and a song that, though not written for Olivia, she was the first to record and release. The song was called "I Honestly Love You," listed on the first MCA pressings of the album as "I Love You, I Honestly Love You."

"I Honestly Love You" reached Olivia and John Farrar, who produced the record, via a demo sent to them in the mail by the song's publisher. Jeff Barry and Peter Allen wrote it. Barry had been one of the most successful songwriters at Don Kirshner's famed New York City Brill Building complex in the 1960s ("Da Doo Ron Ron," "Do Wah Diddy Diddy," and "Leader of the Pack" were among his cowritten songs). Peter Allen, whose life and career became the basis for the stage musical and the movie *The Boy from Oz*, would later cowrite smash hits such as Melissa Manchester's "Don't Cry Out Loud" and Christopher Cross's "Arthur's Theme (Best That You Can Do)," which won an Academy Award for Best Original

Song of 1981. (Allen came up with the latter song's chorus line, "When you get caught between the moon and New York City" while waiting for an airplane that he was on, which was in a holding pattern, to land at the John F. Kennedy Airport in New York City.)

Neither Barry nor Allen had had Olivia in mind as a potential recording artist for "I Honestly Love You." "I had this idea for a song I thought would be great for a man to sing," Barry said of the song's genesis. Allen certainly didn't think it would be a hit for her. "When Olivia told me she was going to put it out as a single, I begged her not to," he told Australian music journalist Glenn A. Baker in 1988. "I said, 'Don't be crazy, it will be the end of your career. It doesn't even have a drum on it!'" Barry recalled that MCA didn't even want to release it as a single, but "radio demanded it."

Olivia felt differently. "I flipped out when I heard it," she told an interviewer for *Billboard*. "I was terrified that I would find out it had already been done." Allen had, in fact, planned on recording and releasing the song himself, but he held off to make way for Olivia and didn't put out his own version until 1975. The song would remain a favorite of Olivia's throughout the ensuing decades. John Farrar said, twenty-five years after she first recorded it (and one year after she recorded it again with a different arrangement), "I think that meant a lot to her, that song." When Olivia appeared on *The Rachael Ray Show* in 2008, she told Rachael that "I Honestly Love You" was still her "very favorite song" from her catalog.

MCA released "I Honestly Love You" as a single in North America on August 10, 1974. By then, Olivia had resumed touring in the States. She performed as the opening act for Charlie Rich at the Las Vegas Hilton for two weeks in July; it was both performers' Vegas debut, booked as a replacement after Elvis Presley canceled a scheduled engagement there. Later in the month, she shared the bill with the Smothers Brothers for two nights at the Greek Theatre in Los Angeles. Then she and the band got back on the bus to tour fairgrounds and amusement parks, mostly in the South and the Midwest.

"It was great," Bernie Pershey said of his year and a half of touring as Olivia's drummer.

> Because she was being marketed country, we did a lot of Midwest fair shows with bands like Charlie Rich, Porter Wagoner, Tammy Wynette. It was good to get to see how really good country musicians play. And it was the first time meeting people from all over the country—from Miami to Texas to Los Angeles. Eyes got opened to other elements of culture.

Members of thisOneness also recalled the fun atmosphere of touring with Olivia and the sense that she and the band became almost like a family, which would be common themes among musicians who toured with her in later years as well. Pershey told journalist Jon Bream that during downtime they would sometimes go horse riding with her, and he recalled a funny story from when they were on tour in the Southwest.

Once in a while Olivia would make what she called a Dingo cocktail, half champagne and half orange juice. One day while she and the band were traveling on the bus, she had a stiff Dingo or two, and then she picked up the CB radio and started singing something like "Nobody wants to play rhythm guitar behind Jesus / Everybody wants to be the leader of the band." When she told a trucker who heard her who she was, he didn't believe her. She replied that he could see for himself by pulling into a truck stop down the road.

He did, and so did many others. "There were over one hundred truckers there; she didn't realize she was speaking on an open channel," Pershey recalled. "So she sat there and dutifully signed cowboy hats and stuff. I remember the steamed look on the road manager's face because of how far off schedule we were from that incident. She was a nice person."

Pianist Gregg Inhofer described Olivia as being "as sweet as her image." In 1975 she gave him a digital watch—a fairly new and trendy item at the time—with the inscription "I dishonestly love you." In later decades, he and Olivia would keep in touch via text messaging, and he would come see her whenever she performed at theaters and casinos in Minnesota. He has held on to the watch.

The band gave Olivia and John Farrar, inadvertently, a different sort of gift. In explaining what inspired him to write "Have You Never Been Mellow," which became the title track of Olivia's next album, Farrar said, years later, "I remember being on a tour with her in America; all the guys in the band were using 'mellow' as their favorite word." What Farrar was recalling was how Robyn Lee's bandmates would often say to him, "Mellow out, Robyn!" when he became too intense about his work. The guys in the band explained to Farrar how Americans used "mellow" as a verb, and that became his inspiration when he soon found himself "just desperately trying to come up with a song I hoped Olivia liked."

In September 1974, Olivia returned to England to record that next album. "I Honestly Love You" kept climbing the US charts during her absence. It reached No. 1 on the Hot 100 on October 5, three weeks after it had already done so on the adult contemporary singles chart. It peaked at No. 6 on the country singles chart, although on the country chart of one of *Billboard*'s chief competitors, *Record World*, it reached No. 1 on November 2. It also became her third-straight gold (which then meant million-selling) single in the States. "I Honestly Love You" also became a No. 1 hit in Canada, Australia, and Sweden.

In addition to recording sessions at Abbey Road Studios and a three-day vacation in Spain, Olivia made an appearance on an episode of *It's Cliff Richard*.

She sang "I Honestly Love You," which had just been released in Great Britain, too, and she and Cliff sang two duets, "I'm Leaving It Up to You," a 1963 US number one hit by Dale & Grace which Donny and Marie Osmond had just revived as a big international hit, and the oft-covered Everly Brothers classic hit "All I Have to Do Is Dream." (Olivia would later work, closely and for a long time, with Dane Bryant, whose parents, Felice and Boudleaux Bryant, wrote that song.)

Meanwhile, the pointless and rather silly brouhaha about whether or not Olivia was a "real" country singer continued to escalate in the United States, particularly in Nashville. Another journalist for the *Tennessean*, Jerry Bailey, reported in the edition of September 17 that "Olivia Newton-John, an Australian vocalist who couldn't drawl with a mouth full of biscuits, has a good shot at becoming the Country Music Association's most lauded singer this year." Bailey added that Olivia "ties with veteran entertainer Charlie Rich," who obviously felt that Olivia was enough of a country singer to open for him in Las Vegas and at other concerts, for nominations in the most categories (four). Rich had given her an early birthday gift, a heart-shaped pendant with her birthstone, an opal, in the center of the heart.

By this point, the British press was well aware that Olivia's records were being better received in the United States than in the United Kingdom. "Olivia Newton-John, who has Cambridge connections, is hot property on the pop music scene in the United States, where she is also recognized as a top country-and-western singer," noted the *Cambridge Evening News*. "Expect her latest single, 'I Honestly Love You,' to soar to the top of the American charts… but will it achieve similar success in this country?"

British reporters were also frequently asking her if she'd be moving away from her native country (she'd been away for almost half of 1974 to that point) to become a resident of the United States. "There's so much work out there, and my records are selling so well, that I'm seriously thinking of going to live there," she told a reporter, adding, "[but] I love London." The fact that "I Honestly Love You" reached only No. 22 on the British charts, in October, could only have served as a further nudge to move to America full time.

She certainly had not forgotten about Australia, as she made clear in a number of interviews in 1974. "I could easily live in Australia," she told a reporter for *Record Mirror* in January. "The climate is so much better [than in England], and Australians are much more open and forthcoming than people here." But an article published in Australia's *TV Week* at the end of March reported that Olivia "has told friends that she considers America the real 'big time,'" and quoted her as saying, "My career did not get going until I left Australia." In another interview for *Record Mirror* in July, she said, "I like going back to Australia each year but it's the long plane journey. I feel like a gypsy nowadays and sometimes I wish I could just sit down and put my feet up more often—then again, I'm fortunate to be in the position I'm in I reckon." It was becoming clear that America offered her the career she wanted, and the comparative lack of success of her recent records in Great Britain further underscored the point.

More evidence of her superstar status in the United States came on October 14, when the Country Music Association held its annual awards ceremony in Nashville. Presenters Roy Acuff and Chet Atkins made what the *Tennessean* would call "the surprising announcement that newcomer Olivia Newton-John is the Female Vocalist of the Year winner." Her first name, one writer noted, was "botched during the ceremony [by Acuff, who said '*Oliver* Newton-John'] and it almost seemed a little bit intentional." Olivia accepted the award via a videotaped message from London, in which she told those gathered at the CMA ceremony (and those watching on TV), "It's a long way from London to Nashville, but I'd like to take this opportunity to say a big hello to all the friends I made on my last visit there. And I hope to see you all soon when I fulfill an ambition of mine to record an album in your hometown."

Her implicit praise for Nashville did nothing to douse the firestorm of controversy that followed. Press criticism was fairly mild. The *Charlotte Observer* said that Olivia and Ronnie Milsap were "good choices" for vocalists of the year, yet added that Olivia's albums were "not true country" and that her selection as the CMA Female Vocalist of the Year was "surprising" given that she was a relative newcomer to the field. "The fault was with the voters," wrote columnist Harry Morrow.

The sharpest backlash, by far, came from some established country music stars. On November 13, 1974, the *Tennessean* published an article by Jerry Bailey, the writer who had made the derogatory remark about Olivia in September, about the formation of a new group that was meant to be a rival to the CMA. "About 50 prominent country music singers voted to unite into a new organization last night and formed a screening committee to verify qualifications of new members," wrote Bailey. "Meeting at the home of George Jones and Tammy Wynette, the artists dubbed themselves the Association of Country Entertainers (ACE)." An attorney retained by ACE told Bailey that membership would be restricted to individuals who "basically make their living in country music as a country music entertainer."

"Much of the current controversy," Bailey added, "erupted around this year's CMA awards show [on] Oct. 14. In 'street talk' on Music Row, many of the award winners without strong country roots were critically attacked." Olivia, Bailey noted, "is the victim of many of the complaints, though she is far from being alone." ACE's lawyer "refused to speculate" as to whether Olivia would be allowed to join the organization. "That will be up to the screening committee." (There is no evidence to suggest that she ever tried to join ACE.) Among the country stars that joined Jones and Wynette in the new organization were Bill Anderson, Johnny Cash, Merle Haggard, Brenda Lee, Barbara Mandrell, Dolly Parton, Johnny Paycheck,

Hank Snow, Mel Tillis, Conway Twitty, Porter Wagoner, Billy Walker, Dottie West, and Faron Young.

"Our gripe, if we have one, is that these people want to come in and take our music away," Anderson told the Associated Press, adding that he was referring to artists, presumably including Olivia, "not willing to stand up and say, 'I am a country artist.'" Walker complained, "These people came in and prostituted our business and watered down our music. This was done by big money on the East and West Coast." When Nashville-based journalist and broadcaster Bill Williams suggested that crossover artists such as Olivia and John Denver were actually "bringing new fans into country music," Paycheck retorted, "If there's any justification or truth in what he said, then I don't care to be a part of it."

It took a while for Olivia to learn of the controversy that her CMA Award had sparked. "I heard there was a lot of resentment down there [in Nashville] to her," John Farrar said years later. "But we were in England and sort of isolated from it at the time." She heard more about it after she went back to the United States two months later. She would later express much the same opinion as Williams, telling Associated Press music journalist Peter J. Boyer in 1977, "My music's opened the doors for a lot of people who've never listened to country before.... They're now listening to standard type country singers." She also told another writer that "I was hurt a little bit in the beginning" when she learned about the backlash.

Nevertheless, the backlash by the country traditionalists against the newcomers seemed to continue and find a new target at the 1975 CMA Awards show, when the association named John Denver the winner of its Entertainer of the Year Award. After presenter Charlie Rich opened the envelope and saw Denver's name on the slip inside, he set the envelope on fire with his cigarette lighter. Charlie Rich Jr. later suggested that his father was feeling the effects of alcohol and painkillers at the time, but many who were watching viewed it as an unsubtle expression of Rich's opinion of the CMA giving Denver the award. His son's explanation seems plausible, though, given that Rich had seemed glad enough to have Olivia tour with him in 1974 and that his own eclectic brand of music often didn't fit the traditional country mold. Nor did he get involved with ACE. "I know the last thing my father would have wanted to do," Rich Jr. said, "was set himself up as judge of another musician." Waylon Jennings chimed in sarcastically in a way that left no doubt, though: "John Denver won Entertainer of the Year... now that's what I call country."

According to Oxford University Press's *Encyclopedia of Country Music* (2012), the country artists "most active in ACE were all connected with the Grand Ole Opry." Many of the twenty names that the author of the entry on ACE, Paul W. Soelberg, mentioned among that group would be known today only by knowledgeable fans of country music from fifty years or more ago. ACE disbanded in September 1981—by which point Olivia had moved far from the country field except for performing her early to mid-1970s hits in concert—and according to Soelberg, the organization "never had adequate funding" to accomplish much.

It should be noted that while Dolly Parton was involved in the founding of ACE, she did not get particularly involved and, moreover, she offered her support to Olivia immediately. Mark Beckett, who began playing drums in the Grand Ole Opry's Opry Band in 2009 and joined Olivia's band two years later, remembers Olivia saying that at the time of the CMA controversy, Dolly was "one of, if not the only one," among the Nashville country stars "that was nice to her." Dane Bryant, who worked with Olivia on and off from 1995 until the end and produced her last recording—her and Dolly's duet of "Jolene"—recalls that when Olivia won the CMA Award, "Nashville was still not very welcoming to outsiders, as they put it, *except* for Dolly and Loretta [Lynn], and Dolly took her to dinner" not long after that.

Soon Dolly's younger sister, Stella, offered Olivia a very clear public expression of support. Stella was in the process of writing songs for her debut solo album, the 1975 release *I Want to Hold You in My Dreams Tonight*. Amid the ruffled feathers around her in Nashville following Olivia's CMA Award, Stella and her producer, Bob G. Dean, wrote a song called "Ode to Olivia." It began with the line "We ain't got the right to say you're not country" and essentially apologized to Olivia for the Nashville establishment's treatment of her while also cleverly working in or referencing the titles of Olivia's songs "You Ain't Got the Right," "Let Me Be There," "Have You Never Been Mellow," and "I Honestly Love You."

"I was a huge fan of her music during that time and continued to be for the rest of her career. And I was upset that the Country Music Association was so disappointed that someone in Nashville didn't win the award when she had more chart action that any of the other females in country music at the time," she says today. "And so I just wrote a song to kind of reprimand the CMA," she laughs, "for allowing that to even be an issue. But it probably wasn't necessarily the association itself; it was more the artists that got disgruntled…. It [the song] was just a little rebuttal to the industry, like, 'Really, guys? You guys are stupid, you know, really?'" Stella thought the backlash against Olivia was "really ugly behavior."

In writing, recording, and releasing "Ode to Olivia" (both on her debut album and as the B-side to the title track as a single), "I was just trying to say, 'Olivia, some of us love you a lot, and some of us love your music,'" she reflects. "And I just felt bad, because I know what it feels like to be an underdog, and an outcast, and I didn't want her to feel that way." When Stella played the song for Dolly, Dolly told her, "Don't let Porter [Wagoner] hear that." "I said, 'He can piss off. I don't care what he thinks!' And that's still what I think."

Stella's album sold fairly well, and "I Want to Hold You in My Dreams Tonight" made the Top 10 on the *Billboard* Hot Country Singles chart. Even though "Ode to Olivia" was the B-side, it got some airplay as well as notice in *Billboard*. "Flames of controversy of the past may be fanned again with [the] release of a song by Stella Parton, sister of singer Dolly Parton, called 'Ode to Olivia.' The song, directed toward Olivia Newton-John, is an out and out tribute to her," noted a brief article in the April 12, 1975, issue. "Miss Newton-John, who is scheduled for a concert here [Nashville] in the near future, was the subject of some criticism by individuals in country music recently when she swept most country music awards [which might have been a reference to her Grammy as well as the CMA Award]." "Miss Parton," the article added, "takes the other stand: that she is not only welcome, but a refreshing breeze in the country field."

When Olivia heard the song, she called Stella and told her how much she appreciated it. "She asked for copies to send to her family, which I was honored to do," Stella recalls. The two became friends for the rest of Olivia's life. "Anytime she was in Nashville, she would always request my presence…. We were always very kind and caring of one another." During the Covid-19 pandemic, Stella began doing a podcast, and Olivia called her and told her "that she wanted to be on it so she could publicly thank me again, 'cause I think she knew she was not, you know, gonna make it, and she had wanted to again reiterate how much that meant to her. And it was very touching that she would do that."

Stella began to cry recalling the podcast itself. "I tried to keep it lighthearted, but my heart was breaking that she would make such an effort while not well. But it was so… that was just what she was about, who she was as a person. And so I was very touched by that and cherished that interview with her." It was the last time they ever spoke. Stella managed to laugh recalling something that she learned: "I didn't know this, but she had, her dog that she loved very much, she named Stella. And I thought that was the sweetest thing. I thought, 'Oh! Well, how sweet is that?' So, she could say my name every day. I loved it."

"If I'd ever met an earth angel, I would say that Olivia Newton-John was one of those. She was definitely an earth angel in every sense of the word, her looks as well as her demeanor," Stella says of her friend of nearly half a century. "She just had that spirit of goodness in her, and so to me she will always be an earth angel. She was just a sweet, sweet angel, and that was how I will always remember her. What a blessing to have known her and her gentle soul."

5 COME ON OVER

"The one thing that I found in England was that I had to work much harder than in Australia," Olivia told a reporter in August 1975. "In Australia, the competition wasn't that tough, so you didn't have to work hard. But in England, the competition was very stiff, and I had to be quite strict with myself." But as Olivia returned to the United States in December 1974 to appear in a Bob Hope holiday TV special and *Dick Clark's Rockin' New Year's Eve*, she realized that it was now time to make America her home base if she wanted to maximize her career opportunities there. In February 1975, *People Weekly* reported that Olivia "rents a Malibu beach house [in the neighborhood of Trancas] with Lee [Kramer] but protectively maintains her flat in London, with the furniture under dust covers." She also bought a brand-new Volkswagen Beetle convertible.

Her return to California—this time as a more-or-less full-time resident for the remainder of her life—coincided with the release of a new album. MCA Records released *Have You Never Been Mellow*, Olivia's third North American album, on February 12, 1975. In addition to the title track, John Farrar contributed another original song, written with his bandmate Hank Marvin, an upbeat, bouncy number titled "It's So Easy," which featured Mike Sammes's trademark bass vocal backing. (This was two years before Linda Ronstadt revived the Buddy Holly song with the same title.) The album's cover versions included two John Denver songs; a gentle, country-tinged ballad that her MCA labelmate Rick Nelson had recently written and recorded ("Lifestream"); and the Albert Hammond/Hollies classic "The Air That I Breathe." The album also featured a cover of a country song so few people had heard that almost everyone thought it was an original. Bruce Welch and John Rostill wrote "Please Mr. Please," which used the classic country song motif of a breakup and a jukebox, shortly before Rostill passed away. Welch recorded it and released it as a single on EMI Records in Great Britain in 1974, but disc jockeys and record buyers alike overlooked it.

In the summer of 1974, Olivia had told interviewer Mary Campbell that she preferred recording to touring. "I like recording best. I think I like it best because it means I can sing a lot," she said. "Usually, I go in in the afternoon and work through until I finish. It could be one in the morning. Sometimes there are days when I sing six or seven good tracks in the same day. Another day I can only get through one or two. It all depends." She knew that touring was necessary, but she wasn't crazy about it. "I don't want to be on the road forever. I want to be able to get in a position where I can work so many weeks and be off so many weeks."

Nevertheless, Olivia embarked on an American tour interspersed with TV appearances, including *The Midnight Special* and Johnny Carson's *Tonight Show*, each of which she had also performed on in 1974. Her schedule kept her from appearing on the Grammy Awards show in Manhattan on March 1, 1975, which turned out to be unfortunate as she won two awards: Record of the Year and Best Pop Vocal Performance, Female, both for "I Honestly Love You." She and Anne Murray became, at the same time, the first two women to win a Grammy in pop as well as country categories, a feat that wouldn't be duplicated until much later by Taylor Swift and Kacey Musgraves.

News of Olivia's Grammy wins quickly reached Australia, where a reporter contacted her father for a comment. Brinley Newton-John, who had retired the year before from the University of Newcastle and had been awarded Emeritus Professor status, said that he was "tickled pink" and that Olivia had succeeded in an endeavor in which he had not. "I trained as a singer myself once," he told the journalist, "but I gave it up and went back to the academic life again. The competition was too tough." The brief newspaper article didn't indicate how much he listened to Olivia's records, although it did say that he "spend[s] at least three uninterrupted hours a day listening to Wagner, Verdi, and Strauss."

The recognition from the industry continued to be matched by commercial success; the new album sold half a million copies in the United States in its first two weeks, and the title track became a number one hit on the pop and adult contemporary charts and reached No. 3 on the country chart. Yet on top of the backlash from traditional country music artists (which, one suspects, derived from envy and fear that the country field was changing), pop and rock music critics didn't give her much respect either. Robert Hilburn, a well-known *Los Angeles Times* scribe, wrote in the summer of 1974 that "while her voice is capable of a bit more range and emotion than is shown on the hit singles, her arrangements are so simple, fluffy and virtually Muzak that she is never really challenged…. The music, I'm afraid, consistently seems to take second place to her own 'cuteness.'" Robert Christgau, the influential and self-proclaimed "dean of American rock critics," reviewed the *Have You Never Been Mellow* album and gave it a D+.

Even some fellow pop recording artists piled on. Singer-songwriter Randy Newman, who would become best known for his 1977 novelty hit "Short People," told an interviewer that he couldn't understand how some records became hits: "Olivia Newton-John, for instance. Good Christ, what is that all about? For the life of me, I can't understand the vast appeal of a song like 'I Honestly Love You.' I mean, it's *boring*, even." When Ben Fong-Torres relayed that statement to Olivia, she replied, in a tone that he described as both hurt and firm, "Well, obviously if I thought there was some truth in that, it would upset me. I actually believe 'I Honestly Love You' is a great song. Whether he likes the way I sing it or not, that's his personal taste."

She also suggested to Fong-Torres that she wasn't particularly interested in what the so-called expert critics thought of her hit albums and singles. "It annoys me when people think [that] because it's commercial, it's bad," she told him. "It's completely opposite: if it's commercial, people like it, and that's what it's all supposed to be about."

Furthermore, she told him that she resented it when critics insinuated that her success stemmed more from her beauty than her talent (a perception that, to the degree it existed, was hardly helped by some of her record label's promotional materials). "I find the whole question embarrassing. I don't think of myself as pretty—that sounds maybe stupid, but I mean, if someone said to you, 'Do you think you're successful because you're handsome?' would you feel uncomfortable? It's half a compliment and it isn't," she said. "The one great thrill I had in America was that my music was accepted before I was ever seen, before I was on television, before I did live appearances; therefore, I had to hope it was my music and not my face, you know?"

Regardless of what the critics thought of her records and her success, the awards kept coming as quickly as the hits. At around the same time that she won the two Grammy Awards for "I Honestly Love You," she also won a People's Choice Award for Favorite Female Artist (she would win another of those in 1977 and yet another in 1979) and four American Music Awards, for Favorite Pop/Rock Female Artist, Favorite Pop/Rock Song ("I Honestly Love You"), Favorite Country Female Artist, and Favorite Country Album (*Let Me Be There*). When Johnny Carson rattled off her list of awards on his show, she laughed, put her head in her hand and said, "It's embarrassing!" She had also won awards from all three of the major US record industry publications (*Billboard*, *Cash Box*, and *Record World*). She told longtime syndicated Hollywood columnist Marilyn Beck, "Earning so many [awards] does make me feel a bit guilty—but not guilty enough to turn any back."

Her choice of the word "earning" was sincere. "I'm not a manufactured person who's been made by these moguls.... I've read in lots of articles that they think, obviously, some clever businessman has given her this song and done these things," she would say in an interview in 1978. "*I* have done it. With help from other people.

But it's a career that's taken me ten years. It isn't an overnight sensation, and I like what I'm doing… and I believe in what I'm doing."

Peter Gormley, one mogul whom Olivia credited for helping get her career off the ground, willingly stepped aside when she chose to live in and concentrate on performing in the United States. He still wasn't interested in leaving London, and he still had Cliff Richard as his client. Lee Kramer became her full-time manager. By February 1975, Olivia felt comfortable enough to refer to Lee as "my guy" in an interview with *People* journalist Robert Windeler, but she was still tight-lipped about her personal life when Johnny Carson raised that subject on his show a few weeks later.

In an interview not long after her appearance on Carson's show, Olivia explained why she wouldn't open up to him (and his vast national television audience) about such matters. "I'm old-fashioned, I guess," she said. "That's one phase of my life I like to keep private. I never discuss my sex life or personal relationships with other people. There's so very little of your life that is private; what you do have, you keep protected."

In March 1975, Olivia bolstered her band by adding an acoustic guitarist and background singer named Skip Griparis. From 1972 until the end of 1974, Skip had been playing guitar and singing lead vocals in the soft rock band New Colony Six, which had racked up ten Hot 100 hits beginning in 1966. By the end of 1974, the hits had dried up and the band, for the time being, called it quits. When Bernie Pershey, an old friend of his from Joliet, Illinois, called Skip and asked him if he'd be interested in joining a backing band, Skip had doubts at first. "I had just ended what I thought was going to be my last band ever," he recalls. "I was just sick of it all—until he said it was [for] Olivia Newton-John, and then, 'Okay, alright. Yep, I'm in!'"

Skip joined the band about five days after he got the phone call, and he met Olivia during a sound check in Little Rock, Arkansas. "I got a lot of help from John Farrar," he notes, as did many other of Olivia's guitarists through the years. "Sometimes he would tour with us, and he would teach me all the [acoustic guitar] parts that he'd played on the recordings." Skip had to do a lot of fingerpicking for Olivia's show, to the point that he sprained a finger learning the songs. He used high-strung tuning (also called "Nashville tuning") on his acoustic Ovation, with four lighter-gauge strings tuned an octave above normal, crucial for playing country songs like "Please Mr. Please." Skip would spend nearly the next four years playing and singing in Olivia's live band.

One of Skip's first shows with Olivia was in Nashville, where, after her first visit the previous summer, she took the concert stage for the first time on March 23, 1975, to what the *Tennessean* reported was "a full Municipal Auditorium." Her opening act was Billy Joel, who at that time was known primarily for "Piano Man." Reporter Lynn Harvey couldn't resist taking a swipe at Olivia's country credentials in her review of the concert, writing that "Olivia danced her way through songs such as the old Beatles nostalgia sound of 'Honey Pie' on her way from steel-guitar backed renditions of her 'country' hits to what could have been a stirring finale."

Harvey's only problem with the finale, however, did not concern Olivia's performance of the song she chose, "I Honestly Love You," but rather the "waves of wolf whistles and yells of 'I love you, too' emanating from the evidently too-young audience." "It was," Harvey concluded, "a disappointing ending to an otherwise pleasant evening," as she found both Olivia's and Joel's performances to be strong.

Another reporter named Harvey—this time Peter Harvey of England's *Record Mirror*—caught up with Olivia a few days later during a weeklong, two-shows-per-night engagement at the Diplomat Hotel in Hollywood, Florida. "It is a bit strenuous playing two really full gigs every night," she told him, "but it's fabulous to be here. The Americans treat me really well. Honestly, I get incredible treatment— I'll probably find it hard to readjust when I get back." The article made it clear, though, that she meant getting back to visit and record her next album. "Shadows man John Farrar," Harvey reported, "and his wife [Pat] are on an extended stay in the States so that John—Livvie's producer—can help her choose songs." Harvey wrote that "the volume of work [for her in America] makes it virtually impossible for her to return to England" as a resident.

Left unsaid in the article, although it was certainly implied, was how Olivia's success in the United States had by this point considerably surpassed her success in her native country. The reception that radio stations and record buyers in each of the two countries accorded her next single further widened the gap. In the States, "Please Mr. Please" became her fifth consecutive million seller, a tragic hit (given the premature death of one of its writers, John Rostill) as well as an ironic one (for its other writer, Bruce Welch, it was inspired by his breakup with Olivia). Like Olivia's other American hits, it also proved to be a big crossover hit, Top 5 on the pop and country charts and No. 1 on the adult contemporary chart in the summer of 1975. In the United Kingdom, EMI Records passed on "Please Mr. Please" as a single and released her cover of John Denver's "Follow Me" instead. It only reached No. 57 on the UK singles chart.

None of her million sellers in the United States from 1973 to 1975 did very well in the United Kingdom. "I Honestly Love You" didn't quite reach the British Top 20, "If You Love Me (Let Me Know)" stalled outside the Top 50, and both "Let Me Be There" and "Have You Never Been Mellow" missed the singles chart altogether. "Long Live Love," not released as a single in America, was her biggest British hit of this period, and it peaked just outside the Top 10. Whereas the album *Have You Never Been Mellow* topped the US chart, it only reached No. 37 in the United Kingdom. Her success in Australia during the same time frame came much closer to matching her success in the States, but "Please Mr. Please" was an exception, only reaching No. 35 on the Australian chart. Her strongest market was Canada, where she racked up three straight No. 1's with "I Honestly Love You," "Have You Never Been Mellow," and "Please Mr. Please."

Nevertheless, and despite her taped message for the CMA Awards show in which she had said she looked forward to recording an album in Nashville, she still wasn't ready to break away from London as her recording base. On May 24, 1975, the London *Daily Mirror* published a photo of a broadly smiling Olivia upon her arrival at Heathrow Airport from LAX, with the headline "Olivia's Return" underneath. The article reported that it was her first time back in England in six months. "It's a wonderful feeling to be back," she told the press. "I really miss London." She would only be staying, the article reported, for ten days, though, to record her next album and to promote the "Follow Me" single.

Before she went back to the United States, journalist Geoff Barton interviewed Olivia for *Sounds*, a weekly pop/rock music newspaper. In the article that featured the interview, he noted that she'd had two Top 10 hits in Britain in 1971 but that "she has never equaled that success since." Barton pressed her for her thoughts on why her subsequent records hadn't caught on in Britain like they had in the States.

"I don't think that my music was taken all that seriously" in Britain, she told him, "and perhaps it was a case of releasing the wrong songs at the wrong time, there's an awful lot of that involved." "I really don't know," she added. "I don't think you can ever say why. If I knew why then I'd be able to have number ones all the time. It might be the wrong songs, it might be the wrong sound or timing… I just don't know."

When Barton asked her if she had any plans for a concert tour in Britain, she "bluntly" replied, "No, not at the moment. There's not much point until I have some record success, otherwise no one will come." He then asked her if she hoped that "Follow Me" would give her another British hit. Her reply suggested that she had lost confidence when it came to the British market. "I'd love it to happen," she told him.

> I'm not always this pessimistic, but I don't have great hopes, because I've really had bad luck with the songs I've really wanted to be hits. "Have You Never Been Mellow" and "I Honestly Love You" I really believed in as songs. In America they happened and here they didn't, so I don't know. But I'd really love it to happen. Maybe it will. If I'm not too conscious of it, maybe it'll happen.

The single's failure to crack the Top 50 could hardly have bolstered her confidence in her career prospects in the United Kingdom; nor could the "thumbs-down" review it received from *Record Mirror*.

Given Barton's line of questioning, it was hardly surprising when he asked Olivia if she had now become a resident of the United States. "Yeah," she told him.

All my work is there at the moment, so I don't see any point in commuting. It was much simpler to pack my bags and move places, I couldn't keep two homes going. I've given up my residency in Britain now, so I'm only allowed back three weeks a year, which isn't long. But I still regard Britain as my home country, even though I am Australian.

She obviously still felt attached to Abbey Road Studios as her recording base, even though she and John Farrar would both recall that Studio No. 3 had barely proven large enough to record "I Honestly Love You" when they had to fit a string section into the cramped studio. It wasn't just the studio itself that drew her back, though, but some of the English musicians as well. While Bruce Welch didn't play on the new album, others who had played on her previous records did, such as drummer Brian Bennett, bass guitarist Alan Tarney, and guitarist Terry Britten. Aside from Farrar, who also played on this and her earlier albums, she would need a new studio band if she moved her recording sessions to America as she had most of her other career activities and, by now, her residency.

Not only did Bruce Welch not play on or have a hand in producing this album, but he didn't contribute as a songwriter, either. Nor, apparently, were any more leftover songs written by John Rostill available. In an interview for *Radio and Records* in August 1975, weeks before the new album's release, Olivia said that she, Farrar, and Lee Kramer had listened to records and demos and discarded songs they deemed unsuitable until they had whittled the potential track list down to about fifteen. (Years later, though, after her personal and professional relationship with Kramer had ended, she told an interviewer that he hadn't really played a role in choosing her material.)

Farrar wrote two of the eleven songs that made it onto the album, including its first single, "Something Better to Do." Another song, "Slow Down Jackson," was, as Olivia explained in her memoir, an ode by songwriters Michele Brourman and Karen Gottlieb to an Irish setter that a fan had given her after a concert in Jackson, Mississippi, which Olivia then named after that city. Louisville-based folk singer-songwriters Diane Berglund and Jim Phillips, a couple who were married for a time, wrote the album's title track, the ballad "Clearly Love," which built from a gentle lilt to a soaring climax.

As was the case with her previous albums, *Clearly Love* also contained an assortment of cover versions. These included country songs such as "He's My Rock," a version of which by Olivia's MCA labelmate Brenda Lee was in the US country Top 10 around the very time Olivia recorded it, as well as Mickey Newberry's "Lovers" and Linda Hargrove's "Let It Shine." (The latter, according to Farrar, "was something that came in the mail, unsolicited.") Olivia also covered a Hollies hit once again—this time it was "He Ain't Heavy... He's My Brother."

"I think Olivia wanted to do that," Farrar told an interviewer. "We both like it, thought it was a great song."

Olivia raided the late '50s rock-and-roll songbook again, too, by recording the tragic rocker Eddie Cochran's classic "Summertime Blues" for the album. While Olivia's covers of rock-and-roll oldies, such as this one and "Just a Little Too Much," were well produced, played, and sung, she didn't reinvent them like Linda Ronstadt would with her Peter Asher–produced covers of oldies such as "When Will I Be Loved" and "It's So Easy." Olivia told *Radio and Records*, "I don't want to be another Linda Ronstadt. I want to be me." Years later, however, she would enter the studio with Asher in the producer's chair to cover Brenda Lee's 1960 number one hit "I Want to Be Wanted."

One afternoon while Olivia and Lee were in England during May to June 1975, Lee phoned a friend of theirs named Stephen Sinclair. Sinclair, then twenty-three, had been a child star in England and had made records as a child. He came from a family of musicians, but during his teens he entered the fashion industry in London and did very well. (That was how he met Lee, who subsequently introduced him to Olivia.)

During their telephone conversation, Stephen told Lee that he had left the fashion industry and was writing songs. Lee invited him to come to his and Olivia's hotel suite and play him a song. Only Lee was there, but he was sufficiently impressed that he told Stephen, "Hey, that's really good. Come to Abbey Road tonight. Olivia's down there. Play her that song!"

Olivia was impressed, too. She and Lee suggested that he come to California the next week, which was when they would be returning. "We'll put you up at the Sunset Marquis, and we'll take you to MCA and see what they say," they told him. He arrived in Hollywood on June 18, and the next night Lee and Olivia invited him to their house. "We played Scrabble, we had a bite to eat, we hung out," Sinclair recalls. "It was great."

Olivia and Lee were unaware that Sinclair would be coming out to Malibu from his hotel in a taxi. "Just stay over," they told him, "and we'll all go in [to MCA Records in Universal City] tomorrow." He recalls walking on the beach with Lee and Olivia and their dogs the next morning. "It was so movie-like. It was gorgeous… and they had a whole stable of cars, including this beautiful Rolls Royce Silver Shadow, which we took in [to Universal City]." While they were in the car, they heard one of Olivia's records on the radio.

Later the three of them went to the Palm Restaurant on Santa Monica Boulevard in West Hollywood. "At that time," Sinclair recalls, "it was very hot and very new… it was *crazy*. There were photographers and fans, and you couldn't get in the place. It was packed. We kind of sailed in." It was an eye-opening experience for him. "I knew she was popular, but I didn't know what it meant to be really, really big in the United States." Olivia and Lee helped Sinclair get a recording contract with MCA, and Lee signed him as a songwriter to Lee Kramer Music. Over the next four years, Olivia would record three songs that had been written or cowritten by Sinclair. He remains eternally grateful to her. "It was unbelievable. She was great. *She* got me in [into the music business in the United States]. And she loved any success I had. She was really a good friend."

About a week after Sinclair arrived in California, Olivia (and Lee) hit the road again with thisOneness. (During their performances as Olivia's backing musicians and singers, with Skip Griparis now onboard as, in his words, an "adjunct" member who didn't participate in their shows or recording activities without her, they now called themselves the Dreamlovers.) During the weekend of June 27–29, 1975, she drew a crowd estimated at 15,200 to her first show, followed by 14,800 and 17,500 for the next two shows. A month later, her two concerts in one night at the Allentown Fairgrounds in Pennsylvania drew a combined audience of 14,271, setting a one-night box office record of $82,330 for that venue.

Local reporter Dan Pearson wrote a very favorable review of Olivia's first concert of the evening, noting her "exceptionally clear voice," "perfect" pitch, and "considerable" range. "She may not be back next season," he wrote, "but when she does return the fans will have the welcome mat out." Another article written by Pearson in the same edition of the Allentown *Morning Call*, however, served as an archetypal example of how the press focused as much on Olivia's looks as her talent. Under the headline "Newsmen Did Share of Gaping at Singer," Pearson wrote, "Pardon the cliché, but singing star Olivia Newton-John can accurately be described as a 'living doll.' She has such attractive, pristine features that her face appears to have been carefully sculpted in ivory."

While Olivia expressed her unhappiness with this sort of press coverage, she wasn't willing to join the feminist movement for which her friend Helen Reddy's 1972 number one hit "I Am Woman" served as an anthem. Dennis Hunt of the *Los Angeles Times* wrote in July 1975, "Some may think Miss Newton-John may have been driven to embrace feminism because of her experiences fighting the 'pretty singer' stereotype and climbing to the top of a business that, until recently, had few woman stars. But she is not a feminist."

"I don't associate what I went through with the feminist movement," Olivia told Hunt. "I don't really know that much about the feminist movement because I haven't paid that much attention to it. I agree that equal pay for equal work is a good idea, but that's where my interest ends." "That's probably a very narrow-minded view," she added, "because there are a lot of women who have problems with getting jobs and being independent. But I don't have those problems, so I haven't bothered to get involved in the feminist movement."

She then seemed to realize how those words might strike some readers, particularly less fortunate women who *were* struggling with those problems. Hunt wrote that she "shook her head solemnly." "I've probably come across," she told him, "as an unconfident little nervous wreck who is anti-feminist and very wrapped up in her own silly little problems. That's not really me. But that very sweet image I have is not really me either. The real me is somewhere in between." Olivia would become an activist for many worthy causes—just not in 1975, when most of her time and effort were consumed by a career that was as active as it was successful.

Those who worked with her during this period still recall how hard she worked. "When she hit the stage, she gave it her all... even when she was not feeling well," says Rick Ruskin, who joined her live band as a second acoustic guitarist in the spring of 1976. "She was a pro," Skip Griparis concurs. "[She was] just very consistent, always gave the folks a great show." "There was only one night I ever heard her falter," he adds, "and that was after she had an argument with Lee [Kramer], and then she was just not as, you know, no one in the audience would have noticed it, but working with her every night, I was like, 'Okay, something's not right.'" Greg Mathieson, who played piano and keyboards on Olivia's 1977 album *Making a Good Thing Better* and on her *Grease* recordings as well as on tour with her, says that in his experience working with her, "she didn't make mistakes, she knew exactly what she was doing.... It was a pleasure to play behind her."

Even hard work and talent don't guarantee a nonstop string of chart-topping records, though, and the *Clearly Love* album marked the beginning of a slump in record sales that didn't turn around until *Grease* came out in the spring of 1978. After back-to-back number one albums, *Clearly Love* fell just short of the *Billboard* Top 10, and after five straight million-selling singles, "Something Better to Do" failed to reach the Top 10 on the pop or country chart, although it did reach No. 1 on the airplay-based adult contemporary chart. Although John Farrar had already written one Hot 100 No. 1 for Olivia and would write two more, this album lacked anything as commercial as "I Honestly Love You" or Farrar's "Have You Never Been Mellow."

Farrar himself, whom Greg Mathieson describes as "a real talented cat and a real nice one, too," later expressed surprise that MCA had even released "Something Better to Do" as a single. "I do not know where that [song] came from," he told an interviewer more than twenty years later, describing it as "sort of a stage, 1940s song," and, with his typical self-effacing modesty, as "one of those stupid songs I guess." "I don't think I expected it to be a single," he added. "I expected it to be a silly song." But he found one thing to like about the record—how its fairly sparse arrangement keeps the listener's focus on Olivia's vocals. "She had this lovely, pure quality that was great to hear at the time."

Before MCA released a follow-up single, Olivia appeared on John Denver's next single. For the recording of "Fly Away," a song that he had written, he asked Olivia to sing the title phrase after him in the song's call-and-response refrain. She squeezed in the time to do it in July 1975, and later that year she sang the song with him on his ABC-TV special, *John Denver's Rocky Mountain Christmas*.

While some press wags suggested that the two might be more than friends, Denver dismissed that in an interview (although he added, jokingly, that it was "not a bad notion"). He and Olivia were indeed friends, though, and he invited her to spend her first Thanksgiving in the United States with him and his family. "Fly Away" just missed the pop and country Top 10, and it reached No. 1 on the adult contemporary chart.

Olivia then ended up with, in a way, four straight weeks at No. 1 on *Billboard*'s adult contemporary chart in January 1976 with two different records. "Fly Away" was No. 1 for the weeks ending January 10 and 31. In between, her own single—a rare double A-side (although those had been common in previous decades), with "Let It Shine" on one side and "He Ain't Heavy… He's My Brother" on the other— held the top spot on the chart. Farrar was surprised that the latter got nearly as much airplay as the former on adult contemporary and pop radio stations. On the more sales-oriented Hot 100, though, the single only reached No. 30. Country radio stations only played "Let It Shine," but it reached No. 5 on the country chart.

By the time that single hit the market, Olivia had already cut her next album. During brief trips back to her native country in October and November 1975, she recorded *Come on Over* at Abbey Road Studios. MCA would release the album in early 1976, barely five months after the release of *Clearly Love*.

The album included cover versions of several very well-known songs: "The Long and Winding Road," which Olivia had sung in concerts; the traditional English folk song "Greensleeves"; the old country classic "Blue Eyes Crying in the Rain"; and "Jolene," which perhaps at that time was too new to be considered a country classic, but certainly became acknowledged as one. (It would also become, four and a half decades later, the last song Olivia ever recorded, this time as a duet with its composer, Dolly Parton.)

The album also included cover versions of some lesser-known songs, such as "Smile for Me," a Lynn Anderson Top 20 country hit from 1974, and obscure ones such as "Wrap Me in Your Arms." "[I] wrote it ['Wrap Me'] on a snowy Minnesota afternoon in front of a toasty fireplace in about 30 minutes when I was 25," recalls singer-songwriter Harlan Collins. "My publisher, Lionel Conway at Island Music, pitched it to Olivia and her producer John Farrar, and they liked it enough to cut it. I never met either one of them, as is often the case in these situations." Olivia's version "is lush orchestration balladic waltz to my ears," he says, whereas "both my version and [Welsh singer Mary] Hopkin's are waltzes with a bit more swing, more band-like." Collins's own version was not released until after Olivia's. Hopkin recorded the song after Olivia did and released it in 1977.

A song written by two of Olivia's "mates" in the Bee Gees, Barry Gibb and Robin Gibb, served as the album's title track.[1] The Bee Gees had released the song on their album *Main Course* in June 1975. This album revived the trio's nearly moribund recording career with its combination of funky songs and falsetto, a sharp departure from the slower, often melancholy songs that they'd had great success with between 1967 and 1972 before their record sales and airplay took a nosedive. The first single from *Main Course*, "Jive Talkin," became the Bee Gees' first number one hit in four years. Olivia played the album a lot on her tour bus that summer, and it was her idea to record "Come on Over," a song that didn't resemble "Jive Talkin'" or the album's other Top 10 single, "Nights on Broadway," but rather was a midtempo, piano-driven ballad with a powerful lead vocal by Robin Gibb.

While Olivia put her own stamp on the song, it was the chance to sing in a more powerful voice than on her soft hits like "Have You Never Been Mellow" and "Please Mr. Please" that made her decide to cover it. "I really love that song—and I'm getting confidence in doing songs like that," she told Gerry Wood in an interview for *Billboard*. "In each album I try to add something different. But I'd also like to keep what I established myself with. Because I don't use all my voice, people think that I have much less voice than I actually [do]. On the next album [*Come on Over*] I show more voice than ever before."

The new album didn't restore Olivia to the top of the charts, though. Like its predecessor, it earned a gold record, but it didn't quite crack the Top 10. The "Come on Over" single reached No. 1 on the adult contemporary chart and No. 5 on the country chart, but only No. 23 on the Hot 100. Neither of the two albums, nor their singles, found much commercial success in Australia or, especially, Great Britain.

In addition to producing the *Come on Over* album, John Farrar composed one song for it and cowrote another with his former bandmate Hank Marvin. Farrar later told writer Wesley Hyatt that both the album and that period of his and Olivia's long collaboration were ones that he would rather forget. When Hyatt asked him what he thought was behind the gradual slump that beset Olivia's recording career starting in the fall of 1975, he replied, "I think the material. It was like we had this huge peak and went into a valley for a while."

6 DON'T STOP BELIEVIN'

" set up the whole first album that she ever recorded in the United States," recalls singer-songwriter and record producer Chris Christian. "They [Olivia and John Farrar] had just decided to do an album in the United States, and not only that, but to do it in Nashville." Given that Olivia was now living full time in the United States and that her last two albums had been a bit disappointing in terms of sales, she didn't see the sense in recording at Abbey Road anymore. But despite what she had said about looking forward to recording in Nashville, that wasn't the initial plan for her spring 1976 recording sessions. "When I first came to America," Farrar told an interviewer years later, "we went to record in Los Angeles, and I had the wrong players. Larry Carlton [a top LA session guitarist] said, 'You need to have the right players.'"

Given Olivia's track record of pop and country crossover success (more so in the latter field recently), she and John then decided that they should try recording in Nashville instead. The only problem, Christian recalls, was that "they didn't know who to call." Olivia had met Owen Bradley, the head of MCA Nashville, during the luncheon he held for her on her visit there in August 1974, but apparently she didn't think to contact him.

Instead, it was Olivia's and Farrar's connections within the "Gum Leaf Mafia," a group of young Australian adults living in Los Angeles, that led them to Chris Christian. This coterie of Aussies included, among others, Steve Kipner, who would later cowrite Olivia's biggest hit; the clothing designer (and Olivia's close friend) Fleur Thiemeyer; and Fleur's boyfriend at the time, singer-songwriter Darryl Cotton. Cotton would become a member of Olivia's touring band in 1976, and he also belonged to a group called Cotton, Lloyd, and Christian. (The member whose name was in the middle was Michael Lloyd, who was about to find immense success as the record producer for Shaun Cassidy, who had three gold singles and three platinum albums in 1977–1978.) Fleur told Farrar that Christian was based in Nashville, so Farrar gave him a call.

Christian agreed to find a studio for Olivia and a band as well. He picked Buzz Cason's Creative Workshop in Nashville's Berry Hill section, a studio that opened in 1970 and quickly became one of the most popular in the city. "I picked the best studio, the best musicians, the best of everything in Nashville, because she obviously deserved that, and John needed that." Christian, like many in the Nashville music business, thought that Olivia "was *not* a country artist. She was a pop artist, really, and so the question was, which musicians to use that would do the kind of pop record she wants to do, even though it was in Nashville." Christian therefore picked musicians who had experience working with pop as well as country artists: bass guitarist Joe Osborn, drummer Larrie London, keyboardist Shane Keister, guitarist Steve Gibson, and Bergen White to do the string arrangements. "They were the A-team," Christian recalls, Nashville's equivalent of the famed Los Angeles Wrecking Crew of top studio players. Osborn went back-and-forth between both groups, playing on countless hits in Los Angeles and Nashville, and London played behind Elvis Presley as well as country legends such as Merle Haggard and Waylon Jennings. Christian played acoustic guitar on the album, and Farrar played electric and acoustic guitars, as he had on previous records for Olivia.

Christian and his wife Shanon invited Farrar and Olivia to stay at their house, which included a recording studio in the basement, and they both accepted. "They lived with us for about three or four weeks," Christian recalls. "We became good friends." The studio basement came in handy on at least one occasion. "One night Olivia was talking to Shanon upstairs, and I said, 'I've got an idea for a song, John.' So we went downstairs and wrote 'Compassionate Man' in about two hours." That song not only ended up on the *Don't Stop Believin'* album, but it was released as a single in Japan and became a hit. "I think I got a gold record from Japan" for the single, Christian says.

Christian and Shanon soon discovered that going to restaurants or supermarkets posed a bit of a problem for Olivia because "she got too many people coming up to her." Nevertheless, on one occasion they went to dinner at Medieval Times in Nashville. Shanon became nauseated during dinner. After she went to the restroom, Olivia followed her. "Olivia's back there with a cold towel, down by the toilet with Shanon with a towel on her head for forty-five minutes." Christian still marvels at the memory. "Isn't that *unbelievable*? [She] didn't even think twice about it. This was a friend, her friend who she wanted to help. That really showed her character." But when Christian and Shanon saw how fans approached Olivia everywhere they went, they "just ate at the house pretty much after that."

About one month or two after the album was finished, Christian and Shanon went to dinner with Olivia while visiting Los Angeles. (They would later buy John and Pat Farrar's house in Beverly Hills.) When Olivia arrived at the restaurant, a steak house on Beverly Drive, she told them that another friend of hers from Nashville would be joining them. Soon Dolly Parton arrived, and the foursome spent about three hours together.

When John and Olivia arrived in Nashville to record, they didn't have a set song list for the album. Christian wasn't sure if "Compassionate Man" would be on the album when he and Farrar wrote it, "but of course, John was really looking for songs at that point." Even though Olivia was finally recording in the United States, she was still relying on, in addition to Farrar, English songwriters, some of whom had contributed to her previous albums. Farrar wrote "Don't Stop Believin'," which *Billboard* would name one of its country "top singles picks" the week it was released in July 1976, praising its "brilliant choral harmony and clear, bright instrumentation." "Newton-John," the review continued, "expands her vocal range and capabilities impressively."

Farrar also cowrote three songs: "Love You Hold the Key" with Olivia, "Compassionate Man," and, with Hank Marvin and English lyricist Dan Black, "Sam." Black cowrote another song on the album, "Every Face Tells a Story," for Cliff Richard, who didn't release his first recording of it and then used his second version as the title song for an album in 1977. Bruce Welch returned as a songwriter for Olivia with two cowritten songs, "A Thousand Conversations" and "Hey Mr. Dreammaker," which Cliff Richard also recorded and released in 1976.

Olivia would fondly remember her first experience recording in Nashville. She said more than forty years later that "the time with Chris and Shanon in Nashville was a short but wonderful time creating *Don't Stop Believin'*." When Chris asked her after all that time what her memories were of those several weeks in Nashville besides the recording sessions, she replied, true to her love of nature, that she remembered them all sitting on his and Shanon's back-porch steps, overlooking the garden, and seeing fireflies for the first time in her life.

In addition to recording in the United States for the first time, Olivia also found herself with a new touring band in 1976. The members of thisOneness stopped performing with her after her last fall 1975 shows, which were sandwiched around her trips to England to record the *Come on Over* album. Skip Griparis, the "adjunct" band member who was hired in March 1975 and who stayed on with Olivia, recalls "some debate as to whether they quit or were fired…. They wanted more money, and Olivia and/or her manager, Lee Kramer, wouldn't pay it."

The conflict came to a head during an engagement at the Riviera in Las Vegas. "I remember," Griparis says,

they had kind of a big blowout, I think before our second show one night in Vegas, and it was a disaster. Right before going on, somebody had knocked my guitar down, it went completely out of tune, so I grabbed a spare guitar that I had that wasn't the right kind, it was electric rather than acoustic. And the band just kept getting quieter and quieter during the set. It was just a horrible show.

To make matters worse, Ben Fong-Torres of *Rolling Stone* was in the audience; he would be interviewing Olivia after the show. This interview, as Fong-Torres explained in the article that finally appeared in the magazine in July 1978, became a saga in and of itself. It took numerous interview sessions, with long periods in between them, and he watched Olivia's career go from hot to somewhat cold to red hot with *Grease* by the time he finally wrapped it up and submitted it for publication.

The timing for a bad show proved inopportune, particularly since Olivia didn't seem very comfortable about being interviewed for *Rolling Stone*. "I feel it must be strange for you interviewing me," she told Fong-Torres when they met at the Riviera, "because I must be so alien to the paper. When I found out I was doing the interview, I thought, 'Why the hell would they want to talk to *me*?' I'm so out of everything the magazine seems to represent." Griparis walked into Fong-Torres's interview with Olivia and "put the blame on me having the wrong guitar… so that he wouldn't think that her group or her show was weak." Half a century later, Fong-Torres recalls not the show but rather that Olivia was "one of the nicest performers—and persons—I profiled for *Rolling Stone*." At the Riviera, he introduced her to his soon-to-be wife Dianne, and "shortly after returning home, I got a bouquet of flowers from her and her partner (perhaps also her manager, name of Lee, I think) to congratulate us on our wedding."

The split between Olivia and the members of thisOneness did not result in any lasting acrimony. In 1980, when she was recording songs for the *Xanadu* soundtrack, John Farrar called Gregg Inhofer, and he asked him to play keyboards on "Suddenly," Olivia's duet with Cliff Richard—the only time Gregg ever got to play at one of Olivia's recording sessions, as thisOneness only performed with her onstage. When she came to Minneapolis on tour in September 2012, Gregg, Robyn Lee, Bernie Pershey, and Dale Strength and his brother Bob Strength all met with her; a photograph of the occasion shows a clearly happy reunion. (Only bass guitarist Doug Nelson wasn't there—he passed away in 2000.) Gregg would continue to stay in touch with Olivia via text messaging.

The replacement band, besides lone holdover Griparis (who now took over the bass vocal duties previously handled by Robyn Lee), consisted mostly of Los Angeles session players. John Farrar returned to the live band as the lead guitarist, and Pat Farrar would join as one of the background vocalists, a role that she played on some of Olivia's records as well. The band, recalls, Griparis, was "truly excellent."

Olivia's group enjoyed nice perks while touring the United States with her in 1976. She rented a Boeing 720—in fact, the first one ever built, in 1960, which, after being retired and sold by United Airlines in 1973, was rented by Led Zeppelin for two North American tours. Other artists who rented the jet, named "the Starship," for tours included the Rolling Stones, Elton John, and Peter Frampton. The jet included a lounge and bar, a bedroom, a shower, and a study. The band members could drink on the plane after shows for free (meaning out of Olivia's pocket). "I don't know if she made *any* money on that tour between the

Starship, the bar tab, and the limos. It was crazy, but it was sure fun for us," says Griparis. "We had a few nights off in the French Quarter, I remember, in New Orleans. Great time on that tour." Playing for Olivia, Rick Ruskin says, "was the best gig I ever had." Yet most of the new band members, after a couple of tours, left to tour with Seals and Crofts, who offered them more money. Griparis and Ruskin remained onboard.

Some of the people who worked with Olivia during this period questioned Lee Kramer's competence as a manager, although they generally thought he was easy to get along with. "I think that Lee Kramer didn't do her any favors," reflects Rick Ruskin. "There were some things with the management… that sort of pissed me off." Steve Binder directed, produced, and cowrote the 1978 ABC-TV special *Olivia*, for which Kramer was credited as executive producer. Binder recalls that Kramer "never added two cents to anything. I mean, he was just her boyfriend, and a nice guy." Binder met Kramer when he went to Olivia's house to discuss making the TV special with her, but, he says, "I don't believe I ever saw him when I actually did the special."

A neutral observer couldn't help but wonder: Was Kramer a legitimate manager, or did he just parlay his status as Olivia's boyfriend into getting that position? "I think you just hit it there," Skip Griparis says with an audible sigh. "I don't know whether she just trusted him, thought she could trust him. I don't know why she didn't go to somebody that had experience. He was… a shoe salesman in England. What made him think he could be her *manager* is beyond me."

"He was nice to me," Skip adds. "[I] never had any personal problem with him, but I don't know that he made the best decisions for her." Sometimes he seemed to even lack common sense. Skip recalls what happened when Olivia bought Lee a new motorcycle for his birthday one year. "He parked it outside their office or whatever, and it got stolen! I thought, 'I don't know, did it mean so little to you, or did you not know that things get stolen in America, or what's the deal?'" Skip found Olivia's professional and personal relationship with Lee to be puzzling. "I don't know what he was worse at, boyfriend or manager. You know, that's a tossup. I always thought she could do better, like, why, why him? I don't know."

Stephen Sinclair, who was a close friend to both Lee and Olivia, but knew Lee first, says,

I'll tell you, he was a *really* good businessman, and very successful. *But*, it is very difficult—you can be a pretty cool guy in your town, and a big player in your community or in your city or your business. But when you come to LA, and suddenly you are the boyfriend/manager of the biggest female singer in the world, you are a huge target… that's tough, man, let me tell you. It is tough. And in the end, I think, in many ways, it got the better of him… he was coming from a good place.

Olivia could have perhaps benefited from more astute management in her dealings with MCA Records at this time. She signed a new contract with the label on April 1, 1975. The contract required her to "record and deliver to [MCA] master recordings for two albums per year for an initial period of two years, and, at [MCA's] option, further similar recordings for three additional periods of one year each." The contract also stipulated that

> if [Olivia] failed to deliver a recording when due, [MCA] would become entitled to extend the term of the agreement. In return, [MCA] would pay [Olivia] royalties and a nonreturnable advance of $250,000 for each recording received during the initial two years, and an advance of $100,000 for each recording received during the option years. The cost of producing the recordings would be borne by [Olivia].

Olivia's albums weren't as expensive to make as more elaborately (and slowly) produced albums by recording artists such as Pink Floyd and David Bowie, but they featured top-notch session players and orchestras or string sections, and these musicians earned higher wages in the United States than in England. Her albums in the 1975–1977 period cost around $150,000 each to record, mix, and master before being delivered to MCA.

The two-albums-per-year stipulation proved to be the biggest flaw in the contract, from Olivia's standpoint. Her busy touring schedule, TV appearances, and trips to England and Australia all cut into her time to make albums. Skip Griparis recalls that during 1976–1977, Olivia would "tour for two months at a time, maybe three tours per year." In 1976 she returned to Australia to perform with Glen Campbell in his CBS-TV special *Glen Campbell Down Home, Down Under*, and later in the year she starred in her own TV special, her first of four for ABC. Not only did this schedule mean that she had to make her albums quickly, but she and John Farrar were always scrambling to find good songs, the factor to which Farrar attributed her slipping record sales starting in the fall of 1975.

A two-albums-per-year contract was anachronistic by this time, a relic of the 1960s when groups like the Beatles and the Beach Boys made albums at that pace. Olivia's close friend Karen Carpenter and her brother Richard recorded one album per year for A&M Records from 1969 through 1978, except in 1974 when they released no album. Helen Reddy made nine albums for Capitol Records from 1971 through 1977.

Moreover, executives at some record labels helped recording artists find good material and producers (although Olivia certainly had no problem in the latter regard, being produced by Bruce Welch and John Farrar and, subsequently, just Farrar). Clive Davis at Arista Records, for example, became famous for matching recording artists with the right songs and the right producers. Mike Maitland, the president of MCA Records, paid a visit to Olivia in Nashville while she was recording there, but he didn't offer her any songs or other creative input.

MCA was not a well-respected company in the recording industry. Musician Charles "Bud" Dant had worked for Decca Records as a producer and A&R executive for seven years before MCA bought Decca in 1962, and he stayed on for about seven more years before he decided he'd had enough of the company and left. In an interview in the late 1980s, Dant told writer Philip Bashe, "MCA didn't understand or care about the record business. They acquired Decca only because they wanted Universal Pictures, which Decca owned."

Dant's departure from MCA preceded Olivia's arrival at the MCA subsidiary Uni Records, but, by many accounts, things didn't improve much when MCA consolidated Decca, Uni, and its other record labels into the new MCA Records label in late 1972, with Maitland at the helm. Joel Selvin, who began a long career covering music for the *San Francisco Chronicle* during that year, recalls a comment that summed up the label's problems with a twist of '70s humor: "Back in the day, Journey manager Herbie Herbert told me, 'If Richard Nixon really wanted to get off, he should have given his tapes to MCA because then nobody would have heard them.'" The label, Selvin says, "was a mess." Those in the industry began calling it "Music Cemetery of America." Tom Snow, who wrote songs for Olivia and sometimes played on her records from the late '70s through the mid-'80s, offers an equally blunt assessment of MCA. "They weren't really a record company," he says, noting that the company's attention seemed more focused on films (via Universal) and its amusement parks.

Don't Stop Believin' didn't reverse Olivia's gradual but ongoing commercial decline; in fact, while the album earned a gold record, it barely cracked *Billboard*'s Top 30. The title track and "Sam" both became number one hits on the adult contemporary chart, with the former also reaching the country Top 20 and the latter just making it into the Top 20 on the Hot 100. This was all a far cry from her massive success from late 1973 through summer 1975.

But good news beckoned from a part of the world that even Olivia, who could call three different countries on three different continents home, had never seen. The album *Have You Never Been Mellow* had reached the Top 5 in Japan (even though the single didn't), and *Clearly Love, Come on Over*, and *Don't Stop Believin'* all did the same. The Carpenters had already toured Japan with great success, and with her records now finding more favor there than anywhere else in the world, Olivia decided that she would take her band there for a tour in late 1976.

She did not, however, take Lee Kramer on the Japanese tour. In the spring of 1976, around the time that Olivia was recording *Don't Stop Believin'* in Nashville (also without Kramer), the gossip columns started reporting that the pair had ended their relationship. Ben Fong-Torres, who wrote a syndicated newspaper article on Olivia in the summer of 1976 based on his ongoing interview with her for *Rolling Stone*, reported that "Kramer has acknowledged an end to their business relationship." Kramer also told Fong-Torres that he had felt pressure being Olivia's manager, having been new to the music business when he assumed the position, and that it had been hard not to carry business matters into their home. (They were still living together in Malibu.) "I live, sleep, eat, everything else, Olivia," he told Fong-Torres. Now, Kramer said, he was relieving himself of business duties regarding her career, although he implied that their personal relationship was still solid.

Stephen Sinclair saw the problems in their relationship up close. "He was a very traditional guy," Sinclair reflects. "He wanted her to come home on Fridays and spend the weekend with him" if she was away working without him. "He actually sort of expected her to come home on a Friday and make dinner." Sinclair still chuckles incredulously at the notion. "Olivia said to me one day, 'I told him he could have 100 percent of the part of me that I can give to anyone, but he can't have 100 percent of *me*.' It was really powerful."

Dan Cleary replaced Kramer as Olivia's manager. Cleary was a seasoned veteran whose other clients included Natalie Cole and the Commodores. Cleary, Skip Griparis recalls, "helped [Olivia] with getting *Grease*. You know, if Lee had been there, I don't know if that would have happened."

The concert promoter for Olivia's December 1976 tour of Japan was the legendary Tats Nagashima, who had brought the Beatles to Japan a decade earlier and more recently the Carpenters. Rick Ruskin recalls Nagashima fondly. "[He] was six foot four, Japanese-born, of Samurai descent, and he was, I think, educated at UCLA. He treated the band *royally*." Olivia and the band and crew traveled with Nagashima by car, in caravans, to some shows, and he would treat them all to wonderful meals for lunch at restaurants along the way. "It was great," Ruskin recalls. "[Olivia] was *beloved* in Japan…. The Japanese people were wonderful to us."

John Farrar led a mostly new touring band to Japan as lead guitarist and musical director. In addition to Griparis on rhythm guitar and bass background vocals and Ruskin on acoustic guitar, the rest of the band consisted of Abe Laboriel on bass, Doug Livingston on steel guitar and synthesizer, Greg Mathieson on piano, and Peter Donald on drums—a quite accomplished group of session musicians. Farrar and Olivia had scooped up Mathieson after he had suddenly quit Helen Reddy's band after a concert in which "she walked… over to me and spit [a] whole mouthful [of water] in my face in front of a full audience of people." When the band performed with Olivia on an episode of *The Tonight Show* hosted by Reddy (substituting for Johnny Carson) in February 1977, Mathieson brought his wife along. He still recalls clearly what happened. "Helen throws a fit. She says she won't do the show while my wife is in the studio. Pretty funny. I'm laughing. I don't care. Well, Olivia, being the great woman she is, tells my wife to sit in her dressing room, and the show goes on." Mathieson would soon be contributing to Olivia's records as well.

The backup singers on the Japanese tour were Pat Farrar and two of the backup singers on the *Don't Stop Believin'* album, Donna Fein and Muffy Hendrix. Skip Griparis laughs remembering an incident during the tour that demonstrated John Farrar's perfectionism. "He wasn't happy with the three girl singers. They weren't singing in tune. And he said, 'Either you guys start singing in tune, or Skip and I are gonna do it.'"

In most countries—although not the United States, Australia, or New Zealand— EMI Records released Olivia's recordings. EMI Japan wanted a live album from the Japanese tour. John Farrar brought Bill Schnee along on the tour to be the recording engineer, after Schnee had mixed the *Don't Stop Believin'* album at Cherokee Studios in Hollywood. Schnee has nothing but fond memories of the Japanese tour. "It was a great tour," he recalls. "She was a huge star there then." Olivia sang to audiences of from about three thousand to five thousand. "They were very, very vocal, that's for sure, but they were usually incredibly quiet while she was singing, and then as soon as she was done, you know, then there's the outroar," he says, chuckling at the memory.

Schnee also remembers that Olivia and her entourage arrived in Japan a few days before the tour started, which meant they were there during Thanksgiving. "So she treated us all to a beautiful Thanksgiving dinner at the hotel we were staying at. She treated everybody with incredible respect. Can't say enough about what a sweet and honestly beautiful girl she was." Rick Ruskin recalls the band getting together with her on that tour and playing charades and parlor games.

Olivia's concerts at Festival Hall in Osaka on December 3 and 4, 1976, would be used for the live album, which was released only in Japan and South Korea (and, oddly, only five years later) as *Love Performance*. The photos on the album cover came not from this tour but from a Japanese tour that she did two years later. Bill Schnee didn't even know that the album had ever been released until the author of this book told him while interviewing him.

Not long after Olivia returned to California, her relationship with Lee Kramer, for the time being at least, came to an end. Olivia split with Kramer in February 1977 and began dating a thirty-year-old songwriter named Jamie Carr, who told a reporter, "I love her. She's the sweetest person I know." Kramer, meanwhile, told the press, "We both love each other dearly and it's not going to change."

Greg Mathieson recalls an instance during a rehearsal with the band when some of the guys were talking about the difficulties of dating when they were on the road a lot. Olivia walked in and heard them talking. "Well, I have a hard time getting dates," she said, "because guys think I'm too pretty or something. I scare them off." "I thought," Mathieson reflects, "that was interesting that she said that.

She could take care of herself with guys, you know. She knew what was going on… she knew how pretty she was and her effect on men, as she should know."

As her relationship with Kramer came to what turned out to be a hiatus rather than an end, Olivia returned to the recording studio. While no one recalls her saying that she didn't want to, the two-albums-per-year stipulation in her MCA contract necessitated it regardless. "John [Farrar] called and asked me to help him with her new album," Bill Schnee remembers. "He wanted to record it in Los Angeles, and he didn't know musicians [there]. So he asked me to put the band together, which I was very happy to do." Farrar and Greg Mathieson (who was about to become a much-in-demand session player in LA) both played on the record, along with an all-star cast assembled by Schnee: guitarist Jay Graydon, whose credits included Steely Dan records; Toto drummer Jeff Porcaro; James Taylor's bassist Leland Sklar; and the legendary pedal steel guitarist Sneaky Pete Kleinow, along with other session aces who made contributions to a track or two. Most of the sessions were held at Sound Labs on Argyle Avenue in Hollywood. Schnee engineered and mixed most of the album.

While the sessions went smoothly, the album suffered from the problem that Farrar was already well aware of during this period: the lack of songs of the caliber of "If You Love Me (Let Me Know)" and "I Honestly Love You," with only the exception of cover versions of songs that were already well known, such as "Ring of Fire" and "Don't Cry for Me Argentina," or, in the case of "Slow Dancin' (Swayin' to the Music)," one that was about to become well known, as Johnny Rivers was climbing his way to the Top 10 with it before anyone heard Olivia's version. Farrar and Olivia each wrote one song for the album.

In late March 1977, with recording sessions for the album finished, Olivia set off on an American tour, beginning with a one-week engagement at the Riviera in Las Vegas followed by a week at the Sahara Tahoe. Rick Ruskin recalls an unsettling incident from the stint at the Riviera. One day he went to the stage early.

> I get down there and there's this guy, he flashes me some bogus FBI badge, and he's saying that he needs to get into the dressing room because he's doing an investigation. And I went, "I don't know how the hell you got in here, but you'd better get out of here *now* before I call security because this is bullshit."

Afterward, Ruskin "did mention it to somebody, and I said, 'Hey, your security is lax if a guy like this can get into the runway backstage without the proper credentials.'"

Before the first show that night, security had Ruskin walk through the showroom, instructing him, "See if you see the guy." Sure enough, he did, and security ejected the man from the premises. "Things like that would happen," Ruskin laments, "and there were people, I mean, a guy came up to me after we did a show in Griffith Park" in Los Angeles. As Ruskin was walking into the parking lot, the man approached him.

"Are you the guitar player?"

"Yes."

"These songs, let me ask you something, those songs Olivia's singing?"

"Yeah?"

"Who's she singing them to?"

"She's singing them to the *audience*," Ruskin replied incredulously.

"I thought," the man replied earnestly, "she was singing them to *me*."

Ruskin sighs recalling the bizarre encounter. "So those crazies are out there. You know, they're just, they're just out there, and the minute you get out there in the public eye, unfortunately, they're going to be attracted to you… if you get any kind of notoriety, there's gonna be some crazy that's gonna get fixated on you." Olivia, even more unfortunately, would have to deal with this problem again and again, eventually beefing up her security considerably. Rick recalls yet another worrisome incident that occurred while he was touring with Olivia: "There was a bomb scare during one of the shows, and the auditorium had to be evacuated."

Stephen Sinclair sometimes traveled on tour with Olivia and Lee and their entourage, and he remembers troubling incidents as well. "They arrested people at [her] concerts who were armed and said they were coming. You know, this is a rule of thumb: the nicer you are, the more they want to kill you."

Sinclair also recalls some alarming and bizarre episodes that occurred at Olivia's home during this period. He stayed with her and Lee at the Trancas house for a brief spell in 1975, "looking after the dogs and just hanging out" while waiting for his MCA recording contract to be finalized. "One morning I came out and there was a vial of blood, right outside where the gate opens, with a note that said, 'Are you alive in there?'"

In 1976 Olivia bought a house on McAnany Way in the Big Rock neighborhood of Malibu. One Sunday morning shortly after she and Lee moved in, Sinclair was sitting in the dining room off the kitchen with Lee and Lee's brother Mike when a man that none of them recognized suddenly walked in through the kitchen door.

"Hi," he said, "is Olivia here?"

Lee replied, "Yeah. Who are *you*?"

"Well, the angels sent me."

There was a long pause. Sinclair wondered whether the man was armed.

Lee told the intruder, "Oh, great! Well, look, she might want to come out and see you. I'll go and get her. I think she has just washed her hair and is getting out of the shower." The man sat down at the dining-room table. Lee went into another room and called the police. "In ninety seconds, they were there," Sinclair recalls.

Sinclair was at the Big Rock house when further trespassing incidents occurred. "We heard somebody on the roof one night… and by then Lee had a gun." When

Lee went outside holding it, the man jumped off the roof and ran away. "She had a lot of *weirdos*," Sinclair exclaims, still sounding perplexed and vexed thinking about it nearly half a century later. As Gavin de Becker, who would later become a friend of Olivia's and a security services provider to her and other celebrities, put it, "Everybody who is in any kind of media will have some kind of approach or encounter that is inappropriate." Olivia, unfortunately, had more than her share.

After her early spring 1977 stints in Vegas and Tahoe, Olivia set off to the South, Midwest, and Northeast. She was once again traveling by jet, which, among other benefits, offered more security than traveling by bus. A member of her entourage told *Atlanta Journal-Constitution* music journalist Bill King that, while Olivia was only playing one night in Atlanta, at the venerable Fox Theatre on April 18, she would be staying in the city for about ten days, taking the jet to other southern cities such as Huntsville, Alabama, and Raleigh, North Carolina, for concerts and then flying back to Atlanta and the hotel where she slept for that week and a half. Olivia told King that she thought Atlanta was "a lovely city, but unfortunately I haven't had the chance to see much of it other than the airport and the hotel, because we don't get back here until around 2 [a.m.] and then don't get to bed until about 5."

Despite the grueling schedule, Olivia was beginning to enjoy touring more than she had earlier. "I like recording best because you're creating something new," she told King, "but I like live work when I'm doing it. A year ago, I would have said I just liked recording and television but now I like performing live. It was hard at first because I was very nervous and when you're nervous, you don't get anything back from the audience and they don't get anything and it's a vicious circle."

She added, "I think sometimes that I could give up singing… but I don't know what I would do… maybe have a family. I don't know if I want to be doing this until I'm 40. And if I have a family, I'll want to stay home with them." When King joked that there were undoubtedly plenty of "volunteers" who would be willing to start a family with her, she laughed and said, "[I'm] not that serious about it. I don't think I'm quite ready for it now. Not yet."

King, who now recalls Olivia as "the nicest star I ever met," and his wife Leslie were able to talk with her in person at a reception held for her in the hotel across from the Fox Theatre after her concert. She was "as personable and chatty" in person as she had been when he had interviewed her on the phone days earlier. King also says, "I don't remember any 'minder' being with her as she circulated around that reception after the concert in 1977." But, he adds, "a year or two later she was in town briefly for some sort of radio or TV station birthday party. I do recall a large entourage around her at that one, and it was very restrictive. They wouldn't let us take pictures of her."

Olivia's spring 1977 US tour came to a climactic end on Sunday night, May 8, at Manhattan's famed Metropolitan Opera House. "The venue was sold out," Greg Mathieson remembers, but Olivia seemed a bit nervous. At the end of the show, she received a standing ovation, and then she came back for her usual encore, "I Honestly Love You." "The performance was going great," Mathieson says. "She was singing great. Then, right near the end of 'I Honestly Love You,' her voice started to crack, and I realized she was starting to cry. It just made the song and lyrics work better. Then I started to cry, and I barely managed to make it to the end of the song."

Music critic Stephen Demorest reviewed the concert for the New York *Daily News*. "There were tougher beats in the naked city than mine Sunday night," he wrote. "I watched a frisky blonde named Olivia Newton-John make butterscotch out of more than 3,500 New Yorkers at the Metropolitan Opera House."

7 SANDY #1 AND SANDY #2

"Olivia's [new] album is just as slick as all its predecessors," wrote Bill King, a self-avowed Olivia Newton-John fan, "and her voice is, if anything, stronger than it was in the early days of her career. But producer John Farrar (who has been in charge of all her recordings) has chosen a group of songs that are, for the most part, forgettable." That was a pretty typical review of *Making a Good Thing Better*, which MCA released in June 1977. The public wasn't thrilled with the album either. It reached only No. 34 on the *Billboard* chart, and it broke her string of six straight gold albums. MCA only released one single from the album, the title track. Olivia had given the audience at the Metropolitan Opera House a sneak preview of that song, and Stephen Demorest called it "a Bee Gee-ish dance tune." But while the Bee Gees' younger brother Andy Gibb spent four weeks atop the Hot 100 that summer with "I Just Want to Be Your Everything," a "Bee Gee-ish dance tune" written by an actual Bee Gee (Barry Gibb), Olivia's single stiffed at No. 87—her least successful single in four years. In Australia, "Don't Cry for Me Argentina" was the single, but it was not a big hit, only managing a chart peak of No. 32.

The album also created problems between MCA and Olivia. The finished, mixed and mastered, release-ready album had not been delivered to the label by April 1, 1977, as required by her contract. Nevertheless, MCA exercised the first of the three one-year extensions that the contract allowed, but the missed deadline would later become the label's first piece of evidence for charging that Olivia had failed to meet her obligations. For her part, Olivia would claim that MCA failed to adequately promote the album (not an uncommon complaint among MCA recording artists during this period).

Whatever the reasons, it was starting to look like Olivia's run of five straight million-selling singles and back-to-back number one albums between late 1973 and mid-1975 might well have been her heyday. By now, *Rolling Stone* was starting to lose interest in the story that Ben Fong-Torres had started interviewing her for in the autumn of 1975. As he wrote when the article finally appeared in July 1978, when he first spoke to her at the Riviera in Las Vegas, she had been "selling lots of records, something she stopped doing in late '75, just around the time this story was getting started." Her hit singles, he noted, just didn't "keep coming" after that. "And without the hits, without the constant reminders of her pop power... there just was no story." *Rolling Stone* was only interested in publishing an article about her if she was topping the charts.

At this critical juncture in Olivia's career, a fresh and significant opportunity arrived. In mid-April 1977 she had told Bill King, "I've achieved a lot of the things I always dreamt of, and some I never dreamt of, but, in the future, I think I might like to do a film, maybe. I'd like to act if I can find the right film. I'd never thought about it, but I keep getting sent scripts." (She rarely mentioned *Toomorrow* in interviews by this point; as she told Debbie Kruger in 1994, "Well, it wasn't something I wanted to rave about.")

Weeks later, the "right film" came, even though she wasn't so sure at first. "It all started at a 1977 dinner party at the home of singer Helen Reddy, the 'godmother to Hollywood's Aussie colony,' as *People* magazine called her at the time," wrote Australian music and pop-culture journalist Paul Donoughue years later. Reddy sat Olivia across from Allan Carr, who along with the red-hot Australian/British music mogul Robert Stigwood, was producing a movie adaptation of the hit Broadway musical *Grease*. The seating arrangement was deliberate on the part of Helen and her manager/agent husband Jeff Wald, and Carr spent the evening trying to persuade Olivia to accept the starring female role in *Grease* opposite John Travolta, who had just starred in Stigwood's film *Saturday Night Fever*, which would be released in December 1977.

Olivia didn't jump at Carr's offer. "I was very anxious about making another film, because my music career was going well," she recalled nearly forty years later, "and I did not want to mess it up by doing another movie that wasn't good." Randal Kleiser, directing his first film at age thirty, had his doubts about whether Olivia was right for the role. "I remember meeting her for the first time at that party," he later told *Vanity Fair*, "and thinking, well, 'Have You Never Been Mellow?' How is that going to work? How is she going to become this slut?" Carr and Travolta had no such concerns, though. "She had a brilliant voice, and I didn't think there could be any more correct person for Sandy in the universe," Travolta said in 2016. He likened the choice of Olivia for the female lead in *Grease* to "putting Taylor Swift in that role today." "I never let up on it," he added. "I insisted that she be met and that we cast her." Despite her misgivings, which included her belief that she was too old to be playing a high schooler (which was true of the entire cast, really), once Olivia met Travolta, she decided to do it. "There was great chemistry" between them from the start, she recalled.

Near the end of May 1977, Olivia went to England "for a few days to do some TV shows and appear at the Jubilee thing at Windsor with Elton [John] and co.," reported *Record Mirror*. While she was there, according to American gossip columnist Liz Smith, she "drove the British press nuts giving out interviews about a major film she was going to do but refusing to tell the name. So of course, it turns out she is going to make her first [*sic*] movie as Sandy… in the film of *Grease*." Allan Carr gushed about Olivia's performance in her screen test. "She couldn't have been more adorable on screen. She'll be a big movie star!"

Filming began on June 27, 1977, at Venice High School in West Los Angeles, about one and a half miles from Venice Beach, another filming site for *Grease*. Paramount only budgeted $6 million for the film, barely more than half the $11 million budget of *Star Wars*, which was released in May 1977 and was considered a low-budget film itself. (Dan Cleary managed to negotiate a fee of $125,000 for Olivia, plus a percentage of earnings that would later raise her take to over $2 million.) In addition to Stigwood, Carr, and Kleiser, Bill Oakes of RSO served a vital role in the making of the film: music supervisor. When Oakes saw the *Grease* stage musical, he "wasn't knocked out" by the songs. The film contract allowed him to "punch things up" by bringing in new songs. Nearly half the songs that made it onto the soundtrack (ten of twenty-three) had not been in the stage version.

Robert Stigwood phoned Barry Gibb and asked him to write a title song for the movie (which the stage musical lacked). As Barry would recall, the conversation went something like this:

"Can there be a song called 'Grease'? I have another song called 'Grease' by another artist who I won't mention, but it doesn't work."

"What do you want?"

"I want a hit record that's called 'Grease.'"

"How can anybody write a big hit record called 'Grease'? I mean, do you write about combing your hair, do you write about Brylcreem, or what? How can you make that romantic?"

Barry also struggled to think of a word that rhymes with "grease." Ultimately, he decided that "'Grease' is the word." "If you write a song about the word 'grease,'" he said, "it would work, and that's all I did." He wrote it and recorded a demo with the backing of only a piano and hands slapping a thigh. The recording of the song by Frankie Valli would open the movie, along with a cartoon sequence conceived by Allan Carr.

In the fall of 1977, just after the filming of *Grease* wrapped, the Bee Gees were in Los Angeles filming a Stigwood movie of their own, an ill-fated cinematic take on the Beatles' album *Sgt. Pepper's Lonely Hearts Club Band*. The movie also starred Peter Frampton. During the filming, Barry met Valli, who as the lead singer of the Four Seasons and as a solo artist had achieved legendary status in his own right. Valli played a cameo role at the end of the *Sgt. Pepper's* movie. "Barry told me," Valli later said, "that he was involved in a project, and it was something that he was sure was right for me. I had no idea what it was, because he said he couldn't talk about it. A month later, he sent me the song, and I flipped." Valli gladly accepted the offer to record it, feeling sure that it would be a hit. Barry coproduced the record and contributed backing vocals, and Frampton played guitar.

Oakes recalls backlash from executives at Paramount when he let them hear the movie's title song. "They reacted in horror. They said, 'This is a disco song!'" Oakes laughs at the recollection. "They didn't know what they were doing." Stigwood, he says, wanted the soundtrack to be a contemporary, hit album. "Stigwood wanted to duplicate what we did with *Saturday Night Fever*, really, and do a double-album with songs that weren't sort of Fifties or outdated."

Oakes had agreed to serve as the film's music director before Olivia was cast, and when she signed on, he "was very happy.… I thought, 'Not only will we have the luxury of having a proper singer playing Sandy, but also I'll be able to get my hands on John Farrar.… This will help, because I need some new music.'" Oakes recalls Farrar being "very modest" when he asked him to come up with a couple of new songs for the movie. "I'm surprised you're asking me," Farrar told him. "Why would I ask anyone else?" Oakes replied. Oakes, of course, was well aware of Farrar's role in producing and, in some instances, writing Olivia's hits.

Farrar wrote two songs for the movie: "Hopelessly Devoted to You" for Olivia and "You're the One That I Want" as a duet for Travolta and Olivia. Oakes was unhappy with the fact that the stage version of *Grease* included no song for Olivia to sing solo. "So I put John to work on it. I gave him a copy of Skeeter Davis's song 'The End of the World,' [a hit in 1963]… which I thought had the right flavor to it, and he copied the beat *exactly*." Farrar asked Oakes what the lyrics should be about. "And honestly," Oakes laughs, "I just said, 'Well, you know, it's when she's got all her girlfriends saying, "You should give up on him," and she decides she's *hopelessly devoted to him*.' So, he writes this down in longhand and came up with 'Hopelessly Devoted to You' the next day!"

"A similar thing happened," Oakes remembers, "when we had to do a duet" for the scene where "Sandy #2" bowls over Danny. There was no song for it in the stage version of *Grease*. Oakes once again turned to Farrar

> because he was the obvious guy. And he said, "Well, what's happening here?" I said, "This is where the two leads have fallen out with each other, having fallen in love, and now they've decided they're the one that I want." So, he wrote "You're the One That I Want." So, it was a double win for John [Farrar] and Olivia, those two songs.

Randal Kleiser wasn't sure about "Hopelessly Devoted to You," which he first heard as a demo performed by Farrar himself, and the first time that he heard

"You're the One That I Want," he thought it "sounded awful." But Olivia loved both songs. She recalled, nearly forty years later, the first time she heard "You're the One That I Want." "He [Farrar] came into my trailer at, like, six in the morning, because he had been up all night," she said. "He played it for me and said, 'What do you think?' I went, 'Oh, God, it's amazing.' It just had this fantastic energy."

Farrar hadn't written a smash hit for Olivia since "Have You Never Been Mellow" three years earlier, but with these two songs, he began a hot streak as a songwriter that would initiate a second hot streak—a longer one than the first—for Olivia as a recording artist. (Farrar would write or cowrite several of the biggest hits of that second hot streak, although not *the* biggest.) In addition to "You're the One That I Want," Travolta and Olivia duetted on "Summer Nights," a Warren Casey–Jim Jacobs composition from the stage musical.

For Olivia, the "You're the One That I Want" scene played a pivotal role not only in the movie but also in her career. She began using the terms "Sandy #1" and "Sandy #2" to refer her transformation from the demure "Sandra Dee" who forlornly sang "Hopelessly Devoted to You" in the film to the cigarette-smoking, black-clad Sandy who shoves Travolta's Danny backward with her foot before they launch into "You're the One That I Want." She still referred to "Sandy #1" and "Sandy #2" in her autobiography four decades later.

Right up until the scene was filmed, Randal Kleiser still had doubts. "I knew she was perfect for conservative Sandy," he told the *Sydney Morning Herald* following Olivia's passing. "But I was privately worried that she wouldn't be able to pull the transformation off. But of course, I didn't need to worry." Kleiser also said, "'Tell me about it, stud,' was not in the script; Olivia came up with that on the spot. And when she said it, everyone on set just stopped; it was like Sandy the character had taken over Olivia the actress."

The film's casting director, Joel Thurm, would share a humorous memory related to the scene. "I happened to be just outside her trailer," he wrote in his memoir,

when she first stepped out as [Sandy] in her skintight black [sharkskin] pants and the new hairdo. I laughed as our costume designer, Albert Wolsky, sewed her in and out each time she had to pee. Those now iconic pants were actual 1950s trousers he found in a thrift shop. The zipper was gone, so sewing in and out was required.

Olivia knew that "Sandy #2" was at odds with the wholesome, "Miss Goody Two-Shoes" image that the public held of her. (It wasn't just the public, either. Her sister Rona, according to Rona's son Emerson, "would call Olivia 'Pollyanna' all the time, and Olivia hated it, absolutely hated it.") Even on the set, she got a sneak preview of how transformational "Sandy #2" would be for both her image and her career. "All through production," she told an interviewer, "the crew treated me like I was Sandy [#1]—this seventeen-year-old naïve lady." "[Then] I walked around the back of the crew as Sandy Two, all dressed up with a cigarette dangling from the side of my mouth and they all turned around and I got this incredible reaction from the men. I got a lot of offers. No one knew it was me."

The *Rolling Stone* feature by Ben Fong-Torres that appeared in the July 27, 1978, issue, just under six weeks after the movie reached the theaters, demonstrated how that scene (and "You're the One That I Want") had already changed her image. When Olivia's first run of big hits dried up following "Have You Never Been Mellow," *Rolling Stone* lost interest in even running a story based on Fong-Torres's ongoing interviews with her. But *Grease* and "You're the One That I Want," and the instant success of the movie, that single (a number one hit before the movie even came out), and the soundtrack album (which would spend twelve weeks at No. 1) revived that interest immediately. Olivia understood. She remarked to Fong-Torres that she was suddenly not "so alien to the paper."

Fong-Torres certainly saw what had just happened. "The record with Travolta," he wrote, "is a sexy, rocky piece of pop. It's Olivia Newton-John, pop-folk, pop-country, and pop-ballad purveyor, rocking and rolling for the first time in her thirteen-year career." "Sandy #2" had not only revived Olivia's career but had also given her a sexier, slightly risqué image that paved the way for her later success with hits such as "Physical," "Make a Move on Me," and "Heart Attack."

Greg Mathieson, the piano and keyboard player that Olivia had hired almost immediately after he left Helen Reddy's band, played an unheralded role in the creation of "You're the One That I Want." John Farrar, who produced the record, had just laid some basic tracks for it when he phoned Mathieson. "He called me to play on that track," Mathieson says. "There were no vocals on it yet; it was just a track… there might have been a scratch [vocal] or something." (A "scratch vocal" is a guide vocal for the musicians to play to when they record their parts.) "But anyway, the chorus goes, 'You're the one that I want,' and the guitar goes [*mimics guitar*], and then 'ooo, ooo, ooo.' The 'ooo, ooo, ooos' were not [at that stage of the recording] background vocals. That's my piano part," he laughs.

"And so, after I left," he adds,

and after they started doing overdubs, they doubled [with background vocals] that hook that I came up with that day on that session. And so it's a running joke between him [John Farrar] and I because, well, *that's the hook!* And I played it on piano because there were no backgrounds [vocals] there. That was my piano lick. And so, you know, he [Farrar] always kind of, like, halfway apologizes for it.

Mathieson laughs, recalling Farrar saying to him, "Well, I'm sorry, man, but it was a real good lick. We had to double it with the background singers." Farrar "brings this up every time I see him, and he says thanks." Mathieson also played piano on "Hopelessly Devoted to You," which was produced by Farrar, but not on "Summer Nights," which was produced by Louis St. Louis, coauthor of the Travolta solo number "Sandy."

Olivia was not present when Mathieson added his part to "You're the One That I Want," but he saw her, for the first time since their spring tour had concluded at the Metropolitan Opera House in New York City, soon enough. About a week and a half after he had laid down his piano and the "ooo ooo ooo" hook, "I got a phone call from Olivia's management saying that she really wanted me there for these [*Grease*] rehearsals." Mathieson was both puzzled and reluctant. "I'm not a rehearsal piano player, you know. It's not fun doing that. But once I got there, I figured out why she wanted me there. I had become an actual friend of Olivia's. And so, once I got there and saw what was happening, I could see why she needed an ally."

John Travolta "was real, real nice to her and to me," but Mathieson could sense tension on the set.

> If you don't know, the movie business can be very, shall we say, "cutthroat." All of these actresses wanted to know why they didn't have the lead role in this movie. So right away there's tension there. Then there are ten real dancers. They are uptight because it took longer for Olivia and the three actresses to learn their dance steps.

"Olivia wanted me there," Mathieson reflects, "so she had an ally. On the breaks, she would come over and sit on the piano bench next to me. She just needed a friend to be there with her. Somebody to talk to. Actually, I totally understood why I was there."

Mathieson got a bird's-eye view of some of the making of the film.

> For me, I had never seen a choreographer start from scratch and build a dance scene. It was really interesting. To me it seemed like he was making it up as he went along. I was impressed! In the end, Olivia held her own. She fought through the "bad vibes," worked hard, and pulled it off. I was proud of her. I couldn't have done it. I think it took two weeks to perfect it. I wasn't there when they filmed it. I think they filmed it to the real track of prerecorded music.

Olivia addressed the challenges of dancing for the movie in an interview about a month after filming wrapped. "I went in cold to the dancing," she admitted.

> I had done some in a double-act with another girl [Pat Carroll] when I was 17, but I always considered myself a bit of a klutz—a girl with two left feet—but the choreographer, Pat Birch, says I move very well. I was self-conscious until I saw

some of the early "rushes," and [then] I thought, "Hmmm. John and I look like Fred Astaire and Ginger Rogers."

One particular piece of choreography stuck in her mind. "There was one smashing 'lift' when I soared above his head. I was around in the fifties but far too young to remember very much. Did they really dance like that?" The "You're the One That I Want" scene took seven hours to film.

The *Grease* soundtrack album would be released by Robert Stigwood's RSO Records in April 1978. Although the label's demise in the early 1980s would be just as dramatic as its rise had been during the latter half of the 1970s, no other record label in history has ever been as dominant as RSO Records was in 1978. Six of the Top 10 singles of the year (as ranked by *Billboard*) were RSO releases—three by the Bee Gees, two by Andy Gibb, and one by the band Player. (From the *Grease* soundtrack, the title track ranked as the year's eleventh-biggest hit, and "You're the One That I Want" was the thirteenth-biggest hit.) RSO also had the two best-selling albums of the year, the *Saturday Night Fever* and *Grease* soundtracks, each of which were higher-priced two-record sets.

RSO Records worked out a deal with MCA Records—Bill Oakes says that, as well as he can remember, RSO paid "an override royalty to MCA for Olivia's services on the *Grease* soundtrack, probably about 1 or 2 percent"—and it certainly paid off for both labels. In MCA's case, the benefit, in addition to the royalty cut-in, would be how *Grease* dramatically reversed Olivia's sagging record sales. MCA wouldn't be the primary beneficiary of this reversal until almost the end of 1978, though, and by then the conflict between the label and Olivia, exacerbated by her not giving MCA any new recordings for about a year and half, had become the matter of lawsuits between the two parties.

In the meantime, as the *Making a Good Thing Better* album was finishing its disappointing chart run, becoming only the second of Olivia's US albums not to earn a gold record, MCA released a *Greatest Hits* album for her in October 1977. Sometimes record companies did this when a recording artist's string of hits had come to an end, which at that time seemed to perhaps be the case for Olivia. Then again, sometimes labels did this when a popular artist was in the middle of a long delay between albums, as Asylum Records did with enormous success in 1976 by issuing an Eagles greatest hits album during the year-and-a-half-long gap between the release of the group's albums *One of These Nights* and *Hotel California*. This situation may have also influenced MCA's decision to release the greatest hits album, since the months were rolling by without Olivia recording anything for the label.

Occasionally a greatest hits album would contain a newly recorded song or two, a way to get a new single on the radio and on the charts to promote the album. MCA didn't have that option in this case, but, as an article in *Billboard* discussed right after Olivia's *Greatest Hits* hit the market, radio stations and record labels had recently begun engaging in the process of "passive research" to determine if an old single might do well if it were rereleased. Typically, this meant rereleasing and vigorously promoting a single that had not been much of a hit the first time around. MCA, however, "commissioned," according to *Billboard*, "the Scotti Bros., an independent promotion and artist firm," which spent a month researching the appeal of "I Honestly Love You" as a rereleased single. The Scotti Bros., who also owned a record label by that name, concluded that Olivia's number one hit from three years earlier "hadn't burned itself out in its first release."

Thus, MCA rereleased "I Honestly Love You," this time with "Don't Cry for Me Argentina" on the B-side, concurrently with *Olivia Newton-John's Greatest Hits*. The single did well enough to prove the Scotti Bros. reasonably correct, as it cracked the Top 50, and the album peaked at No. 13 on the *Billboard* chart, her best showing since *Come on Over* during the spring of 1976. The album achieved platinum (million-selling) status within two months of its release, becoming Olivia's first million-selling album since *Have You Never Been Mellow* in spring 1975. The greatest hits album went on to sell another million copies by 1984, by which time it had been supplemented by the equally successful *Olivia Newton-John's Greatest Hits, Vol. 2*.

In a way, *Grease*, even though it was months away from release, may have helped sell copies of the greatest hits album. The movie began generating considerable press attention as soon as Olivia was cast, and the wave of publicity never let up. For better or worse, a great deal of the publicity focused on whether Olivia and Travolta were involved in a romantic relationship—a topic of speculation that never really went away, regarding, that is, their time together making *Grease* and for a while after that.

Neither Olivia nor Travolta was romantically attached to anyone while the movie was being filmed. Olivia told a reporter that she was living alone on her four-acre ranch in the hills above Malibu with her horses, cats, and dogs. Travolta had been in a relationship with the actress Diana Hyland, eighteen years his senior, since meeting her in 1976 when she played his mother in the television movie *The Boy in the Plastic Bubble*. Hyland died of breast cancer in March 1977. During the filming of *Grease*, *People* magazine published an issue that mentioned Hyland's last days on the cover; someone brought a copy onto the set. Travolta saw it and, in the words of Randal Kleiser, "just went ashen."

When asked by a reporter, while the movie was still being filmed, about her relationship with Travolta, Olivia replied, "I like him and we're good friends, but that's all." This might have been true, but Olivia also liked to keep her private life private, and some of the people who knew her then thought (and still think) that the relationship between her and Travolta may have gone a bit further than that. In 2018, Didi Conn, who played Frenchy in *Grease*, told journalist Stephanie Nolasco that she thought that Travolta had been genuinely attracted to Olivia and that the chemistry between the two in the movie was real. Recalling an alternate ending that was filmed for the movie, when Danny and Sandy engaged in a "juicy" kiss, Conn said, "They weren't acting at that moment… it was real, it really was." Bill Oakes thought that "they were sort of like kids when they were doing the scenes together. They were, like, giggling…. I thought it was very sweet."

More than twenty years after *Grease* was filmed, a musician who had been married to a Scientologist joined Olivia's band and became friends with her. He says that Olivia and Travolta "were very, very close. Almost *that* close." He also recalls a conversation that he once had with her.

"Can I ask you a personal question?" she said to him. "Because you were married to a Scientologist."

"Sure," he replied.

"Obviously, you know John is a Scientologist."

"Oh, yes."

"I know the Church of Scientology really reveres him as a very valuable follower," Olivia said. "If I had married John, would he have expected me to become a Scientologist?"

"It would not have been mandatory, but it would have been encouraged, put it that way."

"Thank you," Olivia replied. "That's all I want to know."

By March 1978, Olivia was telling reporters that she was once again "with" Lee Kramer, while describing Travolta as "a dear and platonic friend." Olivia and Kramer had reunited, both personally and professionally, before *Grease* wrapped. Bill Oakes met Kramer a number of times. "Lee was not an easy guy," Oakes says. "He wasn't a barrel of laughs."

The media speculation about a romance between Travolta and Olivia, regardless of whether it bore any merit, proved good for publicizing *Grease*. Allan Carr, in addition to being coproducer, "was basically the PR guy for the movie," according to Oakes. "Robert [Stigwood] and he really never hit it off… [they were] so different. They were absolute chalk and cheese. Allan was self-promoting all the time, and Robert always tended to stay in the background. And when they did meet," Oakes laughs, "Robert would say to him, 'Can you please wear men's clothing this time, Allan?'" Both Stigwood and Carr were gay, but Stigwood was much more conservative in public.

Carr helped keep the publicity for *Grease* rolling during the spring of 1978, as did Olivia and Travolta with interviews. The popular magazine *Rona Barrett's Hollywood* published a "Super Special" issue with the two stars on the cover and a four-page spread inside filled with photos from the movie. When Olivia returned to performing at the Riviera in April, she gave the movie additional promotion. "I remember in '78, before it came out," recalls her longtime band member Skip

Griparis, "we played Vegas. In the middle of the show, a screen would roll down, and they would show 'Summer Nights' to the audience. That was their first peek at *Grease*, and then we'd come back and finish the show." Travolta joined her at the end of one show to sing both of their *Grease* duets with her. "The audience went wild," Olivia told *People* magazine, "and we remembered all the dance steps. It was the kind of show you wish all your friends had seen." Griparis remembers it well. "It was phenomenal!"

"Summer Nights" would become a Top 5 hit and a million seller that summer, but it wasn't the first single from *Grease*. RSO Records released "You're the One That I Want" in March, and it was climbing up the Top 40 by the time Olivia began her engagement at the Riviera. The April 29, 1978, issue of *Billboard* featured a full-page color ad for the soundtrack album, with a photo of Olivia and Travolta, cheek-to-cheek, with big smiles on their faces and an arm around each other, and each holding a gold record for "You're the One That I Want," which, the ad reported, had been certified gold (meaning sales of one million copies) in just twelve days. It reached No. 1 on the Hot 100 for the week ending June 10, 1978, just before the movie came out (although the chart dates in that era reflected data from about two weeks earlier).

"You're the One That I Want" only spent one week at No. 1, and then it was knocked off the perch by another RSO single—Andy Gibb's "Shadow Dancing," which spent seven weeks at No. 1 and would be named the biggest hit of the year by *Billboard*. Nevertheless, RSO Records president Al Coury, who had previously been the vice president of Capitol Records, said that "You're the One That I Want" was "one of the fastest selling records I have been associated with in the past five years." By July, the single had sold another million copies in the United States, earning a platinum record.

On May 17, 1978, ABC-TV aired *Olivia*, her second special for the network. Olivia sang some of her past hits but also sang "Hopelessly Devoted to You," which would be the third single from the soundtrack, a million seller that reached No. 3 on the Hot 100. ("Grease" was the second single, a number one hit and platinum record.) About a month later, ABC aired another TV special called *Grease Day USA*, a one-hour broadcast from the movie's Hollywood premiere. John Travolta showed up in Danny garb, and Olivia in a Sandy #2-ish tight, pink spaghetti-strap dress. She didn't sing, but Robert Stigwood interviewed her briefly. Frankie Valli sang "Grease," and Andy Gibb sang "Shadow Dancing," which he'd also sung on the *Olivia* special. The *Billboard* chart dated July 1, 1978, which reflected sales as the movie premiered, had the *Grease* soundtrack album at No. 14 and rising— and already certified platinum based on shipments to retailers. Valli's single was also climbing the Top 40 at this time.

In 2018, in an interview with *Forbes* magazine for the movie's fortieth anniversary, Olivia said,

We believed in what we were doing, but I don't think anyone could have imagined that would be still so popular 40 years later. Of course, we were hopeful that the movie would do well, and it did, but I don't even think Paramount was that excited about it in the beginning. It just took on a life of its own. Making it was fun, but you never know with movies if audiences are going to go with it or not, even if you love it.

She expressed stronger doubts in private shortly before the film's release. She took Steve Binder, who produced, directed, and cowrote the *Olivia* TV special, and television producer Nick Vanoff to an advance screening of *Grease*. "We went to a little screening room to watch it at the studio, and she *hated* it," Binder recalls laughingly. "She brought a bottle of liquor with her and drank the whole thing while she was sitting there watching," he says, chuckling again. "And she was convinced it was a disaster.… Little did she know!"

8 *OLIVIA, ABBA, AND ANDY GIBB*

"Though I wasn't aware at the time when I entered Olivia's life, I learned later that she was tired of her image as the sweet girl next door and wanted a much harder edge," reflects Steve Binder, who met Olivia in the spring of 1978. "When I did the show, and we got ABBA to agree to guest star… and Andy Gibb, it was exciting for me because I was a true fan of all of them." Olivia chose those guests, both of whom were major attractions to a broad swath of pop fans themselves at the time: ABBA, little over a year after topping the Hot 100 with "Dancing Queen," was climbing the chart with another million seller ("Take a Chance on Me"), and Andy Gibb's "Shadow Dancing" was on its way to giving him three No. 1's with his first three US singles. Binder readily agreed to both choices.

ABC, with Olivia's approval, had asked Nick Vanoff, whom Binder remembers as "a really terrific television producer," to helm the making of the *Olivia* special. Vanoff had worked with legendary entertainers such as Julie Andrews, Perry Como, and Bing Crosby. Vanoff declined the offer but recommended Binder, who had directed, a decade earlier, an Elvis Presley special for NBC that became famously known as "The '68 Comeback Special." Binder, accompanied by Vanoff, drove to Olivia's Malibu Beach home to discuss the project, meeting with her as well as Lee Kramer, with whom Olivia had reunited both personally and professionally. "I remember it vividly," Binder says, "because I had just gotten a new car, and we drove up to Olivia's home off of the Pacific Coast Highway, and it was raining like cats and dogs. And my car got stuck in the mud for a week at her home. I had to have it towed out. But anyway, Olivia agreed that I should produce and direct."

Olivia had first crossed paths with ABBA at the 1974 Eurovision Song Contest. The group reached the American Top 10 with the song that won that contest, "Waterloo," but didn't have another Top 10 hit in the United States until "Dancing Queen." In this pre-MTV era, American television audiences hadn't seen ABBA a great deal, although the quartet had appeared on some well-known shows such as *The Mike Douglas Show*, Dick Clark's *American Bandstand*, and NBC's *The Midnight Special*.

Andy Gibb performed on all of those shows himself in 1977, when "I Just Want to Be Your Everything" launched his career into a meteoric rise that would be followed by a tragic and much-publicized downfall. Olivia had known Andy, the youngest of the four Gibb brothers (and nearly a decade younger than Olivia), since he was a boy. When asked in 2021 when and where she met Andy, she replied, "I can't remember exactly when or where—it's so long ago—but I most likely met Andy with the [older] Gibb brothers."[1] After Andy recorded his debut album, the 1977 release *Flowing Rivers*, in Miami in October 1976, he moved to West Hollywood with his wife Kim, who would leave him just as his first single was climbing the charts.

Upon his arrival in Los Angeles, Andy joined the "Gum Leaf Mafia" of Aussies in the area (like Olivia, he was born in England but spent many of his early years down under), socializing with Olivia and other Oz transplants such as Fleur Thiemeyer, who would soon be designing his clothes for public appearances and photo shoots, and Steve Kipner, who was born in the United States but grew up in Australia. "I knew Andy," Kipner recalls, "actually since he was a baby in diapers in his parents' house when his older brothers were still living there in Brisbane, Australia." Kipner's father, Nat, had worked with the Bee Gees in their early, pre-fame years.

This special lacked all of the nonmusical TV stars that had been a part of Olivia's first effort for ABC in 1976; this time the focus would be on the music. Binder had two cowriters, film and television scriptwriter Susan Elliot and Alan Thicke, seven years before he found fame and success as an actor on *Growing Pains*, but Binder came up with the concepts for the various scenes. Looking back nearly half a century later, he recalls some fondly but wishes he could redo or at least re-edit others.

Olivia sang a new Jimmy Webb song, "Grow Young," to begin the show. Then the enormous stage doors opened behind her, and she entered a set that featured Andy Gibb and the members of ABBA surrounded by children in a playground for an ensemble performance of the Cat Stevens song "(Remember the Days of the) Old Schoolyard." Binder still considers this scene to be "the strongest segment" in the show. "I had asked and was able to cover the entire stage at CBS with actual sand, and it was a gigantic sandbox," he recalls laughingly.

And as I realized since, I was going *live* live with the entire segment, including the orchestra and as well as my stars, I conceived this segment where they would all interact with each other, that when Olivia was singing, ABBA and Andy would do the backgrounds, and when ABBA was performing I would have Olivia and Andy do the backgrounds for them, and so forth.

"And it was *all* live," he emphasizes. "The orchestra was actually onstage in the sandbox, which was horrendous because what I didn't realize is that sand was getting into all their instruments and it was so uncomfortable," he chuckles,

for them to play live in this gigantic sandbox. But I think the segment really came off well, that they *nailed* it musically, had a lot of fun doing it, and it was not nonstop. I did reshoot some of those songs. I think I stopped maybe once, at the most twice, to do pickups, but the end result was it was totally live, and people don't realize, you know, most of these types of endeavors are all prerecorded and over-rehearsed, and the directors usually try to eliminate any mistakes, especially musically.

"And what was really great about it," he reflects,

was that all of the cast were really perfectionists when it came to their music, and it turned out to be a fantastic segment, in my opinion, of all of them showing what they could really do without, you know, having to go and fix things technically and so forth and so on…. There was no such thing in those days as an auto tuner, etc. So that really proved, beyond a shadow of a doubt, just how talented all of them were.

Olivia, he says, "was a true perfectionist when it came to her vocals and so forth." The musical director for the show, chosen by Binder, was the singer-songwriter Jimmy Webb.

Binder has regrets about the next scene, though—a schoolhouse scene. "I had actually brought Olivia and ABBA and Andy to the grammar school where we filmed it," he recalls.

The whole concept was to integrate the real cast as a surprise on these kids, and I still regret it because in the editing it just didn't turn out that way…. I sent the teachers the actual script to the show well in advance, thinking they would have the kids do the actual script of the scene that I sent to them, and they didn't. They made up their own little scene, and that sort of threw me in terms of how I was going to integrate and surprise the kids on camera with Olivia and ABBA and Andy Gibb. That's a segment that I would love to get my hands on and redo.

He has similar feelings about "The Game of Life" segment, which included ABBA singing "Money Money Money." "I kind of regret today," he says, "as I look at it, having Olivia dress as a princess and, you know, it just, I think that could have been a much stronger segment." It was the only segment in the show where a song was lip-synched rather than sung live.

The show also featured a live segment that reminded some viewers of the "in the round" setting in which Elvis Presley and his musicians performed in the 1968 special that Binder directed. In this case, Olivia, ABBA, and Andy were gathered in a similar fashion, with Andy and Björn Ulvaeus playing acoustic guitars, Benny Andersson playing a keyboard, and Olivia behind a small drum kit. "I've used that [setup] a few times in some of my specials," Binder says, "if I felt the talent warranted it."

A couple of humorous moments involving Andy occurred during this segment. One, most likely scripted, was when Björn asked him, "Do you have any musical sisters or brothers, Andy?" Andy, playing along with the joke, mentioned that his brothers "have this group together they've started up." Olivia asked, "Oh yeah? How's it doing?" "I don't know," Andy replied. "They've got this album they're trying to get off the road." Olivia then said, sounding skeptical, "Oh, it's not that *Fever* thing? It'll never take off." "I'm telling them," Andy said in agreement. "But they won't listen." At another point in the segment, the group was performing the old Regents/Beach Boys hit "Barbara Ann," and Andy, blessed with the trademark Gibb falsetto, sang the high notes, leaving Olivia to sing the low notes. She gestured at him and said, "It's the wrong way around," and laughed. The song broke down a few seconds later, and she asked him in mock exasperation, "How come you're doing the high part and I'm doing the low part?!"

Even though parts of the segment were scripted, some of it seemed spontaneous. To Binder,

It was important… to prove that it wasn't superficial relationships. These people really, really respected and liked each other and had so much fun working together. I mean, you could feel that the entire time we did the special. It wasn't just, you know, show up on Monday from nine to five and do your job. It was much more emotional than that. They really enjoyed backing each other up, and even in the rehearsals and what have you, there was a camaraderie there of friendship.

"It was a lot of fun while doing the show and having my team together to share. You know, we were all a family. There was no division between the artists and [those] behind the camera. I mean, we were all striving to make the best special we possibly could." He remembers Olivia being "totally [into it]… she just executed whatever I asked her to do…. I enjoyed it, I think she enjoyed it, I think all the guest stars enjoyed it, and we had a lot of fun, and we loved doing the show."

Benny Andersson certainly did. "The whole thing was a beautiful experience," he would recall decades later.

> It was one of the best shows we've ever done. Olivia was a very lovely, warm person, and we all had a lot of fun doing the program. Of course, we've done the usual quota of TV talk shows in America, but this one with Olivia was an important step for us. Besides presenting our music for large audiences of thirty to forty million viewers, we all sat down for a ten-minute "rap" session, which gave the whole thing more intimacy.

Stephen Sinclair, who says he "lived full time in the ON-J bubble for six to seven years from 1975," remembers ABBA, particularly Frida and Agnetha, being among Olivia's circle of friends after the TV special. Frida showed up at one of Olivia's concerts in Las Vegas in 2016, and she visited Olivia backstage afterward. When Olivia passed, Frida and Agnetha each issued a statement mourning the loss.

Binder could see that Olivia and Andy Gibb were good friends. "Andy was actually a lot of fun to work with," he says. "Super talented." This was the first time that Olivia and Andy worked together, but they would do so quite a bit more over the next several years, on television and also at Criteria Recording Studios in Miami on a pair of duets. They would cross paths again not long after making the special, in late July 1978 when Andy played a concert in Honolulu, where Olivia just happened to be on vacation with her friend Karen Carpenter. Both of them attended Andy's concert and the after-party in his suite at the Hilton Hotel. Olivia, ABBA, and Andy each performed at a benefit concert for UNICEF in New York City in January 1979, and each appeared on the benefit album that was released from the concert. Olivia and Andy each sang one song solo as well as a duet together.

Binder says that when he and the cast and crew were making the show, which was taped on May 8, 1978, and aired only nine days later after a marathon thirty-six-hour editing session, he had no idea that anyone would still be watching it nearly half a century later. The only commercial release that it saw after its one and only television airing was by MCA Discovision in the short-lived laser disc format. But in the twenty-first century, *Olivia* found its way onto YouTube—not just the complete special, but also twenty minutes of live performance footage of all the stars, some of which was not in the special itself, and in true stereo. As of this writing, it has received 12 million views on YouTube.

Binder himself has contributed to that enormous total. "I thought it was one of the best specials for sure that year, if not one of the best specials that I had done, and I am to this day very proud of it…. I try and watch it every once in a while. You can hardly miss it because it's on YouTube, etc."

"All that matters," Binder says, "is the public, and the public response to it. And I have looked at comments on YouTube on the special, and it's *amazing* not only how many fans she had but how they love what we did on the special, so I'm very gratified by that." The show was also a ratings hit when it aired, coming in as the seventh most watched program of the week, ahead of hit series such as *M*A*S*H*, *The Incredible Hulk*, and *The Love Boat*. It also ranked eight notches higher in the ratings than a Carpenters special that also aired on ABC on the same night.

Perhaps because *Grease* hadn't been released yet when *Olivia* was taped and aired, Olivia came across more in her old "Sandy #1" image than "Sandy #2," in how she dressed, in the nature of the skits, and in the songs she sang. She performed her old country-pop hits "If You Love Me (Let Me Know)," backed by ABBA and Andy; "Have You Never Been Mellow"; and "Please Mr. Please." She also sang "Hopelessly Devoted to You," but that was a "Sandy #1" song that was actually a comfortable fit with those early hits. In fact, in addition to reaching No. 3 on the Hot 100, that single also reached number seven on the adult contemporary chart and No. 20 on the country chart—her final Top 20 country hit. Then again, since John Travolta was not a guest on the show, she couldn't perform her other two songs from the movie, "You're the One That I Want" and "Summer Nights." One has to think that Travolta would have appeared on the special had she asked him to, but, despite having had a Top 10 hit himself in 1976 ("Let Her In"), he wasn't in the same league musically as ABBA or Andy Gibb. The ensemble performances that continue to delight Olivia's, ABBA's, and Andy's fans wouldn't have been the same.

Despite the success of the special, Olivia didn't ask Binder to work on her next one, *Olivia Newton-John: Hollywood Nights*, two years later. She asked Alan Thicke, "a social friend" of Binder's until his death in 2016, to produce it, which Binder says "kind of surprised me… but it didn't affect our friendship [meaning his and Thicke's]. I've never taken that attitude. I'm a freelancer, and the stars are free to choose whoever they want to to work with." Binder attributes Olivia's choice of Thicke to produce her next special to her desire to be "more hard-edged… more contemporary than the goody two-shoes" after the success of *Grease*. *Hollywood Nights* would feature a much larger cast of guests than *Olivia* had, although Andy Gibb would be a repeat guest.

Binder only ever saw Olivia once again after they completed the special. "We were driving down Sunset Boulevard and she pulled up alongside of me, and we looked at each other and realized who we were and waved at each other and blew some kisses at each other, and that was it. [But] I kept up with her career to the very end."

Making the *Olivia* special "was a great experience," he says. "It was a lot of fun. I loved working with *all* of the artists on the show. It was a great memory for me."

9 TOTALLY HOT

"British-born 'Grease' star Olivia Newton-John was mobbed and almost crushed by fans when the film opened in Chicago last weekend," reported the June 24, 1978, issue of London's *Record Mirror*. "The drama occurred as 28-year-old Olivia arrived for the premiere with 'Saturday Night Fever' star John Travolta who also appears in 'Grease.' As hundreds of fans converged on the couple Ms. Newton-John's dress was ripped, and Travolta battled to keep the crowd at bay. Neither stayed to watch the film."

The article also reported that Olivia "suffered bruising." While stardom was certainly not new for her, clearly *Grease* was taking it to another level. "It was like being caught in a rugby scrum," she said, "except they wanted to use me as the ball. It was the most frightening experience of my life." She subsequently became sick. "I'm just getting over the flu out here," she told *Record Mirror* journalist John Shearlaw by phone from her home in Malibu Beach. "I've been in bed since the premiere." "Now I've got to do it all over again in New York," she added, where another premiere event for the film would be followed by a party at Studio 54.

Clearly, she was delighted with the instant and enormous success of *Grease*. She admitted to Shearlaw that she had been "hesitant" to accept the role, "but what really swung it was that there were two parts for me. Sandra Dee, who I play, starts off as a pretty boring person really. Someone who doesn't dance, a goody two-shoes character… which I suppose is what my image is, or was!" She giggled while making that observation, and then added, "At the end though I'm the complete opposite. I'm a real greaser and," she added after a deliberate pause, "a tarty lady! It's great! I think that my image after that is in for a bit of a shock, but that's what's so good about it. I've always been seen as a perpetual teenager, too good to be true, but I've grown up now. I just count myself extremely lucky to be able to do it."

She made it clear to Shearlaw that she was thrilled about something else, too: "You're the One That I Want" had just reached No. 1 in the United Kingdom when they spoke—it would spend nine weeks atop the British chart. "Sam" had been a Top 10 hit in the United Kingdom in 1977, her first there in six years, but this was the first time she had reached No. 1 in the nation of her birth. "The hit in Britain has really thrilled me," she said. "I was beginning to give up on England, but now the record might encourage things a little." In her typical generous manner, she made sure to give Travolta credit for his role in the duet: "It was great working with him, he gave me so much." "You're the One That I Want" also became Olivia's first number one hit in Australia since "I Honestly Love You."

Whether the success of "You're the One That I Want" was the determining factor or not, EMI Records, which released Olivia's records in the United Kingdom and other foreign markets, renewed her contract at this very time—but only after missing the deadline to renew under the company's own terms, for which Lee Kramer made the label's execs pay. "When EMI in the UK forgot to pick up [extend] Olivia's contract," Stephen Sinclair recalls, "they thought she'd just sign late. Kramer said no. EMI went crazy, but he made them pay a very substantial amount of money to get her signature. Olivia, who was not one to litigate, was ambivalent, but she went along with it." Olivia told Shearlaw that she'd be starting work on a new album the following month (July 1978).

But while the renewal with EMI (which Olivia had been concerned might not even happen) turned out well for her, her difficulties with MCA Records came to a head. As "You're the One That I Want" was approaching the number one spot in the United States (for RSO, not MCA), newspapers reported that Olivia had just "filed suit against MCA Records, asking a court to free her from her contract with the company." Her lawsuit contended that MCA "did not put enough effort into promoting her records." *Rolling Stone* soon reported that Olivia was seeking $10 million in damages. She and Lee Kramer hired attorney Donald Engel, whose long roster of other clients included Frank Sinatra, the Beach Boys, and Rod Stewart. Engel would be assisted by a younger attorney, John Mason, who would remain Olivia's lawyer for the rest of her life.

Olivia was neither the first nor the last recording artist to publicly express dissatisfaction with MCA Records. At the end of 1975, Rick Nelson had accepted a buyout of the remainder of the twenty-year, guaranteed million-dollar contract that he had signed with Decca Records, the corporate antecedent of MCA Records, at the beginning of 1963, frustrated with the label's lack of promotion of his follow-up releases to his 1972 million-selling hit "Garden Party," and signed with Epic Records. And in 1981, Elton John filed an $11.3 million breach-of-contract suit against MCA Records, charging the company with "reneging on an album contract."

MCA immediately fired back at Olivia. The company filed a countersuit for $1 million, charging that she had failed to deliver albums on time starting in the spring of 1977 and that she still owed the label an album under her last contract extension. MCA also asked the court to prohibit Olivia from signing on with another label.

Just before Donald Engel filed Olivia's lawsuit, Ben Fong-Torres visited Lee Kramer at his office—in which, he noted, Olivia's gold and platinum records covered the walls—to interview him again for his long-delayed *Rolling Stone* article on Olivia. Kramer explained his and Olivia's position: "We're dealing now with the ability of MCA to deliver a hit, which is a dubious area." This implication that it was MCA's fault that Olivia had not had a Top 10 hit in almost three years prior to "You're the One That I Want" ignored what John Farrar later observed, or what friendly critic Bill King had also noted, namely that Olivia's material hadn't been as strong in 1976–1977 as it had been in 1973–1975. Then again, both of these things could have been true—the quality of her material could have been declining concurrently with MCA's promotional efforts. Kramer, of course, focused on the latter. He went on to tell Fong-Torres, "They've made a number of significant changes within the company, which suggests they don't consider it was the greatest company, at least in the past year."

Mike Maitland, still the president of MCA Records, seemed reluctant to offer a rebuttal. "There's no way," he told Fong-Torres, "I could get into that without making it worse." But he did say, "Lee's got to do that [accuse MCA of being disorganized] to improve his position." Maitland conceded, however, that over the previous year, "We've been down. But I'm confident it'll be resolved. Marketing is being restructured."

When Fong-Torres asked Olivia, in what he called "a final, final update" via telephone, about the lawsuit, she had little to say. "I don't know what I could say that wouldn't be controversial," she told him in a soft, nervous voice. "There've been a few shake-ups. Hopefully there'll be improvements." Thus, the *Rolling Stone* profile on Olivia, two and three-quarters years in the making, finally appeared with that late-breaking scoop. (Fong-Torres, remembering the flowers that Olivia had sent him and his then wife-to-be, and her kind demeanor, now says, "In my career at *Rolling Stone*, I received thank-you notes from only two artists: Neil Diamond and Diane Keaton. Olivia topped them both.")

Amid the media reports of the Olivia/MCA lawsuits, she and John Farrar entered the recording studio in Hollywood (actually they used three—Cherokee Studios, where Bill Schnee had mixed the *Don't Stop Believin'* album—and two others that no longer exist) to record her next album, her first in over a year and a half. Olivia and Farrar didn't have to struggle as much to find material for this album as they had for at least her last two; between them, they wrote about half the album. Farrar wrote "A Little More Love," which would be the first single from the album and her first for MCA since the rerelease of "I Honestly Love You" one year earlier, and "Totally Hot," which gave the album its name. He also cowrote another song, "Never Enough," along with his wife Pat, Trevor Spencer, and Alan Tarney. Olivia had recorded a song written by Spencer and Tarney, "Living in Harmony," already a UK hit for Cliff Richard, for her second British album half a dozen years earlier. Olivia's compositions for the *Totally Hot* album were "Talk to Me" and "Borrowed Time."

The album also contained, as had her previous albums, some cover versions, in this case "Boats against the Current," which had been the title track of an Eric Carmen album released in 1977, and the classic Spencer Davis Group hit from 1966, "Gimme Some Lovin.'" The choice of these two covers indicated a change in musical direction for Olivia. Absent were covers of John Denver songs or country (or at least partly country) oldies like "Ring of Fire."

While Olivia and Farrar were working on the album, a Los Angeles court ruled that Olivia could not "record albums or perform as a recording artist for anyone other than MCA" before April 1, 1982, pending a settlement of the case. This ruling was a preliminary injunction and a round-one victory for the record company, but it did not mark the end of the legal battle between the two parties. It did, however, ensure that MCA would be releasing the album.

During a break from those sessions, Olivia made an unlikely visit to a small town with the unlikely name of Olivia, Minnesota. The town was celebrating its centennial, and Dave Pedersen, the editor of the *Olivia Times Journal*, decided to invite Olivia to come and be the grand marshal for the parade. His colleagues laughed incredulously when he told them that he was going to invite her, but he sent her a letter anyway. "I said, 'You're the one we want,'" Pedersen recalled with a laugh in 2022. "I knew she could always say no, but you can't say yes unless you ask." He doubted she would even see his letter. "Somehow the letter got to her, that's the biggest miracle. The other miracle is she said yes. I told her we couldn't pay her. Her only reward was fresh baked bread, which she asked for, and two ears of corn, which were from the free corn feed that we had that day."

True to her generous spirit, Olivia said she was glad to come. "The letter was such a kick," she said. "How could I pass it up? This is the only place I've ever heard of with the same name as me." Her visit would mean more to the townspeople than she had realized; on July 12, 1978, just ten days before she came, six prominent local citizens had been killed when their private plane caught fire in a lightning storm and crashed. Landing Olivia's private jet at the town's small airport posed a problem itself, as the runway was not quite long enough for it, but she managed to arrive safely.

Olivia told Pedersen that she didn't want to ride with the parade in an open convertible, but rather on a horse. The organizers found a brown Arabian named Rae, but then another problem nearly ensued. "She's getting on the horse, and it took off across the football field [at] 100 miles an hour," Pedersen recalled. "The sheriff's posse chased her down, brought her back, and they said, 'You can't ride this horse,' and she said, 'Yes I am.' She insisted on it. She said, 'Give me a minute.' She walks up to the horse, grabs him by the head, talked to it, got on, did a little jaunt, and said, 'We're good.'" In the wake of the tragic blow that the tight-knit community had just suffered, the friendly visit from its namesake superstar meant even more to its citizens. "We went from probably the darkest day to maybe one of the brightest days all within a couple of weeks," said resident Joe Dollerschell, who had been one of the security personnel for the event. Remembering the occasion after Olivia's passing, he added, "Everyone in Olivia is an Olivia Newton-John fan." Olivia then returned to Los Angeles and resumed work on *Totally Hot*.

"A Little More Love," released as a single in November 1978, would be the album's biggest hit, reaching No. 3 on the Hot 100 and becoming her ninth release (including the two duets with John Travolta) to sell at least one million 45 RPM singles in the United States. The second single from the album, "Deeper than the Night," would be aimed at the pop/rock market, and the third, "Dancin' 'Round and 'Round," at the country market, which the first two singles appealed to only enough to barely crack the Hot Country 100. (The album's third single had "Totally Hot" on the flip side for Top 40 radio.) Like the hits from *Grease*, "A Little More Love" scored with record buyers around much of the world, also reaching the Top 10 in, among other countries, Australia, Canada, and Great Britain.

"A Little More Love," the *Totally Hot* album, and, not least of all, its album cover all showed that Olivia's transformation into "Sandy #2" was not a flash in the pan that would be limited to *Grease*. *Billboard* reviewed the single as a "top pick" in the issue dated November 25, 1978. "A more sensuous Newton-John emerges in this interesting arrangement underpinned with ominous guitar riffs," the review began. (Steve Lukather of Toto supplied those riffs, and David Hungate, also of Toto, played bass.) "Her vocal strength takes on a new dimension, as does her image considering the graphics on the LP, *Totally Hot*," for which she dressed in black leather and wore stiletto heels.

Insofar as Olivia's biggest complaint against MCA was a lack of promotion for her more recent releases, her lawsuit seemed to already be achieving its goal, although it's just as possible that MCA smelled a buck after *Grease* returned her to the top of the charts. (In fact, to an extent, Olivia would be competing against herself with *Totally Hot*, since the *Grease* soundtrack was still in the Top 10.) MCA Inc., the owner of MCA Records, was now, in a banner year for the American record industry, flush with cash. The November 11, 1978, issue of *Cash Box* reported, "Aided by significant increases on the part of its records and music publishing, MCA Inc., has reported record revenues, net income, and earnings per share for the first nine months of 1978." That same issue of *Cash Box* included a two-page color advertisement for *Totally Hot*, and it also included a favorable review of the album (which did not necessarily have anything to do with MCA having placed the ad, although the trade paper charts in this era could sometimes be manipulated by labels that were willing to pay for hits).[1]

That issue of *Cash Box* also featured an article under the headline "MCA $2Mil Campaign Set for New Olivia Newton-John LP." Bob Siner, the executive vice president of MCA Records, told *Cash Box*, "We are going to spend $2 million on the campaign using all media, including substantial television buys set in segments of high saturation, radio buys, and lots of in-store pieces," such as large posters, window displays, and wall units to be used in record stores. "MCA is totally committed to Olivia," Siner added. "If there's any unhappiness on her side I can't say. The album and our campaign don't solve all the problems between the two parties, but MCA is in the business of selling records and we are very confident that *Totally Hot* will sell very well." He also pledged that the label would provide "more extensive" support for the new album than any of her previous ones. That support included engaging the promotional services of the Scotti Bros. once again.

The article also quoted Olivia's lawyer (Donald Engel, who was not mentioned by name), who said that *Totally Hot* was being released under the terms of an agreement between Olivia and MCA "pending a determination of all the legal claims by each side." Although the dispute wasn't settled yet, Olivia and MCA executives alike had to be happy when the album reached No. 7 on the *Billboard* chart and was certified platinum—a stark contrast to her last album for the label, *Making a Good Thing Better*, which didn't even sell the five hundred thousand copies required for a gold album in the United States. *Totally Hot* also reached the Top 10 in Australia, Canada, Japan, the Netherlands, Norway, and Sweden, but not in Great Britain, where it only reached No. 30.

The second single from *Totally Hot*, "Deeper than the Night," also allowed Olivia to show off the "vocal strength" that *Billboard* had noted as a "new dimension" of her sound in its review of "A Little More Love." "Deeper than the Night" was written by Tom Snow and Johnny Vastano, whose prior songwriting credits, together and separately, included songs for Leo Sayer's 1977 album *Thunder in My Heart*. "We were both at that time signed to publishing deals with Richard Perry," says Snow. Perry was then one of the top record producers in the industry and also had his own label, Planet Records. "I think he [Vastano] might have had a title" for "Deeper than the Night," Snow recalls, "but we just sat down and kind of collaborated, and I hate to use the word 'jammed' on the thing, but it was a pure collaboration, words and music." They didn't write it with Olivia or necessarily anyone else in mind. "It might have been Kathleen Carey, who was representing Richard's writers at the time," who got the song to John Farrar and Olivia. Farrar, who, Snow says, "later became a dear friend and collaborator, liked it, and Olivia liked it, and they asked me to come in and play keyboards on it…. We cut the basic [track] and then John put his, as always, great finishing touches on the song."

"Deeper than the Night" just missed the Top 10 in the States and also hit the Top 20 in Canada. It wasn't a big hit elsewhere, but it became a personal favorite of Olivia's, one that she would perform in concerts for years and include on the US release of *Back to Basics: The Essential Collection 1971–1992* instead of some other singles that were bigger hits for her. Moreover, Snow would remain one of her key songwriters in the years ahead, along with Farrar and Steve Kipner, and he would also continue to play on her recordings of the songs that he wrote or cowrote for her.

Although it was clear that Olivia was leaving behind the pop-country market for the pop-rock market, MCA released "Dancin' 'Round and 'Round" as the third single from the album with the goal of replicating the Top 20 success of "Hopelessly Devoted to You" on the country charts. This song came to Olivia via, indirectly, one of her best friends, the actress Susan George, also a native of England. Adam Mitchell, a native of Scotland who was by then also living in the Los Angeles area, had recently written and recorded a demo of the song. (He would also release a finished recording of it on his 1979 album *Redhead in Trouble!*.) Mitchell happened to be a friend of Susan's. One night in 1978 he was at her house, "just sitting around and playing guitar," he recalls, "and John Farrar was there…. I played 'Dancin' 'Round and 'Round,' and he really liked it and said, 'You know, I think that might be good for Olivia.'"

"Dancin' 'Round and 'Round" would reach No. 29 on the *Billboard* country singles chart during the summer of 1979, her fifteenth and last entry on that chart. Mitchell didn't mind at all that Olivia's recording of the song came out before his own. In addition to earning royalties, he "thought her version was great," he says, "and, you know, that's unusual. A problem for most songwriters [is], I can count on one hand the versions of songs of mine that other artists have cut that I really liked. And I really liked hers." Not long after Olivia recorded his song, he was at Susan George's house again when Olivia phoned. Mitchell, who never met Olivia in person, got to talk to her. "I introduced myself to her and I said, 'I wrote "Dancin' 'Round and 'Round," and thank you for cutting it.'" When MCA released it as a single, the promotional staff plugged the flip side, "Totally Hot," to Top 40 radio, but it stalled at No. 52 on the Hot 100, where "Dancin' 'Round and 'Round" only made it to No. 82. The *Totally Hot* album, somewhat surprisingly given its emphasis on pop/rock, reached No. 4 on the *Billboard* country albums chart; it was her last album to reach that chart for twenty years.

After Olivia finished recording *Totally Hot*, she and Travolta traveled to Europe and England to promote *Grease*. On September 9, 1978, they appeared in Deauville, France, at the fourth annual Deauville American Film Festival, and by that evening they were in London for the British premiere of *Grease*. Susan George, who had accompanied Andy Gibb to the Hollywood premiere, accompanied Olivia to this one. In a tribute that Susan wrote for Olivia, her friend for more than fifty years, after Olivia's passing, she recalled that "our stretch limo was mobbed. She was staggered and playfully humbled by all the amazing attention. Did she ever know how beautiful she was? No, never, and that was part of her magic."

Then Olivia, with assistance from John Farrar, put together a band and got ready to resume touring. The Totally Hot World Tour, which included no shows in the United States, kicked off in Japan in October. She had been set to tour Japan six months earlier, but she canceled "in protest against a fisherman killing a dolphin that broke through a farming net in Nagasaki Prefecture," noted Japanese press reports. Upset Japanese fans gathered signatures for a petition that they sent her, asking her to reconsider. She didn't abandon her advocacy for dolphins, though. At a press conference before the Japanese leg of the tour began, she said, "I want you to think about ways to prevent dolphins from approaching fishing grounds." She donated some concert proceeds to Japan's research center for dolphins.

Nevertheless, her advocacy had negative ramifications for her tour of Japan. "I supported her in this," says Skip Griparis, "but she ruffled some feathers in Japan and that didn't help ticket sales…. We didn't do nearly as well. In '76 she was fairly sold out everywhere. In '78, not as well. It wasn't terrible, but it was a comedown from the previous time."

The less-than-stellar beginning of the world tour in Japan turned out to be an omen for the entire tour to some extent, notwithstanding Olivia's return to the top of the charts on an international level. Part of the problem, Griparis recalls, lay with the band itself, which consisted of several newcomers. "It wasn't our best band for a couple of reasons. Some of them just didn't care for the music that much, and they were just kind of going through the motions. Some weren't good at this kind of music."

Something else about the band still sticks in Griparis's mind. "The drummer they hired was a drunk! He looked like a blond John Travolta, which I mentioned once to Olivia." Olivia replied, "Yeah. Great minds think alike! I caught that too!" That reply made Griparis wonder if that was why she had hired the drummer, whom he felt wasn't up to her standards musically. "The tempos just kept slowing and slowing. Not good, the vibe wasn't good." Nor was the vibe much better offstage. "One night we were traveling in a cab with the drummer… [and] he jumped out of the cab while we were in traffic and got into some parked car that he liked… he just jumped into somebody else's car. I mean, he was out of his fucking mind!"

Surprisingly, ticket sales turned out to be a disappointment beyond Japan. "A lot of the gigs, as I recall, [or] some gigs," says Rick Ruskin,

got canceled because the advance sales were so poor. We were supposed to go to Paris. We never went to Paris. We were in Australia, and the Australian promoter was bitching to everybody within earshot that he put out all this money in promotion and stuff, and so many gigs got canceled that he was not going to do too well.

To Ruskin, some of the blame might have been attributable to Lee Kramer; MCA didn't offer much promotional help, either.

Griparis also remembers the cancellation in Paris "because of low ticket sales." "It's unfortunate," he reflects, "that my final tour with her, and actually her final tour for about four years, was a little awkward. The band was just not… there were some guys that just shouldn't have been there." He cites bass guitarist Bryan Garofalo, a veteran of studio and live work during the 1970s and 1980s, as an example. "He had an attitude. He wasn't into it."

Nevertheless, the tour did have some highlights. Olivia got to see both of her parents, her brother, and her half-brother and half-sister in Australia. (After Olivia moved from London to California, her mother moved back to Australia. Shortly before Olivia did the Australian leg of the tour, an Australian magazine reported that Irene "lives alone in a modestly furnished Melbourne flat.") The tour concluded in England in December. Olivia hadn't played any full concerts in her native country since 1973, and she had told *Record Mirror* in June 1978 how much she was looking forward to rectifying that. The British concerts were not plagued by low ticket sales, and Bob Siner and George Osaki (who designed Olivia's MCA album covers) came to London to present her with a platinum record award for *Totally Hot*. John Farrar was also present, and while the presentation focused on Olivia, he too received a platinum record as the producer of and a contributing songwriter to the album. MCA had an asbestos-clad messenger hand out the awards.

When the tour ended, Olivia told Griparis, who had the most seniority of anyone in her road band (nearly four years), "that she wasn't going to tour for a long time, to not wait around for her." It almost felt like the end of an era for him, leaving him with memories of "how wonderful she was to work for, how nice she was to me." One year she even threw a birthday party for him at the Riviera in Vegas, after having the audience sing "Happy Birthday" to him in the second show that night. "She was just the best."

Olivia's thirtieth birthday had occurred a month before she kicked off the Totally Hot World Tour, and in an interview just before she reached that milestone, she gave a hint as to why she wasn't looking to resume her heavy touring schedule of 1974–1977. "When you're in your twenties, you feel you have a grace period. But with 30 just around the corner, I'm getting frightened," she said.

I'm not obsessed with age, but I can see that my life is nearing the middle. Many of the things I've been avoiding, like marriage and a family, need new examination. I've already had a very happy career, and I want it to continue, but I need more in my life than that. I think the idea of growing old with an armful of gold records and nothing else is horrible…. It's okay if that's all you want, but it's no longer enough for me.

Each of Olivia's parents weighed in on her unmarried status in interviews during the summer of 1978. "I think she'd be absolutely marvelous as a mum," her father said, "but I think she has been very wise about not getting on to the marriage circuit yet. She's seen two divorces in her family and that is a bit off-putting. But she's also seen me in a very happy second marriage and that has cheered her up a lot."

Irene Newton-John told a reporter,

I didn't want Olivia to marry young. I felt her sister had married too young. I think the fact that she hasn't married yet possibly has something to do with the example she has seen in my family where people have changed partners quite often. There's me, my brother and sister, and her sister Rona. Olivia is probably very cautious about marriage. Anyway, she has very little to gain from it unless she wants children.

"She doesn't need a man to provide for her," Irene added, as if it weren't already obvious. "I'm in the same position so I can understand. I have enough to live on and I can make my own decisions and live my own life. Until she finds someone absolutely right, she won't marry. She doesn't want to have any of these traumatic experiences we've had."

Although Olivia and Lee Kramer had reunited, it still wasn't clear that he was "absolutely right" as a potential husband for her. Bill Oakes didn't think so based on what he saw after Olivia and Lee reunited in 1977. Oakes recalls that at times Olivia "seemed to be quite afraid" of Kramer.

I do remember that. She was, at the time, up in Big Rock [in Malibu], her place we'd go to occasionally, and she was very different if Lee was there than if he wasn't. We always noticed that, if Louis St. Louis, the music arranger, and I would go up there. She seemed to be sort of intimidated by him in some way.

It appeared to Oakes that Kramer had

a bit of an ego thing, you know, "I'm with Olivia Newton-John." She was obviously happy, I think she was great, on the set. He wasn't around. But at her house, I do remember there being a bit of an atmosphere there… because we'd occasionally go by there to listen to the stuff we were recording. It didn't seem like a great relationship to me.

Kramer, dressed in a black outfit that called to mind the T-Birds of *Grease*, accompanied Olivia to her first public appearance of 1979. Robert Stigwood, the Bee Gees, and the English television host and journalist David Frost had conceived of and arranged a televised UNICEF benefit concert in New York City that was held at the United Nations General Assembly in Manhattan on January 9. In addition to the Bee Gees, other performers included Olivia's recent television special guests ABBA and Andy Gibb, her friend John Denver, Rod Stewart, Donna Summer, Rita Coolidge and Kris Kristofferson, and Earth, Wind & Fire.

The recording artists who played at the concert were to donate not only their live performance for an album that would be released by Polydor Records on behalf of UNICEF, but also the publishing rights to the song they performed. The Bee Gees donated their current hit "Too Much Heaven," while some other artists, such as John Denver, donated an older song from their catalog. Olivia didn't own the publishing on many of her songs; she hadn't written most of them, and furthermore, Kramer's publishing company, Lee Kramer Music, took a cut on many of the songs she recorded.

About four or five days before the concert, by which time she and Kramer were in Manhattan, she phoned Stephen Sinclair at his home in Malibu. It was about eight o'clock in the morning in California. "Listen," she said to him, "do you think you can come up with something for this concert? We need to transcribe it, we need to rehearse it, so it needs to be like *now*."

Sinclair had an acoustic piano in his cottage. "So, I thought," he says, "you know, I should write something acoustically, because it's more emotional for that kind of event." Within a few hours, he wrote a ballad, called "The Key," with a very complex series of chords. "I phoned her back, and I played it to her over the phone. I played it to her and Lee, and they recorded it on something and that was it." Sinclair and Kramer donated their songwriter's and publisher's royalties, respectively, to UNICEF, and Olivia performed the song at the concert.

Originally, Olivia was scheduled to sing only one song, like the rest of the performers on the bill, but she and Andy Gibb ended up singing a duet together as well. Barry Gibb had written a song called "Rest Your Love on Me" in 1976, and the Bee Gees had just released it as the B-side of "Too Much Heaven." "Rest Your Love on Me" became the only Top 40 country hit that the Bee Gees ever had, compared to thirty Top 40 pop hits in the United States. Conway Twitty would have a number one country hit with the song in 1981. At the UNICEF concert, as Olivia told music journalist Mary Campbell in 1981, "Someone on the production staff… suggested we [she and Andy] sing that song [together]." They performed a gentle and (to use a term that wasn't in use yet in 1979) "unplugged" version of it.

A couple of months later, as Olivia told Campbell, "Andy was doing a new album and asked me down to Miami to record it with him. I didn't have an album currently." Barry Gibb also gave them a second song, "I Can't Help It," which no one had released yet. Much to Olivia's dismay, she found that Andy's escalating drug abuse and insecurities had made him suddenly unreliable. On the day that

Olivia arrived at the studio (Criteria) to record, Andy was a no-show; he was in Bimini and failed to return to Miami in time. Olivia rehearsed the duets with Barry, who was coproducing the session with Albhy Galuten and Karl Richardson. (The same trio produced all the Bee Gees' recordings of this era, Andy's hits, and Frankie Valli's "Grease.") When Andy finally arrived, he was in rough shape, and as Galuten later recalled, "there was a lot of struggle getting a vocal out of [him]."

Andy and Olivia ultimately finished both recordings and also sang together onstage at the annual NARM (National Association of Recording Merchandisers) convention, which was held at the Diplomat Hotel in Hollywood, Florida, from March 23 through 28. Their two studio duets, however, sat unreleased for nearly a year before Andy's *After Dark* album finally came out at the beginning of February 1980. Andy hadn't managed to finish the album before Barry had to abandon the project for the time being to prepare for and head out on a tour with the Bee Gees. *After Dark* wouldn't be finished until just before Christmas 1979. When it was finally released, Olivia, according to *People* magazine, "reportedly complained" that her duets with Andy "were stale" after the long delay. In the album's liner notes, Andy thanked Olivia "for her friendship and patience."

In March 1979, Olivia returned to England, less than three months after the Totally Hot World Tour had ended there, to receive a special honor. She brought her four-year-old nephew, Rona's son Emerson, with her on her flight from Los Angeles to London.[2] On March 13, she went to Buckingham Palace and curtsied to Queen Elizabeth II, who bestowed upon her the honor of being named an Officer of the Order of the British Empire. Australian Premier Malcolm Fraser had nominated her. "I was knocked out to get this award," Olivia told the press. "When I first heard about it, I thought it was a practical joke. I had to check it up with my office people before I believed it. I really appreciate the incredible honor of getting the OBE at the age of 30."

With *Totally Hot* and its singles keeping her on the charts for well over half of 1979 and, she thought, a single with Andy Gibb on the way that year, Olivia turned her focus to her next movie. Allan Carr wanted her to star in his planned follow-up to *Grease*, an "epic music movie," according to *Photoplay* magazine, to be called *Discoland*. Olivia turned him down and he was furious. "I guarantee," he told the press, "I shall *never* ask her to work for me again, even if she begs me on bended knees." A friend of Carr's would later say, "If you disagreed with him, you were betraying him. He had to push you away."

After much reworking, Carr's "epic" musical came out as *Can't Stop the Music* in June 1980, starring the Village People. Valerie Perrine played the female lead. The movie bombed and began a downhill slide for Carr, although he later rebounded when he produced *La Cage aux Folles* on Broadway. For many years Carr wouldn't speak to Olivia, but they did reestablish contact before his death in 1999.

"I had a number of offers for films after *Grease*—straight acting roles as well as musicals," Olivia told a journalist in November 1979. "Time was going on, and I was tempted. But I never had the instinctive feeling that I had for *Grease*." Nevertheless, she said,

> I was on the brink of taking one when my agent said, "This outline just came in and I think it's perfect for you." The script wasn't even written when I said, "That's the one." The music hadn't been set or anything. I really took a gamble, but I believe in the concept so now I just have to hope that my instincts were right because that's all I was going on.

Thus, Australia's *TV Week* noted, "Australia's popular expatriate is focusing on *Xanadu*."

10 *XANADU* AND *HOLLYWOOD NIGHTS*

" t is a film that is partly borrowing from Greek myth, partly a tribute to a 1950s Rita Hayworth movie [actually 1947's *Down to Earth*] with a similar plot, and it is also about the flash-in-the-pan roller-disco craze of the late 1970s," wrote BBC journalist Catherine Bray in her fortieth-anniversary retrospective of *Xanadu*. "These competing elements, each hoping to hook a different demographic sector of the audience, go to war throughout the film. Nobody wins."

Olivia had been wise to stay away from Allan Carr's disastrous follow-up to *Grease*, but unfortunately her own turned out to be just about as disastrous, both at the box office and with film critics. On the other hand, the project would have some significant redeeming benefits for her. She got to act and dance with the legendary Gene Kelly, which, she said forty years later, "was a terrifying proposition but an amazing experience." The soundtrack album, while not reaching the same level of success as that of *Grease*, would sell a million copies in the United States almost immediately and was certified as having sold another million by 1984. It also yielded a number one single in "Magic" and hit collaborations with the Electric Light Orchestra and Olivia's dear old friend Cliff Richard. *Xanadu* also provided Olivia with an introduction to Matt Lattanzi, who would become her first husband, and even though that marriage would end in divorce, she would often later point out that "without meeting Matt on set I wouldn't have my beautiful daughter Chloe."

"*Xanadu*," explained Australia's *TV Week*, "grew from an idea to make a 1980 musical fantasy in the tradition of the great MGM musicals [of the 1940s]. It revives the excitement of those dance-and-music spectacles, while using modern film and sound techniques to dazzling effect." That was the intent, at least. Olivia would play the role of a Greek goddess.

Lawrence Gordon produced *Xanadu* for Universal Pictures. He had recently produced two hit movies starring Burt Reynolds, *Hooper* and *The End*. The director was Robert Greenwald, who would go on to have a long and successful career but did not have much experience at this point. Press reports mentioned that Olivia had "an unknown Australian named Mel Gibson" in mind to play the male lead, but the role went to Michael Beck, an American actor who had just worked for Gordon in *The Warriors*, and whom some reviewers described as "an Andy Gibb look-a-like." Andy had been rumored as a possibility for the role, but those reports were false hype, as were more widespread reports a bit later on that he would star in *Grease 2*.

The legendary actor and dancer Gene Kelly, who was sixty-seven when *Xanadu* was made, was semiretired by then. "I had said," he told *Atlanta Constitution* journalist Eleanor Ringel in August 1980,

> I was never going to do another musical, but *Xanadu* came along and a lot of it appealed to me. They were trying to do some things we'd done in the past, and I like Olivia Newton-John. So, I said I'd do it, but I won't sing or dance. Then when we got into the picture, every journalist who came on the set said, "You can't mean that," and finally, when the picture was over, the producer said, "There's a big hole in the picture—you haven't done anything with Olivia." So, we put together a number.

But while Gene, whom Olivia would describe in an interview in 2015 as "a lovely man and very, very, *very* hardworking and professional," said positive things to the press about *Xanadu*, his widow Patricia Kelly recalls that privately he wasn't too happy about the film. "Gene was not a fan of *Xanadu*. He adored Olivia Newton-John, but he felt that the director and producers were wasting time and money, with no script ready when they began production. For someone who grew up in the [Great] Depression and who, as a professional, respected budgets and schedules, it was completely anathema." Patricia says that Gene, who passed away in 1996, always made "just very positive comments about [Olivia]," though. The feeling was mutual. According to musician and record producer Chong Lim, who worked closely with Olivia and became friends with her beginning in the late 1990s, "She often talked about Gene Kelly, about working with him in *Xanadu*. I think that could have been a highlight [for her]. She often talked about him, about the experience working with him." Olivia would also recall what a thrill it was for her to introduce her father to Kelly.

Martin Samuel, who along with his wife Mary was a dear friend of Olivia's and Rona's, was the hair designer on *Xanadu*. "I got the job through Olivia. Her sister," he reflects, "was our very, very best friend. We met Rona in England. We both lived in the same area and the boys, Emerson and our son, were very close and went to school together." As Olivia was about to start filming *Grease*, she called Rona and told her that she and Emerson should move to Los Angeles to be near her. "So, Rona said," remembers Samuel, "'I'm moving to LA, so I'll see you.' And then, as fate would have it… in 1978 we came over [to LA]… because we wanted to live here." Rona introduced Martin and Mary to Olivia, and in 1979 Olivia asked him if he would like to be the hair designer for *Xanadu*. "It was the second film I had done here as hair designer. I had a big résumé in England."

Samuel recalls much about *Xanadu* fondly. "It was fantastic. A real Hollywood musical." He also got a bird's-eye view, however, of the same problems that irritated Gene Kelly. "The script was kind of, it could have been so much better if it were handled a bit better. The musical numbers were quite good, but… the dialogue things were not handled very well." Kelly, Samuel says, choreographed and "more or less directed" the 1940s dance sequence starring himself and Olivia. "It was a lot of rehearsal for him and Olivia to do that. They were fantastic together… she was very in awe, I think, of him."

The challenges of *Xanadu* went beyond script and production problems. In addition to learning a new style of dancing for the 1940s scene with Kelly, Olivia had to learn how to roller-skate. During rehearsals for skating scenes, she wore knee pads. But while she and Michael Beck were filming the scene where they skate to the song "Suddenly," she took a hard fall on a concrete floor. A medic on the set took her to the Cedars-Sinai emergency room, where she was diagnosed with a cracked tailbone. A doctor gave her painkillers and told her to take a few weeks off, but Olivia wouldn't hear of it and continued working through the pain. Ironically, a photo of a smiling, skating Olivia graced the July 9, 1979, cover of *People* magazine with the headline "Roller Mania."

When the filming of *Xanadu* began in September 1979, Lee Kramer and Olivia were still paired professionally and, on some level, personally, although Olivia wrote in her memoir that their romance came to an end after the Totally Hot World Tour of fall/winter 1978. "They came to our house," Martin Samuel recalls, "and he was on [the] set. But he wasn't, like, *involved* in the shooting or anything like that." (Kramer was, however, an executive producer of the film.) As for the status of Lee and Olivia's personal relationship while the film was being made, Samuel says,

Well, honestly, I can't really remember specifically, uh, what was really going on privately with them, but he was there, around, a lot. I don't know whether they were, what was going on with their personal life at that point. But he was still very much around and, you know, they were great friends. There was never any kind of animosity or anything like that you could pick up, though I don't know where they were at. But then, of course, once she went public with Matt, it was quite obvious what was going to happen.

Matt Lattanzi was a twenty-year-old aspiring actor and dancer, and he had a small role as a dancer in *Xanadu*. "He was young, [a] *very* good-looking dancer," remembers Samuel, "very sweet, lovely man, lovely boy." Matt later admitted that not many years earlier, he'd had a pinup of Olivia on his bedroom wall. When he and Olivia met on the set on August 6, 1979, Michael Beck had not yet been cast, and so she rehearsed some dancing scenes with him. "He was very striking," Olivia would later say. "You couldn't miss him, that's for sure." *Grease* casting director Joel Thurm, who would remain friends with Olivia for the rest of her life, would later laughingly say, "My guess is she took one look at Matt and said, 'Mmm mmm mmm, I want him, he's fresh in town, he's unspoiled. Lock him up and send him over.'"

Skip Griparis paid his friend and former employer Olivia a visit on the set. "There was this guy across the room that kept staring at me, like burning holes at me." Skip chuckles at the memory. "I thought, 'What the hell? Is he gay and he's into me, or what is this?' Turns out that was Matt Lattanzi. So, he was wondering, like, 'Who the hell is that guy that is talking to my girl?' I guess."

Martin Samuel saw the relationship between Olivia and Matt develop. "They just fell in love, and it was, you know, beautiful," he says.

It had to be kept secret. No one knew on the production at all. And so, we used to, in those days at Universal, they still had those little cottages where the actors and actresses would be instead of trailers, all self-contained. And so, Livvy used to have her hair and makeup done in there a lot of the time. That'd be first thing in the morning. And we used to kind of have to get Matt in to say hi and things like that without people seeing, without people knowing, just, you know, us, the little team that were with her.

"He was a stand-in for the leading man," Olivia said of Matt in an interview in 1983,

so I was doing all my dance rehearsals with him, and we just became friendly. We were friends first and that's never happened to me before. Usually when I meet somebody, we start going out. We like each other straight off and become romantically involved, but Matt and I were friends first. I slowly got to know him, which was very nice. He's a terrific person.

Before the filming of *Xanadu* was completed, Matt was (secretly) spending most nights with Olivia in her suite at the Beverly Wilshire Hotel.

By May 1980, Olivia, although she refused to elaborate, admitted to the press that her romantic relationship with Lee was over. So did Lee. He told journalist Colin Dangaard, "There is no longer romantic involvement, but we're still the very closest of friends and, of course, I'm still her manager. We're on the same side of the fence, supporting each other. We're real partners." Olivia told Dangaard that she gave Lee a lot of credit for her success. "He would never let me do something that was not right. He is interested in me as a person. He knew me and worked with me before I made a hit record. And he has a taste which, for him, is instinctive." Olivia didn't mention Lattanzi in the interview.

By now the legal battle between Olivia and MCA Records, after nearly two years, had finally come to a conclusion. The *Los Angeles Times* reported on April 27, 1980, that she had "signed a multimillion-dollar package with MCA after what a recent *Los Angeles* magazine story described as 'a vitriolic period of negotiations punctuated by threats, lawsuits and countercharges.'" The resolution of her case helped her attorney Donald Engel, according to the *Hollywood Reporter*, gain a reputation as a "record contract buster," and he went on to represent recording artists such as Donna Summer, Tom Scholz of the band Boston, and Don Henley in contract disputes with record companies.

Olivia hadn't released anything on the MCA label since the *Totally Hot* album and its three singles, but in February 1980, RSO Records released Andy Gibb's long overdue *After Dark* album with its two Andy-Olivia duets. The first single from the album, "Desire," was still in the Top 10 when RSO released Andy and Olivia's recording of "I Can't Help It" as the second single. The single hit the market just before the March 19 taping of Olivia's third ABC-TV special, *Olivia Newton-John: Hollywood Nights*. Andy was once again one of her guests—he and Olivia sang the new single, although the performance was trimmed for the telecast—but this special featured a much larger roster than her last one. Elton John, Karen Carpenter, Toni Tennille, Tina Turner, Gene Kelly, Ted Knight, and Dick Clark also appeared. "I Can't Help It" peaked at No. 12 on the Hot 100 not long after the special's April 14 airdate, perhaps a little too soft for the tail end of the disco era that saw Blondie's "Call Me" and Lipps, Inc.'s "Funkytown" spend weeks at No. 1. The Andy-Olivia duet fared better on the easy listening–oriented adult contemporary chart, reaching No. 8. It wasn't as big a hit internationally.

In May, MCA released the first two singles from the *Xanadu* soundtrack, the Electric Light Orchestra's "I'm Alive" and Olivia's "Magic." John Farrar didn't have Bill Oakes to offer him any guidance in writing songs for Olivia in this film. For her musical numbers, "I had to write the script pretty much," he later recalled. "Magic" was written for a roller-skating fantasy scene. The record's hypnotic guitars and sound effects, a departure from anything Olivia had done previously, required a lot of effort in the recording studio. "We worked hard on that one," Farrar said. "Quite a while to record, and about three days mixing it." Farrar played the guitars and synthesizers on the record and also added backing vocals, and David Hungate of Toto played bass guitar. Carlos Vega, who had played on the *Grease* soundtrack and had become highly sought after for both session work and tours, played drums and percussion.

Toward the end of May, Olivia and Kramer traveled to Australia. For Olivia it was both a homecoming and an honor: she would be singing at a Royal Variety Performance at the Sydney Opera House before Britain's Queen Elizabeth II and Prince Philip, Duke of Edinburgh. Also on the bill were John Farnham, Peter Allen, Paul Hogan, Julie Anthony, and Helen Reddy. Olivia didn't bring a band—she hadn't toured in almost a year and a half and no longer had a touring band. Rick Lotempio, who was the lead guitarist in Helen Reddy's band, recalls that he and other members of her band played with Olivia as she sang "Deeper than the Night," "Hopelessly Devoted to You," "A Little More Love," and "Don't Cry for Me Argentina." She also joined Peter Allen, the other stars, and a choir to sing Allen's song "I Still Call Australia Home," and she led the ensemble in the grand finale, "Waltzing Matilda," a folksy old Australian "bush ballad."

Olivia returned to Australia in August with Kramer and Joan Bullard, MCA Records' executive vice president of publicity, to promote the *Xanadu* soundtrack and movie (MCA owned Universal Pictures, which released the film). Olivia also attended the Australian premiere with her family. Before the trip, Olivia gave an interview to Phyllis Battelle in Los Angeles for the *Australian Women's Weekly* in which she opened up to an unprecedented extent, at least to any journalist, about her relationship with Kramer. "I'm sure both Lee and I went through every kind of emotion possible," she told Battelle. "When you live with someone for a very long time, it has to be difficult." Battelle then asked her why she and Lee were maintaining their professional relationship. "We've been through a lot together, so why not? It seems such a shame if, after six years together, two people decide never to see each other again. It's too bad, because when a person is part of your life for so long, has watched you grow and shared so many things, isn't it better to be friends?" Olivia thought so. "I thought it might be hard, but, so far, it's worked out well. I hope it can continue." "Lee and I fight, about business decisions," she added, "but I still trust his judgement, his taste; and he cares about me. He'll fight for me, which makes our management-artist relationship a rare one in this town."

Olivia made it clear in the interview that marriage was on her mind. "Right now, I feel like I'm on a freeway, which is straight and going forward. But it has exits. And I can turn off on any side road that I want," she told Battelle. "One exit I could take, if I decide to, would lead to my perfect house. Lately, I've found myself doodling little pictures of cottages, with white-washed walls and picket fences. Very old-fashioned, isn't that? Inside the cottage I see a happy family, children," she said with what Battelle described as "a dazzling grin." "Ah, you see, you have caught me on a good day," Olivia continued. "Sometimes when the world situation is bleak, I am very negative and decidedly against having children—poor things, what's the point? But this week I've got through being depressed, and I definitely want a family." She then paused. "But then, you have to find someone to marry first, don't you?"

When Battelle asked, Olivia told her that she was seeing "a few" men, but "none that she'd care to talk about." Clearly, she wasn't ready yet to go public with her relationship with Matt, but as she continued this (for that period of her life) unusually candid interview, Olivia said,

> You think, when you're 20, that you will never get old, that nothing will ever change. Then you stare into the mirror, a line here, a wrinkle there, and you know it is going to change. It's not just the cosmetic changes that matter. You realize that there is a lot of superficiality in relationships. And you want to find someone who loves you for what's inside, so that when the looks begin to go, it won't matter.

Olivia now seemed to think that living with Lee for the better part of six years without them being married may have been a mistake. "I think about that now," she said, "hesitantly" according to Battelle.

> Now I'm wondering if maybe you should make the commitment to marriage in the beginning, and then work on it rather than live together, testing each other all the time. Because either way, you're going to find things wrong with one another. And I'm not really sure of this, but I do wonder is it possible that you might try a little harder when you're married to keep it together?

Aside from the end of her romantic relationship with Lee and her beginning a new one with Matt, there was another reason why marriage was on Olivia's mind. One of her best friends, Karen Carpenter, whom she had known since they met in London in 1971, and who was about a year and a half younger than Olivia, got married in the summer of 1980. Olivia hadn't been able to accept her friend's invitation to be a bridesmaid because she had been in Australia for the *Xanadu* premiere (August 22), but she made it back in time for the wedding at the Beverly Hills Hotel on August 31, 1980.

Just as Olivia didn't feel ready to bring Matt to any of the premieres of *Xanadu* (for the Hollywood premiere on August 8 she had Martin Samuel escort her, telling him, "I can't be seen with Matt"), she didn't bring him to Karen's wedding either. Instead, she came with Kenny Ortega, who, except for the scenes with Gene Kelly, had been the choreographer on *Xanadu*. Although Olivia would later tell Karen's biographer, Randy L. Schmidt, that she had "wanted the attention to be on Karen," inevitably the bride's other friends were starstruck. When one of Karen's lifelong friends started taking photographs, a security officer walked up to him and said, "Kindly stop taking pictures of Miss Newton-John."

Olivia's friends and associates, of course, became aware of her blossoming romance with Matt sooner than her fans did. A fairly typical opinion was that expressed by Tom Snow: "I liked Matt. I thought he was a cool guy… very friendly." At the same time, the relationship baffled some people who knew her. Skip Griparis, whom Matt had stared daggers through when Skip was catching up with Olivia on the set of *Xanadu*, reflects, "I don't know, again, why she went with, why she was attracted to these schmucks, you know, back in the day. Why would she be attracted to a guy that clearly wasn't suited for her in Matt, or who was an incompetent asshole like Lee?" To Bill Oakes, "Matt just seemed sort of an unlikely prospect." Oakes remembers thinking, "Is this for real?" "I mean, it seemed like an odd relationship. He just didn't seem that much of a formidable person, and you thought," Oakes recalls with a laugh, "'Well, boy, she really picks them, doesn't she?'" "She was such an adorable girl," Oakes says, "you'd think that she'd have had everyone at her feet. [Matt] was a toy boy for her, in a way."

The press, meanwhile, still wouldn't let go of rumors of an affair between Olivia and John Travolta. When she arrived at London's Heathrow Airport on September 15, 1980, for the British premiere of *Xanadu*, a reporter asked her about a boast that Travolta had allegedly made about always having affairs with his leading ladies. "He is always being misquoted," Olivia replied. "We are good friends, and I know he would never say anything like that."

Earlier in the year, when her duets with Andy Gibb came out, *People* and *Us* magazines each ran a cover photo of the pair; the *Us* headline was, "Olivia Newton-John: Her Man Moved Out, but She's Singing Love Songs with Andy Gibb." Andy's friend Scott Paton, who worked for Casey Kasem's *American Top 40* and met and interviewed Olivia a number of times, recalls that Andy seemed to have a crush on her at one point. In 1979, Andy named a racehorse after her (Livvy's Choice). But when *People* asked him about the rumors of a romance between himself and Olivia in April 1980, he said, "I'd like the rumors to be true, but it takes two to tango." "She's my closest friend in Los Angeles," Gibb told an LA journalist, "and I always see her when I'm here. We go horseback riding together in Malibu."

These frivolous headlines about alleged romances with her famous male friends and collaborators were harmless publicity, but all the publicity in the world couldn't help the *Xanadu* film. Neither of the two best-known American film critics of the day, Gene Siskel and Roger Ebert, who reviewed movies together on television and separately in newspaper columns, gave it a thumbs-up. "*Xanadu* is a mushy and limp musical fantasy, so insubstantial it keeps evaporating before our eyes," Ebert wrote. He saw "very few reasons to see" the film: the presence of Olivia ("a great-looking woman, brimming with high spirits"), Gene Kelly ("[he] has a few good moments"), and the soundtrack (particularly "Magic"). Also, Ebert added, "It's not as bad as *Can't Stop the Music*," the Allan Carr production that Olivia had decided to avoid. Siskel wrote that the film suffered from a "pathetically thin script." *Esquire*'s review quipped, "In a word: *Xana*-don't!" Between production and promotional costs, the film lost money for MCA/Universal.

Ironically, given that Olivia had the good judgment to turn down Allan Carr for *Can't Stop the Music*, that film and *Xanadu* became linked in Hollywood history. A young film publicist, a UCLA alumnus named John J. B. Wilson, saw the two movies on a double feature and found them so bad that he created the Golden Raspberry Awards, a sort of Oscars for the worst films. At least *Xanadu* didn't win the first "Razzie." That "honor," announced on March 31, 1981, went to *Can't Stop the Music*. The Golden Raspberry Awards received much fanfare and have continued as an annual tradition ever since.

The *Xanadu* soundtrack was an entirely different matter, though. "Magic" spent four weeks (most of August 1980) at No. 1 on the Hot 100, and *Billboard* ranked it as the third-biggest hit of the year behind "Call Me" and Pink Floyd's "Another Brick in the Wall (Part II)." "Magic" also reached No. 1 in Canada and the Top 5 in Australia, New Zealand, and South Africa. It only reached No. 32 in the United Kingdom, but Olivia's collaboration with the Electric Light Orchestra, the film's title song, reached No. 1 in the United Kingdom, Austria, Belgium, Denmark, Germany, Ireland, the Netherlands, Norway, Spain, and Zimbabwe, and the Top 10 in Australia, Canada, Italy, New Zealand, Sweden, Switzerland, and the United States. Jeff Lynne wrote and produced "Xanadu," and Olivia sang lead vocals. The Electric Light Orchestra played on the record, and Olivia, Lynne, and bass guitarist Kelly Groucutt sang backing vocals. James Newton Howard, who (among other credits) was a member of Elton John's band, played synthesizers.

Although Lynne would go on to produce many recording artists besides his own band, including the Beatles' mid-1990s "reunion" singles "Free as a Bird" and "Real Love," at the time producing someone else was a new experience for him. "It was very strange because I'd never produced anybody else but meself until now," he said in September 1980, "so it was a bit strange… sort of saying, 'Can you just try that bit again,' and all this…. I didn't know how far to go 'cause she was such a nice person that everything I suggested, you know, she tried it." Lynne said in an interview in 2001 on the Los Angeles radio station 95.5 KLOS-FM, "I'd have to say 'Xanadu' [is my favorite song] off *Xanadu* [the album], because I like the chord structure of that and I like the way Olivia Newton-John sings it."

John Lennon had his own favorites from the soundtrack. Defending commercial music in much the same way Olivia had to Ben Fong-Torres for *Rolling Stone*, Lennon told an interviewer, "I love commercial music. I like Olivia Newton-John singing 'Magic,' and Donna Summer singing whatever the hell it is she'll be singing. I like the ELO singing 'All Over the World.' I can dissect it [commercial music] and criticize it with any critic in the business." Lennon made these remarks not long before the release of his first single in over five years, "(Just Like) Starting

Over," which was still climbing the Hot 100 when he was murdered on December 8, 1980, and became a posthumous number one hit.

In addition to collaborating with the Electric Light Orchestra, Olivia also invited Cliff Richard to sing a duet with her for the *Xanadu* soundtrack. By 1980 he had finally had a few big hits in the United States, beginning in 1976 with the million seller "Devil Woman," which Bruce Welch produced. Cliff wouldn't appear in the movie; the song that he and Olivia sang, "Suddenly," written and produced by John Farrar, played while she and Michael Beck roller-skated. But she and Cliff made a video for the song which first aired in her *Hollywood Nights* TV special, and they would perform the song together at concerts on a number of occasions in the years ahead, including Cliff's seventy-fifth birthday concert at London's Royal Albert Hall in 2015.

"Suddenly" became Olivia's third single from *Xanadu*, and it reached the Top 20 in both the United States and the United Kingdom and No. 4 on *Billboard*'s adult contemporary chart. Some two decades later, Olivia told writer Robyn Flans,

I think "Suddenly" is my favorite duet that I sing. Cliff has been a mentor of mine who had me on his television show in England when I was a young girl. He helped launch my career, so I've always had a great admiration and love for him. He's a wonderful performer and singer and I was so lucky that he agreed to sing this with me.

Cliff would speak just as highly of Olivia, telling the Boston DJ and author Barry Scott about a decade after "Suddenly" that he felt "very honored" to have played an important role in the early years of her career. "I feel proud of Olivia, because she's been so fantastic and so huge in America and is such a great artist and a nice person. I don't think she'll mind me telling you this. I love her dearly as a person. She is perfect."

The *Xanadu* soundtrack album, for the most part, consists of Olivia on side 1 and the Electric Light Orchestra on side 2. In addition to Olivia's collaborations with Cliff and ELO, she teamed up with the San Francisco rock band the Tubes on the song "Dancin'," and she and Gene Kelly duetted on "Whenever You're Away from Me," which they did a song-and-dance routine to in the movie. In addition to the Olivia/ELO title track, ELO had two other singles from the movie, "I'm Alive" and "All Over the World," both of which reached the Top 20 in both the United States and the United Kingdom.

MCA released the soundtrack album in the United States on June 27, 1980; in other markets it came out in July. *Billboard* gave the album a strong review, noting that it "has [Olivia] romping through a variety of cuts, ranging from the bewitching ballad 'Magic' to the rock-inflected title cut, written by Jeff Lynne.... The other side of the soundtrack is dominated by four ELO tracks, including the hot single 'I'm Alive.'… It's hard to see how this single-disk package can miss." It didn't. It reached No. 4 on the *Billboard* albums chart and No. 1 on that of rivals *Cash Box* and *Record World*. It also reached No. 1 in Australia, Austria, Belgium, Germany, Israel, the Netherlands, Norway, Spain, and Sweden, and the Top 10 in Canada, Finland, Italy, Japan, New Zealand, and the United Kingdom.

In 1994, interviewer Debbie Kruger asked Olivia if making *Xanadu* had been an enjoyable experience. "Yeah, it was," Olivia replied. "It wasn't a very good movie," she added. "I mean the music was very good. Jeff Lynne is great, and John's music, I thought his integration of the '40s and '80s was really clever.… I thought all the music things were good, but I thought the script was terrible, and it was really a shame, because the premise was really good." She also laughingly remembered a conversation she'd had with director Robert Greenwald. "Halfway through the movie, I asked him what kind of music he liked and he said he didn't like music, which I thought was some kind of an omen."

By 2007, however, *Xanadu* had become a "cult hit," according to *Entertainment Weekly*. In July of that year, a musical comedy based upon the film and its music debuted on Broadway. *Entertainment Weekly* also reported that "this unabashedly flamboyant disco epic has a particularly strong following with women and the gay community. In 2002, a sell-out 'Xanadu Sing-Along' took place at Hollywood's 1,200-capacity John Anson Ford Amphitheatre as part of Outfest, L.A.'s annual gay and lesbian film festival." Olivia still remembered that the reviews "were vitriolic," but she told journalist Clark Collis, "Now I can look back fondly—so many years have gone by. But when it was really close to when we made it, I thought, 'Why did I *do* that?'"

But while Olivia was gratified to see the film enjoy more success in subsequent decades than it did in 1980, *Xanadu* also carried an unfortunate coda for her. A man in Louisiana named Michael Owen Perry, who was twenty-six when the movie was released, became obsessed with it and with her. By 1983, he was living in a trailer in his parents' backyard in Lake Arthur, Louisiana, following his escape from a mental institution. In 1982 he had sent two disturbing letters to Olivia. He believed that she was indeed the Muse, the Greek goddess, that she had portrayed in the movie. "I heard voices," he wrote in one of his letters to her, "and the voices said to me that you are a Muse and trapped under Lake Arthur." It was at this point that Olivia hired Gavin de Becker, security specialist to the stars.

In April 1983, Perry showed up at Olivia's house in Malibu. Her security guards turned him away. Perry subsequently made two more unsuccessful attempts to get onto her property and then returned to Louisiana. On July 17, he murdered his parents, two of his cousins, and a two-year-old nephew. "The victims, all shot in the head at close range," according to a United Press International (UPI) newspaper report, "were found in their Lake Arthur home July 19."

When police officers searched Perry's trailer, they found a piece of paper with three names written on it, including "Olivia" and "Judge O'Connor," which was probably a reference to Supreme Court Justice Sandra Day O'Connor. The officers in Louisiana notified police in California, who began searching for Perry in the vicinity of Olivia's home. De Becker advised Olivia to leave the area. "We know Olivia is the only person he's been writing to," he stated, "and we've been very concerned about her safety."

Perry, however, had fled the scene of the murders in another direction. District of Columbia police arrested him on July 31 for shoplifting a radio from a department store. When they ran a records check on him, they saw that he was wanted in Louisiana on five counts of homicide, and Louisiana State Police officers drove to Washington and brought him back. Olivia, UPI reported, issued a "statement from Australia," where she and Matt Lattanzi took refuge after de Becker had urged her to leave her California home. "The cases [like this] are an unfortunate part of public life and I am just relieved this one has been caught," her statement read. "Because the court case is currently being prepared, the Department of Justice has advised that I not comment further." Brinley Newton-John talked to the Australian press, though, telling reporters, "She was so worried she packed her bags and stayed in a hotel before getting a plane to fly out here." Perry was convicted and sentenced to death in 1985. As of this writing, he is still alive and imprisoned, as courts have denied the state of Louisiana the right to execute him on the grounds that he is insane.

Olivia admitted to being shaken by Perry and other disturbed "fans." She told a journalist that she found the movie *Star 80* (1983), about the murdered *Playboy* Playmate and actor Dorothy Stratten, to be frightening. "It hits a little too close to home." But she insisted, "You can get paranoid if you don't live your life." In 2007 she told Clark Collis, "I guess because I was playing this ethereal character, he [Perry] got reality and show business confused. I left the country for a while. That was a very scary time."

Photo 1 Advertisement for "If Not For You," *Cash Box*, May 15, 1971. Pye International/ Wikimedia Commons

Photo 2 With Peter Leinheiser, guitarist for her opening act The Hudson Brothers, at The Riviera in Las Vegas, 1976. Peter Leinheiser

Photo 3 With Stephen Sinclair, backstage at The Roxy in Los Angeles after a show he played there, 1977. Stephen Sinclair

Photo 4 With longtime band member Skip Griparis, 1978. Skip Griparis

Photo 5 Meeting President Ronald Reagan at the White House during a State Dinner for Australian Prime Minister Malcolm Fraser, June 30, 1981. National Archives, Reagan White House Photographs, 1/20/1981–1/20/1989/Wikimedia Commons

Photo 6 On tour, 1982. Robert Bradshaw

Photo 7 1982 tour; l. to r.: Stephanie Spruill, Kenny Ortega, unidentified woman in shades, Olivia, Carlos Vega (in back), Bob Bradshaw (in red), Bruce Jackson, Kevin Brown, unidentified man (black shirt), Kevin Bassinson; front (kneeling): unidentified, unidentified, prodcution assistant named Mickey. Robert Bradshaw

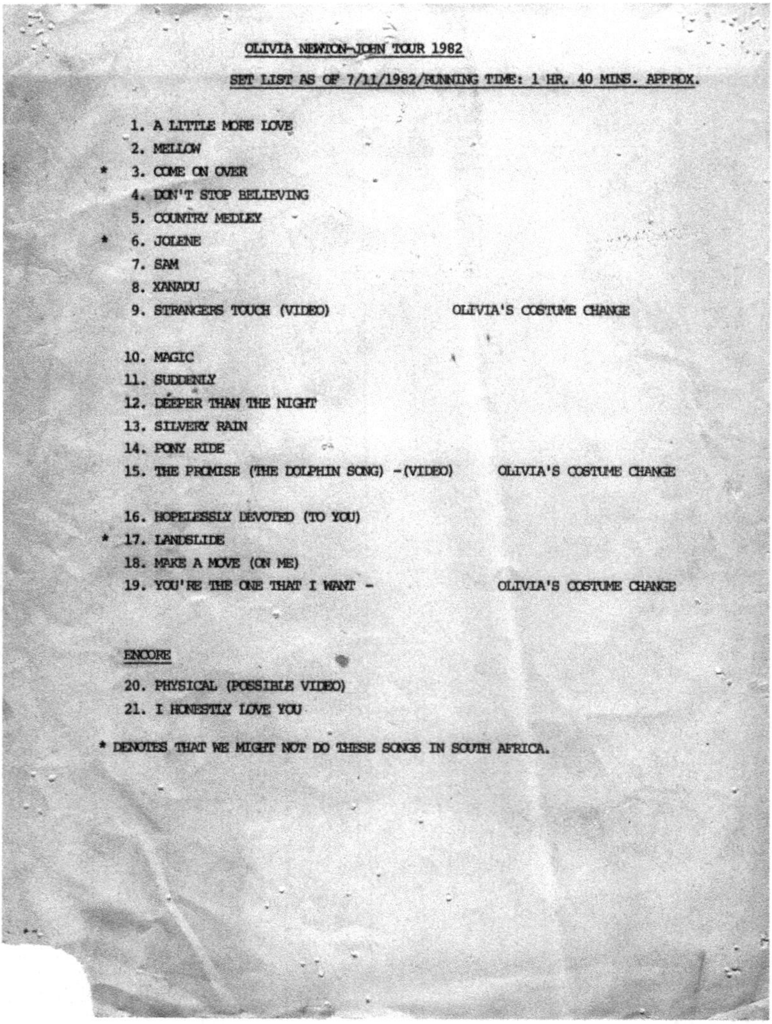

<u>OLIVIA NEWTON-JOHN TOUR 1982</u>

<u>SET LIST AS OF 7/11/1982/RUNNING TIME: 1 HR. 40 MINS. APPROX.</u>

   1. A LITTLE MORE LOVE
   2. MELLOW
* 3. COME ON OVER
   4. DON'T STOP BELIEVING
   5. COUNTRY MEDLEY
* 6. JOLENE
   7. SAM
   8. XANADU
   9. STRANGERS TOUCH (VIDEO)   OLIVIA'S COSTUME CHANGE

  10. MAGIC
  11. SUDDENLY
  12. DEEPER THAN THE NIGHT
  13. SILVERY RAIN
  14. PONY RIDE
  15. THE PROMISE (THE DOLPHIN SONG) -(VIDEO)   OLIVIA'S COSTUME CHANGE

  16. HOPELESSLY DEVOTED (TO YOU)
* 17. LANDSLIDE
  18. MAKE A MOVE (ON ME)
  19. YOU'RE THE ONE THAT I WANT -   OLIVIA'S COSTUME CHANGE

<u>ENCORE</u>

  20. PHYSICAL (POSSIBLE VIDEO)
  21. I HONESTLY LOVE YOU

* DENOTES THAT WE MIGHT NOT DO THESE SONGS IN SOUTH AFRICA.

Photo 8 Courtesy of Robert Bradshaw

Photo 9 With John Travolta and members of the US Navy's Blue Angels flight demonstration team posing in front of an A-4F Skyhawk Aircraft in Salinas, California, October 3, 1982. Wikicommons/PH3 CURT FARGO

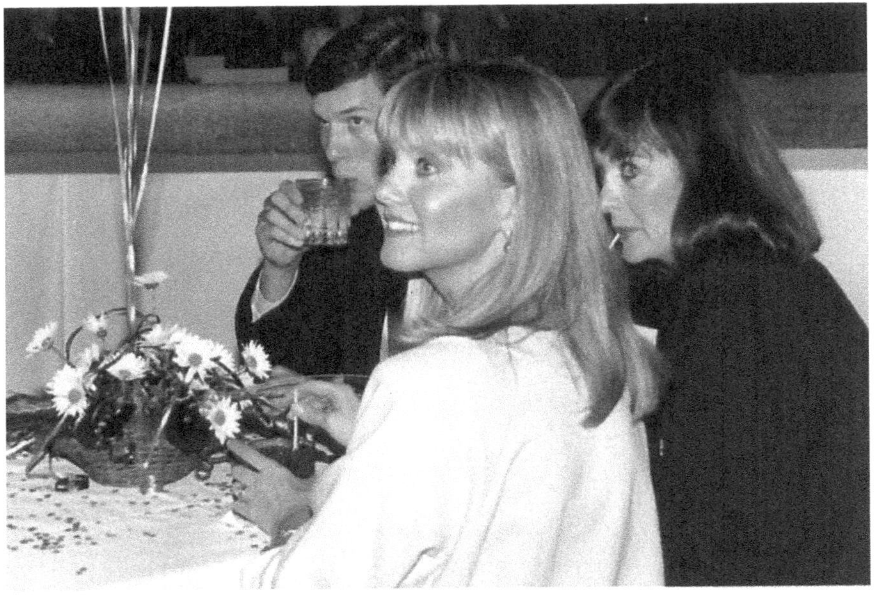

Photo 10 With Pat Farrar and an unidentified man at a fashion show charity benefit in conjunction with the opening of a Koala Blue store at the Aboretum in Austin, Texas, December 4, 1988. Wikicommons/© 1988 Larry D. Moore. Licensed under CC BY 4.0.

Photo 11 With Liona Boyd in Malibu, California, 1994. Liona Boyd

Photo 12 With Chloe at the Los Angeles premiere of the stage musical *Mamma Mia!*, February 26, 2001. Nancy Barr-Brandon

Photo 13 With lighting director Stephen Duros at a Mexican restaurant in New York City, circa 2003. Stephen Duros

Photo 14 L. to r.: Catherine Marks, Marlen Landen (with son), Mark Landen, Dan Wojciechowski, John Gibbons, Olivia, Steve Real, Warren Ham, and Stephen Duros, visiting the Guggenheim Musuem in New York City, circa 2003. Stephen Duros

Photo 15 *Miami Herald* reporter Howard Cohen, Olivia, and John Easterling at the Raleigh Hotel in Miami Beach, during the Pink and Blue Gala to raise funds for breast and prostate cancer research, April 10, 2010. Howard Cohen

Photo 16 With Liona Boyd at Olivia's home in Jupiter Inlet Colony, Florida, December 2012. Liona Boyd

Photo 17 With longtime drummer Mark Beckett in Las Vegas, 2015. Mark Beckett

Photo 18 At lunch with (l. to r.) Glenn Wheatley, John Farnham, Chong Lim, and John Easterling, Santa Ynez, California, June 2016. Chong Lim

Photo 19 With John Farnham at Olivia's ranch in Santa Ynez, June 26, 2016. Chong Lim

Photo 20 With John Easterling at Chong Lim's recording studio in Richmond, Melbourne, Australia, 2016. Chong Lim

Photo 21 With Dane Bryant on a chartered flight from Las Vegas to Arizona to perform at a charity event for workers in the hospice/end-of-life-care industry, July 2016. Dane Bryant

Photo 22 Posing with a kangaroo sculpture–her favorite sculpture in the building–at the Australian Parliament House in Canberra, September 13, 2017. Neil Pharaoh

Photo 23 With Australia's Prime Minister Malcolm Turnbulll at the Parliament House in Canberra, September 13, 2017. Neil Pharaoh

Photo 24 Neil Pharaoh, Olivia, and John Easterling at the Victorian Parliament House, Melbourne, Australia, May 8, 2018. Neil Pharaoh

Photo 25 During a quiet moment of reflection between meetings at the Victorian Parliament House in Melbourne, May 8, 2018. Neil Pharaoh

11 LET'S GET PHYSICAL

"That was the lucky break," Roger Davies told journalist Marc Andrews in 2008. "She [Olivia] asked me to work with her in 1980 at a shaky time with her manager who was also her boyfriend. Daryl [Braithwaite] went to school with Olivia in Melbourne, so that's how I knew her." Braithwaite was the lead singer of Sherbet, one of the most popular rock bands in Australia during the 1970s. Davies was their manager. After the band's effort to crack the US market failed—they had signed with MCA Records and opened for Andy Gibb on the second leg of his 1978 US tour but never managed to crack the Top 40—its members returned to Australia in 1979. Davies, however, settled in Los Angeles.

"I'd been there a month," Davies told interviewer Julius Grafton in 1993,

and Olivia and Lee split on a personal level, which meant he was still the manager, but I became the meat in the sandwich—he'd tell me to tell her things, as the messenger boy. I hardly knew her and a month later I'm sitting on a plane next to her going to Europe to record "Xanadu" with Jeff Lynne in Germany.

It seemed that Kramer had been rather controlling of Olivia, and with their relationship coming apart at the seams, Davies found himself thrown headfirst into his working relationship with her. "I was almost controlling her life; it was so one-on-one, Olivia would ring up and say, 'What will I wear?'"

As Olivia grew closer to Matt Lattanzi, her relationship with Lee became more strained. Finally, one day in early 1981, Olivia decided she'd had enough and fired him. "She asked me to manage her," Davies told Grafton, "which I'd virtually been doing." Olivia was comfortable with Davies, a native of Melbourne who had been mentored by her first professional manager, Peter Gormley.

Kramer also gave Davies another artist he'd begun managing after she'd appeared on Olivia's *Hollywood Nights* special: Tina Turner. Davies paid Kramer an override fee for a couple of years for taking on Turner, but not for taking over as

Olivia's manager, since she had fired Lee. Davies also managed Steve Kipner. The 1980s would be a lucrative decade for Davies.

Stephen Sinclair, who had known Lee longer than anyone else in Olivia's circle, says that he had been a good manager, but he

> wasn't political, you see. Sometimes managers will do things with an artist because they want to be their manager, and they're thinking about politically what is also the right thing in this decision making for *me* apart from them. He wasn't doing that. He was always, he was too much heart, not enough head. Not enough head. And he learned, he learned, but it was very destabilizing, and in the end, it kind of, it wasn't like a fast thing, it was a disintegration… when you're thinking with your heart… he did it all wrong. He wasn't experienced enough to know.… He was a successful businessman and he held his own, but not forever.

Sinclair says that Lee and Olivia, aside from their personal tensions, saw that Davies "could do a better day-to-day job. And he grew into the role of doing a bigger job. But I believe that in many ways, Lee Kramer, because I knew him from being a businessman, was no fool. He was just out of his element and in love." Sinclair was immediately impressed with Davies. "From day one, he was a firecracker and really good at his job."

As the management role passed from Kramer to Davies, Olivia was eager to make her next album. John Farrar had finished an album of his own after *Xanadu*, and in November 1980 he told an interviewer that he was about "to start writing for Olivia's new album.… We'll probably start recording that in a few months." Just before the end of the year, Columbia Records released his self-titled solo debut. Farrar, of course, wrote the entire album, with his old friend and bandmate Hank Marvin as cowriter on one track and with Tom Snow, the cowriter of "Deeper than the Night," on three others. Columbia didn't really promote the album, though, and it failed to crack the *Billboard* album chart, proving once again the well-established music industry maxim that talent and commercial success don't always correlate.

The album did yield some fruits for Olivia, though. Two of its songs ended up on her next album: Farrar's composition "Falling," which became a personal favorite of hers, and the Farrar-Snow composition "Recovery." Farrar and Snow also developed a working relationship that would serve Olivia well over the next few years, including another song they wrote that ended up on the next album, "Make a Move on Me."

The crown jewel of her next album, though, came to Olivia from a longtime friend and fellow Davies client. Shortly after Davies took over as Olivia's manager, Steve Kipner brought him a song that he had written with Terry Shaddick, an English musician and songwriter he had gotten to know in Los Angeles. When

Davies heard their demo of the song, which was then titled "Let's Get Physical," he "wanted Tina [Turner] to record [it], but she didn't like it." He subsequently played it for Olivia and told her, "You should record this." Her reply was, "Really?" Kipner and Shaddick, Kipner later said, had "imagined a male singer like Rod Stewart singing it, but as you know, that would not be the case." Olivia recalled Lee Kramer playing the demo for her; Davies and Kramer had continued working together for a time.

Olivia told Debbie Kruger in 1994 that Davies "encouraged me [to record 'Physical'] because I was freaking out about it, I was very nervous as to what it was going to do. Matt really liked it, 'cause we were together then, and he thought it was a great song." Decades later, John Farrar would laugh recalling Olivia's reluctant decision to tackle the song. "I couldn't imagine Olivia would sing those lyrics, but I'm obviously glad she did," he said. "It was a great song, a very catchy song, but Olivia's image was always very girl-next-door. Even during the final playback, she looked at me and said, 'Do you think I can get away with this?'"

But Farrar and Tom Snow brought her a song that was, at least by early 1980s standards, almost equally risqué. "Make a Move on Me" was bold musically, too, with a distinct, unusual chord progression of F to A minor to E-flat in the chorus. "Normally, it's *four* chords and the truth, right? As they say in Nashville. But John just made the transition to that [chorus]," Snow says, singing the "I can't wait, I can't wait" line. "And he's the one that wrote that. And I thought, 'Wow!' But yeah, I'm pretty proud of that song, 'cause we fooled the audience," he says with a chuckle, "in a certain way."

Snow also remembers the painstaking process of recording the track with the limitations of 1980s technology.

I played the bass line on "Make a Move on Me." It was a loop. We were doing it, John and I and [recording engineer] Dave Holman, we were doing it at [Dave's] home studio, and I kept having to play it *over and over* until I finally got it metrically perfect, you know, and… John would be listening. "One more, mate, just one more."

Snow laughs as he recalls Farrar telling him to play take after take. "But, yeah, that was a pretty cool bass line…. We didn't have the computers in those days, you couldn't correct the timing and everything, you had to actually *play* it." The musicians on the *Physical* album also included Olivia's by then usual roster of session aces, including Steve Lukather and David Hungate of Toto on the title track.

Snow says that Olivia was rarely at the tracking sessions where the musicians recorded their parts. "No, all the basic tracking was done ahead of time, and then she would put on her vocals, and any succeeding overdubs would be done by John. But all the feel and all that stuff, we got that, we did that on our own."

The recording of the album began on April 21, 1981, and finished just over two months later, on June 22. All the sessions were held in Los Angeles, most of them at Holman's studio. The album consisted primarily of original material, but Olivia covered a Cliff Richard single from 1971, "Silvery Rain," written by Hank Marvin. Having already recorded the Bee Gees' "Come on Over" and the two duets with Andy Gibb that Barry had written, she also returned to the Gibb songbook. Barry Gibb and Albhy Galuten, a coproducer of all the recent Bee Gees records and Andy Gibb records (including his two duets with Olivia), wrote "Carried Away" for Barbra Streisand's 1980 album *Guilty*. Barry wrote that entire album with various combinations of his three brothers, except for three songs that he wrote with Galuten. Streisand passed on "Carried Away," but Olivia recorded it a year later and released it on *Physical*. "She got a hold of it somehow," Farrar told writer Christian John Wikane with a chuckle. "I think maybe Barry gave it to her. He's always been a hero of mine from way back when the Bee Gees first started and I was in Australia."

As had some of her previous albums, *Physical* included a song written by Olivia. Upon the album's release, she told journalist Colin Dangaard that the impetus for writing "The Promise (The Dolphin Song)" came from the incident in Japan in 1978, when the killing of a dolphin by a fisherman had led her to cancel a spring tour there. She told Dangaard, "The Japanese were not very pleased" when she canceled the tour, "but it's not just the dolphins I am concerned about; it is sea life in general, and wildlife in the United States. There is so much waste, so much killing that is not necessary. We don't even use whale blubber anymore in cosmetics. There is just no reason to slaughter them."

She explained in an interview for *People* magazine in 1982 how she came to write "The Promise (The Dolphin Song)." In May 1981, she had gone to Hawaii, where Herb Ritts took photos for the *Physical* album cover. For the photo shoots, she spent some time swimming with dolphins in pools at Sea Life Park. "It was strange," she said. "The morning after I was in the pools, I woke up and the words and melody were in my head. I think it was a gift from them."

She told Atlanta journalist Bill King in September 1981 that she would like to write more songs, "but I'm a bit lazy, so unless it comes to me in one burst, I usually don't get 'round to finishing it. I have hundreds of half-finished things." Also, she added, the luxury of having John Farrar writing for her impeded her own aspirations as a songwriter. "I have to get up my nerve to play [my songs] to him, and because I respect his opinion so much, if he doesn't like them, I lose interest in them. I trust him because we've been recording together for ten years."

But she continued to have doubts about "Physical." Before the single was released, she and Davies traveled to England, and "she was really freaked out on the plane," he recalled four decades later. "I felt convinced it was a great record, [but] she said to me that if it didn't work and she got a lot of bad publicity she would never go back to America."

Olivia told *Entertainment Weekly* in 2017, "I recorded it and then suddenly thought, 'Goodness, maybe I've gone too far!' It was a bit raunchier than I realized. I called Roger and said, 'We've got to pull this song!' He said, 'It's too late. It's already gone to radio and it's running up the charts.' I was horrified," she laughed. "I said, 'Oh, wow… um… yeah… okay… well, maybe we should do a video, and it should be about exercise—yeah! That's it! Let's make it about working out!'"

MTV made its debut on August 1, 1981. Olivia and Davies decided even before that to make a full-length video album for *Physical*. MCA wanted to release it on its MCA Videodisc (LaserDisc) label; MCA had already released Olivia's 1978 TV special, the one with ABBA and Andy Gibb, on LaserDisc in 1980, and later released *Xanadu* as well. For the *Physical* LaserDisc, MCA Videodisc president Jim Fielder gave Olivia a generous budget, by the standards of that day, of $800,000. Olivia and Davies assembled a team consisting of London-based director Brian Grant, whose credits included the videos for M's huge 1979 international hit "Pop Muzik" and Queen's "Play the Game," and his associates Scott Millaney as producer and Marcelo Anciano as the writer.

With two movies under her belt (three if one counts *Toomorrow*, which she was sometimes loath to do), Olivia felt confident and enthusiastic about the video album. "I think this is the way albums will go in the future: visuals with the music," she told *Billboard*. "I got to be a different personality and play another side of myself." The dawn of music videos, of course, would favor photogenic recording artists, which was not a problem for Olivia, or for the one previous act that had made a video album, the band Blondie.

Olivia's sound for the *Physical* album wasn't that much of a departure from *Totally Hot*, which had marked her break from her country-pop style of much of the 1970s, but at thirty-two (thirty-three by the time the album was released), she adopted a new look: shorter and slightly darker hair, and a new wardrobe that Bill King wrote made her look "as if [she were] on a visit to the local athletic club." Olivia's close friend Fleur Thiemeyer was the chief architect of her new look, which most people saw for the first time in the "Physical" video. For that video, Fleur dyed a white leotard pink. "Bad taste is timeless," she laughingly told Australian journalist Neil McMahon in 2023. "We put the white t-shirt on and cut the neck out. The neckband of the shirt became the hair band because her hair wouldn't stay right. And the turquoise I put on as a wrap-around because I didn't like the overall shape. And then there were the leggings."

The video featured Olivia cavorting in that outfit, and near the end, in white shorts and shirt and holding a tennis racquet, in a gym with a group of rather overweight men and mock, humorous workout scenes. By the end of the video, the men suddenly look as if they had been working out for years. The final scene, though, ruffled some conservative feathers at the time.

As *Billboard* noted in 2014,

> By the end of the video, even Olivia can't contain her surprise and marvels at her work—but when she seeks out a tennis partner, all the hot guys "play for the other team." Yes, in those days, even a hint of bromance (two men seen holding hands) raised red flags on MTV, which often cut the video short on the air, and some broadcasters banned it altogether.

When journalist Danielle Friedman wrote her book *Let's Get Physical: How Women Discovered Exercise and Reshaped the World* four decades after "Physical," she found something else about the video to be objectionable. "The blatant fat-shaming baked into this story line," she wrote, "was standard fare in the eighties." Friedman also noted that when ABC aired the video on February 8, 1982, as part of the television special *Olivia Newton-John: Let's Get Physical*, the network "cut the video's gay finale for its broadcast." Despite these efforts at suppression, the video, wrote Patrick Kelleher in *PinkNews* after Olivia's passing, became one of several things she did that helped make her "the ultimate gay icon."

Olivia introduced "Physical," just as the single was about to be released, on the season 2 premiere of the syndicated television series *Solid Gold*, which aired (on different dates in different markets) in mid-September 1981. (Andy Gibb and Marilyn McCoo had just become the hosts of the show, and Andy and Olivia sang "Rest Your Love on Me.") When the single reached radio stations, the lyrics that had given Olivia pause and second thoughts about recording the song caused as much controversy as the video would. A UPI newspaper article dated November 9, 1981, reported that "a hit record by singer Olivia Newton-John has been banned by two Utah radio stations, including one owned by the Mormon Church, because it contains 'suggestive' lyrics." KFMY-FM in Provo "pulled the record off the air after receiving complaints about Miss Newton-John's line 'let's get physical.' KSL-AM in Salt Lake City decided not to include the record in its lineup because of the contents."

KFMY program director Jim Sumpter told *Billboard*, "Once the words sank in, it caused an uncomfortableness among listeners." The program director of KSL, which was owned by the Mormon Church, said of his decision not to play the record, "The lyrics are more suggestive than most songs. It goes the one additional step."

The singles charts of the day suggest that, to a minor extent at least, other radio stations may have balked at playing "Physical," if not banning it then at least not giving it as much airplay as its popularity merited. The *Billboard, Record World,* and *Cash Box* singles charts were based on sales and airplay, with more weight given to the former. On those three charts, "Physical" spent, respectively, ten, nine, and eight weeks at No. 1. The charts of two more strictly radio-oriented trade publications, *Radio and Records* and *The Gavin Report*, were based only on what radio stations were playing. On both of those charts, "Physical" peaked at No. 2.

In contrast, the next single from the album, "Make a Move on Me," despite lyrics that were, at least, certainly more suggestive than anything in "If You Love Me (Let Me Know)" or any of Olivia's other early hits, reached No. 1 on the charts of *Radio and Records* and *The Gavin Report*. The single reached no higher than No. 4 on any of the charts that used sales as a criterion; perhaps those radio stations that had balked at playing "Physical" were taking the opportunity to make up for lost Olivia Newton-John airplay. "Physical" was certified platinum, which meant sales of two million singles, while "Make a Move on Me" was certified gold, which meant sales of one million.[1] Tom Snow, cowriter of the latter, laughingly recalls his music publisher Richard Perry telling him, "It's the quietest million seller ever." Nevertheless, since *Solid Gold* used the chart of *Radio and Records* for its weekly countdown of the Top 10 hits, Olivia returned to the show and performed "Make a Move on Me" when it reached No. 1.

Perry had a point, though; the single's success almost paled in comparison to that of "Physical," which, eight years later, *Billboard* would rank as the biggest hit of the entire decade. Forty years after its release, Rob Sheffield of *Rolling Stone* referred to "Make a Move on Me" as the "unjustly forgotten sequel" to "Physical." "It's not as famous," he wrote, "probably because it's not as filthy, but it's a song that can always turn anyone into a *Solid Gold* dancer."

What did Olivia's parents think of "Physical" and the controversy it engendered? "My mom was a very forward-thinking woman," she said in 2017. "She was really open, so she probably thought it was funny." Then she laughed as she added, "My dad may not have. But they were both supportive." Tom Snow recalls, "I remember meeting her mother [in the early 1980s], and she was just delightfully well mannered and, you know, just classy." Of Olivia herself, Snow says, "She was a delight. She was a little bit reserved in some ways, I would say.... She was just always like very down to earth, not, *'I'm Olivia Newton-John and who are you?'* Nothing like that. Anytime I was around her she was always great, always great."

By the time "Physical" reached record stores and the airwaves of (most) Top 40 radio stations, Olivia no longer felt that she had to conceal her blossoming romance with Matt Lattanzi. A newspaper article about her new album began, "Olivia Newton-John's love for a young man—and her passion for dolphins—has inspired her first hit album in more than a year. The album is called 'Physical'—which is exactly how Olivia, 33, feels about Matty Lattanzi, 21." (Actually, he was twenty-two then.) Olivia described Lattanzi to the author of the article, Colin Dangaard, as "a gorgeous, lovely man… unspoiled, nice… and genuine."

That didn't mean, however, that she was ready for marriage. As part of her publicity efforts for the *Physical* album, she appeared on NBC's *Today* show in the spring of 1982 to be interviewed by Bryant Gumbel. He asked her if it was true that she had told a reporter, "Marriage is a thing which frightens me." "Mm-hmm, it's true, I've said that. I've said that a million times," she laughed. "Yes, I think," she paused,

> only because I guess I don't, um, if, *when* I get married, *if* and when, I'll say *if* and when, I'd like it to be a success. Everyone wants that for themselves, but I think it's probably fear of failure in it that makes me so apprehensive, because I see so much failure around me. I'm waiting till I'm really old.

She laughed, "And I can't make a mistake."

Gumbel, who told Olivia that they were born only two days apart (actually, three—he was born on September 29, 1948), then asked her about something else she had mentioned in an interview: her desire to have a child by the time she turned thirty-five. She sort of grimaced when he asked her if it was still true. "Um, I might have to push it a few years now," she said and broke into laughter again.

As "Physical" was making its way to the number one spot in the United States (and also Australia, Belgium, Canada, New Zealand, and Switzerland), Olivia indicated that she still was in no hurry to resume touring. She told Associated Press music journalist Mary Campbell in the fall of 1981, "I haven't toured for three years now. I didn't feel like I wanted to. I don't miss it yet. I'm very fortunate I don't have to tour. I appreciate that." Touring, she told Campbell, "is fun once you get going. But I've had such a nice time being at home, I didn't want to leave for a length of time." She described her home as "a small ranch near Malibu," which sat on between three and four acres, with five horses, eight dogs, and a cat.

At the end of 1981, however, Olivia undertook a one-week promotional tour of Japan, her first visit there in a little over three years. According to *Billboard*, the effort "paid off handsomely and the evidence comes in [Japanese] sales of her 'Physical' album and single." "The product," the report added, "was expected to do well in Japan… but the promotional visit, coming in the year-end holiday season, really sparked sales and emphasized again the value of personal appearances. The singer was interviewed for a dozen major magazines, countless newspapers and nine leading radio stations. She also appeared on three key television programs." By the end of her visit, the album and single had each sold more than two hundred thousand copies in Japan; the album was selling ten thousand copies per day.

Olivia also pulled off what *Billboard* called "a particularly shrewd" promotional move during the trip to Japan: She wore "an orange Japanese kimono for her full press conference. Many visiting artists dress up in kimono style, but Olivia Newton-John looked so much at ease in this national costume that Toshiba-EMI [her Japanese record label] used a half life-size poster of her wearing the garb as its New Year greeting poster." *Billboard* published a photo, albeit in black and white, of her wearing the traditional Japanese kimono at her press conference at the Tokyo Hilton Hotel, with the caption "Japanese John."

In March 1982 she made a similarly brief trip to Australia. She performed at the annual Logie Awards show in Melbourne, and she also visited family members. (Her mother and brother, Hugh, were living in Melbourne, and her father and half-siblings, Toby and Sarah, were living in Sydney.) When journalist Lenore Nicklin asked Olivia if Matt Lattanzi was with her in Australia, she replied, "No, I wish he were. He is visiting his family in Portland, Oregon. He hasn't seen them for more than a year." Olivia also told Nicklin that while in Australia she would be flying to New South Wales (an Australian state), where she owned a farm with sugarcane, custard apples, and avocados, and that she was hoping to return to Australia to live "in perhaps five years."

Even though Olivia had told journalist Vernon Scott in the fall of 1981 that "I have no idea when I will tour again," by the spring of 1982 she had changed her mind. In another interview with Scott to promote the tour, he asked her why. She paused and then told him, "Because it may be my last opportunity. I'm doing this for my fans. Most of the letters I get ask me when I will appear in their part of the country. They want to see me."

She explained to Scott that she had other motives, too. "I've done about everything I could dream of in recording, films, and television. I'm afraid of becoming complacent. So, my personal goal at the moment is to see if I can do it all over again. When you become popular, you also have a growing desire not to disappoint the people who buy your records or see your movies." Hence, Scott, a longtime UPI Hollywood reporter, wrote that Olivia, "the hottest pop singer in the country today," would be hitting the road, "perhaps for the last time, this summer with 50 one-night concerts in a span of two months," with shows on the East Coast, in New England, the Midwest, the South, the Southwest, and the West Coast.

Olivia hired Tom Scott, a jazz musician, saxophonist, composer, and arranger, to be the musical director on the tour. (He would also play saxophone on some songs.) Scott assembled, as would be expected, a stellar band for the tour, consisting of studio aces such as guitarists Michael Landau and Buzz Feiten, bass guitarist Robert "Pops" Popwell, and drummer Carlos Vega, who had played on Olivia's recent records. The backing vocalists included Stephanie Spruill, another veteran of session work, and Dennis Tufano, who had been the lead singer of the Buckinghams, a Chicago-based rock group that had a string of major hits in 1966–1967.

Tufano would not only be a backing vocalist on the tour but would also sing two duets with Olivia, filling in for John Travolta on "You're the One That I Want" and for Cliff Richard on "Suddenly." "I had been kind of taking some time off from music and I was acting at the time in the late '70s and into the '80s, and I wasn't really doing a whole lot of singing," Tufano recalls.

> Tom Scott, the jazz sax player, and I were friends... we knew each other for a number of years, and he called me late one night and said, "Look, I'm doing this Olivia Newton-John tour... I've got two background singer girls and one guy, and he's a great session singer, but he can't sing the duets. He can't act and sing at the same time, and we need to have you be characters in the two songs, and I figured since you were acting that maybe it'll be something that you could slip into." And I said, "Well, I'll give it a shot."

Scott told Tufano to show up at the rehearsal studio early the next morning and audition by singing "Suddenly" with Olivia. Tufano stayed up that night listening to the song on a cassette.

> When we did the thing [the next morning], I was a little shocked because she opened the door and walked in the room. So, I was a little more than nervous now. I've got a roomful of great musicians and now I've got Olivia Newton-John that I've got to sing with... and so I figured, "Well, I have to go for it." So, I really like sang *to her* and really got it together, and her choreographer Kenny Ortega came up to me after... and he said, "Look, there's one other guy that's auditioning, but what I just saw happen between you and Olivia, you're going to be the guy going on the tour."

Soon Olivia came back into the room and told him, "Thank you. Congratulations, you're on the tour."

Olivia also brought "heavy security" on the tour, Tufano recalls. "We had... probably six [security] guys on the tour, and one of them was Gavin de Becker. He was on the road with us the whole time. He was the head of security, and he was great. He was a very funny guy, too, which made it all a little bit less serious." Stephanie Spruill remembers de Becker guarding the door to Olivia's dressing room on the tour "because there were so many weirdos running around, you know, it was just crazy... they were obsessed. They were." Although Stephen Sinclair wasn't present on the tour, he "was very aware of what was going on." "I do know," he says, "that he [de Becker] intervened with people on that tour."

In particular, de Becker and his team had to keep an eye open for Michael Owen Perry and Ralph Nau. Nau had been trying to contact Olivia since 1980, and during the decade that followed, he wrote thousands of letters to a list of female pop stars that included her, Sheena Easton, Cher, and Madonna. He would also travel to Australia and Los Angeles to try to meet Olivia, to Scotland to try to meet Easton, and to Las Vegas to try to meet Cher. All four of the singers hired de Becker for protection, and he later said that he had monitored Nau "on virtually a daily basis from 1981 to three or four weeks before" Nau, at the age of twenty-nine, killed his eight-year-old, autistic stepbrother with an ax and shovel in August 1984 in Antioch, Illinois.

De Becker did let Stephanie and a few select others into Olivia's dressing room, though. Stephanie recalls that one night, before the concert, she was in the dressing room with her and "somebody knocked on the door, and she says, 'Stephanie, will you get the door for me?' And I opened up the door and it was John Travolta! And I'm standing there with my mouth hanging open like," she laughs, "'*Oh my God! John Travolta!*' And Olivia says, 'Let him in, mate!'"

Dennis Tufano remembers Travolta's appearance on the tour, too. Travolta and Olivia "were *very* close. He came to our show in Los Angeles at the Universal Amphitheater and sang 'You're the One That I Want' with her. But I still got to do 'Suddenly,' so I was okay with it," he laughs. "But yeah, it was great. They *were* friends."

Another famous friend of Olivia's turned up on the tour, too. Karen Carpenter remained one of her best friends following what turned out to be her ill-fated wedding; in 1981, Olivia, Matt Lattanzi, Karen, and her husband Tom Burris took a boat trip from Newport Beach to Catalina Island, about thirty-five miles away, and had to stay overnight in a hotel when the boat ran into mechanical problems when they tried to return. On August 13 and 14, 1982, Olivia performed at the Forest Hills Tennis Stadium in Queens, New York City. Olivia regularly did aerobics workouts while on the tour, and anyone else in her entourage who wanted to could join in. Stephanie Spruill did—the show was nearly as physically demanding for her as for Olivia—and in New York she noticed a very thin woman who had joined them but was not doing the routine as vigorously as everyone else. That night after the concert, Olivia took her touring group to a club in Manhattan, which the owner closed to everyone but them. There, Stephanie, who had been a backing vocalist on the Carpenters' 1981 album *Made in America*, recognized Karen, who came and sat next to Olivia. Everyone was feasting on lobster and caviar, with the exception of Karen, who was separated from Burris by then and was staying in Manhattan for treatment for anorexia nervosa. "She was sick. She was very sick," Stephanie sadly recalls. "Olivia was trying to get her to eat… it was bad."

For the most part, though, Stephanie would remember the tour very fondly. Olivia, she says,

> was the biggest thing in the world [then]. And the nicest. And the most *generous*. And when I was going through something, she would come to me and talk to me and hold me and, you know, it was just amazing. I've never been around an artist like Olivia Newton-John. She was the best, ever, and I've been around some phenomenal artists. *Phenomenal.* But she was the most giving.

At the end of the tour, Olivia gave Stephanie a Rolex watch with the inscription, "To Stephanie, From Olivia, 1982." "That was class," Stephanie says emphatically. "She had so much *class*."

Olivia's kindness and generosity also made an impression on crew member Bob Bradshaw. "Olivia," he says, "was a sweetheart." He didn't interact with her much on the tour, "but whenever I did come into contact with her, she was always sweet and nice." After the last concert of the tour, he remembers, she threw a party for her entourage, and "she came up to me and handed me an envelope with a bonus check for $500. Big dough for '82!"

Stephanie and Dennis Tufano both recall, as did musicians who toured with Olivia during the 1970s, how she created a family-like atmosphere on the tour. During lags on the tour, Dennis fondly remembers, "She would put together this big dinner. We did this in New Orleans. We had some downtime… and she put together this big dinner for us… the whole band and the tour guys." The tour, he says, went so well because "we were a family… because of her. She really held the family atmosphere together on the tour" and made everyone feel like "we were all part of the project. That was great, that made it very special…. She had great, great spirit, a great soul."

The concerts on October 12 and 13, 1982, at the Dee Events Center at Weber State University in Ogden, Utah—the state where some radio stations had banned "Physical"—were taped for broadcast on HBO and, subsequently, release on videocassette in 1983. The tour ended on October 23 at the Irvine (California) Meadows Amphitheater. Tufano recalls that Olivia and Roger Davies had planned an Australian tour that was to have begun about four months later, with "the same band and everything, and so we were looking forward to going to Australia with her," but unfortunately she became ill and so that tour was canceled.

About a year after the Physical Tour had ended, the veteran Hollywood columnist (and actor) George Christy asked Olivia if she had any plans to tour again. "No," she said with a laugh.

I really don't have any desire to tour. I hadn't toured for [four] years until this last one. But, I like to keep setting challenges for myself, and after "Physical"'s success, which was such a breakaway from things I'd done before, with the album so well-received, I kind of felt—as a challenge to myself—I should go out on the road and see what I had to offer on stage that was different from what I did [four] years before. So that was very hard but very satisfying, and I'm really glad that we filmed it because it's there forever.

12 TWIST OF FATE

" know a woman can have children right up until she is 40 but I believe it is better to have them earlier and grow up with them. Now that I've traveled and done so much it might be nice to have a child," Olivia told journalist Mike Gardner as the Physical Tour concluded. But, she insisted, marriage would be a prerequisite for her.

I have a traditional instinct about me that says people should be married before they have children. And when I do marry, I want it to be forever. That is extra important for me because my parents divorced. I've seen other people rush into a relationship at my age [thirty-four at the time] because they want kids, only for it to turn sour in a couple of years. I suppose I'm a bit fatalistic about that sort of thing.

Olivia also told Gardner, "I don't like talking about my private life because I have to struggle hard to preserve it as is." Nevertheless, Gardner wrote in his article, for London's *Record Mirror*, that "marriage is in the air" for her. Matt Lattanzi's career wasn't making much progress, and so on the Physical Tour, Dennis Tufano recalls, Matt was, "for the most part," traveling with her on the tour and at most of the shows. "They were great together… they seemed to make a nice couple."

Tufano could see, though, that the superstar status of Olivia put a bit of strain on the relationship. While she was ranked by *Billboard* as the fourth most popular pop artist of the year for 1982, after being ranked sixth for 1981, much of what little work Matt was getting came to him through Olivia. He appeared in the video for a less successful third single from the *Physical* album, "Landslide," and he had a small role in *Grease 2*. "We put Matt in," recalls Bill Oakes, who was the executive producer, "as a favor for her [Olivia]." On the Physical Tour, Tufano observed that Matt "was a little bit jealous of all the attention she got from the moment she left her dressing room. It's tough to have a relationship because… every minute that somebody could see her, there was somebody asking her questions or taking up her time, and she was very generous with her time."

Olivia's generosity with her time extended to people who came to her concerts as well. Atlanta journalist Bill King remembers that after one of her concerts there in September 1982, "she came out afterward and sat on the edge of the stage signing autographs." Stephanie Spruill suggests that these weren't fans from the audience: "The fans that I saw were people like her friends…. I didn't see her going to fans and signing autographs." Given the security concerns around her, that was not surprising. Some of these people were probably radio station personnel and journalists (like King) that Olivia had gotten to know over the years on concert and promotional tours.

Olivia was now at what could arguably be considered a third peak of her career (the first being the "I Honestly Love You" period and the second being the *Grease* period) and, despite her often mentioning her desire to get married and have a child, she wasn't interested in slowing down professionally just yet. She told Mike Gardner that in the past she had wondered what she had done to deserve the flak she often received from critics—the type that Ben Fong-Torres had asked her about in the *Rolling Stone* interview—and, while she didn't use the word "vindicated," that was the implication in the light of her mounting great successes. "Now I'm being more adventurous," she told him. "I don't mind taking chances, and being in my 30s is proving to be the greatest time of my life."

MCA Records decided before the Physical Tour began that it would be an opportune time to release a *Greatest Hits, Vol. 2* album for Olivia once the *Physical* album finally cooled off, so before she set off on the tour, she recorded two new songs to be included on the album and to be released as singles. Steve Kipner, hot off the success of "Physical," cowrote one of the songs, "Heart Attack," this time with the English songwriter and musician Paul Bliss, and John Farrar collaborated with the American jazz guitarist Lee Ritenour to write "Tied Up." "Heart Attack" reached No. 3 on the *Billboard* Hot 100 in November 1982, although it somehow missed reaching gold record status, while the album reached the two million mark in sales by 1984. "Tied Up" proved less successful, barely cracking the US Top 40. Neither of the two singles were big hits in Australia or the United Kingdom.

Kipner recalls the unlikely but very early '80s way that he and Bliss came to write "Heart Attack." "John Farrar," he says, "told us about this new technology where you could play something and the machine would remember it." The machine was the Oberheim DSX, a pre-MIDI digital polyphonic sequencer that came out in 1981. It was "one of the first sequencers," Kipner notes.

It was so revolutionary that I bought it—and literally the first thing we tried on it turned into the song "Heart Attack." What was interesting was that we copied the song's data onto a floppy disk and gave it to John, who copied it into his identical system and used a good amount of it to make the record with Olivia—because of the [new] technology it was one of the first times that happened.

In addition to giving Kipner another (but not his last) major hit for Olivia as a songwriter, "Heart Attack" also marked the emergence of Bliss as a major pop composer. He would go on to write for Janet Jackson and Celine Dion. Kipner, too, would write for other artists—most notably, he cowrote Christina Aguilera's 1999 smash debut single "Genie in a Bottle."

Before Olivia set off on the Physical Tour, Vernon Scott asked her what she planned to do next after the tour was finished. "Movies," she told him. "After *Xanadu*, I didn't want to make any more mistakes. I agreed to do that film when it was only an idea without a script. I won't do that again. Now there are three or four movie possibilities."

"The most exciting thing," she told Scott, "is with John Travolta. It's a comedy with music. We'll play adults this time, not kids. I don't think we could get away with playing teenagers anymore. We've been trying to put together another movie since *Grease*, but nothing good turned up. John developed this story with his own company, and we should begin production next year."

One movie that "turned up" at this time, but without John and Olivia, was *Grease 2*. Bill Oakes recalls being told in the summer of 1980 that Charlie Bluhdorn, who was running Paramount, wanted a *Grease* sequel. "We had no flexibility on schedules," Oakes says. "And it turns out that what they wanted was to have John and Olivia in sort of a cameo."

Olivia told *Record World* in December 1981, "There was some discussion about doing *Grease 2*—a very tentative discussion, there was never an offer or anything—and then I think they decided to go with unknowns. The only person from the original cast is Didi Conn." Oakes recalls that Travolta called Patricia Birch, who was the choreographer for both *Grease* movies as well as the director of the second, and asked her, "Do you want me in it?" Allan Carr (again coproducing with Robert Stigwood) "wanted it desperately. He thought it would be a huge publicity thing for the movie." The plan was to have Travolta spend one day filming a fantasy sequence for *Grease 2*. But Paramount wasn't willing to pay him much for a single day's work. "Nothing could be agreed upon," according to Oakes. "I don't think it was a phone call and then good-bye. I think it was sort of bumbling around," to no avail.

Released in June 1982 on the same day as *E. T. the Extra-Terrestrial* ("No one saw that coming," notes Oakes), *Grease 2* did not fare well with critics or at the box office. Oakes takes pride, though, in casting a then-unknown Michelle Pfeiffer in the lead, and in the "huge online fan club" that the movie has now. Oakes hadn't been so sure about bringing Olivia and Travolta back even for cameo roles in *Grease* 2, let alone making them the stars. "Lightning doesn't strike twice… you never try and do that thing where they bring people back. The magic's often gone." Nor was Frankie Valli invited to record a song for the sequel, and Andy Gibb's friend Scott Paton recalls him saying that Barry Gibb wasn't interested in writing anything for *Grease 2*. (This might have had something to do with the fact that the Bee Gees and Stigwood were engaged in a legal battle over royalties and other financial matters during 1980–1981.)

Oakes's skepticism about reuniting Olivia and Travolta would be borne out by the movie that the two chose to star in together shortly after *Grease 2* flopped. Originally given the title *Second Chance*, Travolta said that upon reading the script, he felt that it would be the ideal vehicle for their onscreen reunion. "I really chose it more for Olivia than for myself," he said. "I felt it would be very good for her. And the best thing was that we were both playing against type—for half the movie we're quite obnoxious."

The movie would be a 20th Century Fox production with, as had been the case with *Grease*, a first-time film director, in this instance John Herzfeld, who also wrote the script. The budget would be $14 million, more than double the budget of *Grease* and also higher than that of *Grease 2* and *E.T.* The plot of the film is succinctly synopsized on imdb.com: "When God decides to destroy Earth, four angels aim to redeem mankind through a young man and woman with their own troubles." The young man, played by Travolta, robs a bank, and the young woman, played by Olivia, is the bank teller who cons the bank robber by giving him a bag full of worthless paper and steals the money herself.

Shooting of the movie, which would be retitled *Two of a Kind*, wouldn't begin until May 1983, so Olivia had some time off during the winter of 1982–1983. After months on the road, she was able to spend time at home in Malibu with Matt Lattanzi, who was busy with a starring role in a "sex comedy film" called *My Tutor*, and with her four cats, nine dogs, and five horses. ("It's like a zoo…. They're fabulous," she told an interviewer.) But she also suffered a deep personal loss that winter.

In mid-November 1982, Karen Carpenter, against the advice of her therapist, ended her treatment for anorexia nervosa in Manhattan and returned home to Los Angeles. (She lived in a three-thousand-square-foot, twenty-second-story condominium penthouse at 2222 Avenue of the Stars in Century City, where Olivia visited her often over the years.) Karen made visits to Olivia's home in Malibu, too. Olivia's friend and, at that time, neighbor, Stephen Sinclair, recalls seeing her there a number of times. Olivia, he recalls, "tried just so hard, tried and tried to help her along and was a good friend to her. And she was a lovely girl, and every time I saw her, she was thinner."

In her memoir, Olivia wrote, "The last time I saw her, we were both staying at the Drake Hotel in New York and she looked so much better." This would mean that she last saw Karen before Karen returned to California. A friend and business associate of Andy Gibb's named Joe Shane says, however, that he was with Andy at his suite at the Beverly Hilton in the presence of both Olivia and Karen shortly before Karen's passing. Karen had become a friend of Andy's after Olivia introduced them in Honolulu in July 1978.

Olivia told Karen's biographer, Randy L. Schmidt, that she had been driving on a freeway in Los Angeles on February 4, 1983, when she heard on the radio that Karen had passed away earlier that day. "It was a terrible shock," Olivia told Schmidt. She told him that she had been on her way to meet someone she didn't know for a business lunch at the Melting Pot on Melrose Avenue, and upon arriving and sitting down, she "just burst into tears."[1] Olivia also told Schmidt that she and Karen had made plans to meet for lunch the next day. Olivia attended Karen's funeral in her hometown of Downey (a Los Angeles suburb) on February 8, as did other famous friends of Karen's including Herb Alpert, Petula Clark, Dorothy Hamill, and Dionne Warwick.

Not even two weeks before Karen's untimely death, she had, according to Schmidt, watched Olivia's concert special, filmed in Utah in October 1982, on HBO. It aired in other countries, too, including Australia where it aired on Channel Seven/the Seven Network. Even now, though, on the heels of so much success, and even in the country where she grew up and got her start, the critics still didn't accord Olivia the respect she deserved. Melbourne music journalist Brian Courtis, writing in the newspaper *The Age*, reviewed the concert under the headline "Physical, but Too Clinical."

"Pelt me with sweatbands if you must," Courtis began his review, "but all the videos in *Countdown* [an Australian weekly music television program] will not convince me that dairy-fresh, born-again jogger Olivia Newton-John is the seductive performer her marketing board would have us believe." Noting that Olivia was still in possession of her "stunning young–Doris Day looks," he added, "Watching her play the siren on stage is like watching Cliff Richard pretend to be a mean rock 'n' roller; the result is just not credible. It can be amusing, and there is nothing wrong with that, but, somehow, I think the publicity machine expects us to take the gyrations a lot more seriously."

Filming of *Two of a Kind* began on May 9, 1983, in New York City for two weeks of location shooting before moving to studios in the Los Angeles area. John Travolta had just finished the filming of *Staying Alive*, a sequel to *Saturday Night Fever* that Robert Stigwood and Sylvester Stallone produced, and which, like its predecessor, included the Bee Gees on the soundtrack. Travolta had just finished making *Saturday Night Fever* when he came to LA to begin the filming of *Grease*, and while *Two of a Kind* was not a *Grease* sequel, the media treated it as, in some ways, more of a *Grease* sequel than *Grease 2* by virtue of its reuniting John and Olivia on the big screen.

In perhaps not a great omen for *Two of a Kind*, the first headline that it grabbed after filming began was one that appeared in newspapers across the United States on May 12: "Dog Takes Nip out of Olivia." While filming a scene on West 74th Street in Manhattan, a dog that was being used in the scene bit her finger. Publicist Gary Kalkin said that Olivia only suffered "a minor scratch" and that she was treated at the scene. At least the injury was trivial compared to the roller-skating mishap on *Xanadu* that had sent her to an emergency room. In this case, she spent three more hours filming that day. "But the scene continued," noted press reports, "without the 11-year-old dog." (Kalkin, who died of AIDS complications at age forty-four in 1995, had also served as press agent for *Saturday Night Fever*, *Grease*, and *Staying Alive*.)

Within a week, though, *Two of a Kind* was getting press attention for a different reason. On May 18, newspapers ran a photo of Olivia and Travolta arriving together at Broadway's Lunt-Fontanne Theatre, on West 46th Street, over the caption "John and John." Soon gossipy press reports were speculating again about the nature of the pair's relationship, even though Olivia's romance with Matt Lattanzi had been public knowledge for about two years by this point and Travolta was in a known relationship with actress Marilu Henner.

In fact, by the end of June, about three weeks before filming wrapped up on *Two of a Kind*, Olivia and Matt's relationship fell once again under the gaze of the nosy tabloid press. London's *Daily Mirror* reported that "the sugary Olivia Newton-John has thrown her boyfriend Matt Lattanzi out of her luxurious home on Malibu beach." The article added that their romance had been "under considerable strain since Matt, ten years her junior, popped up in a variety of steamy scenes in a soft porn movie [*My Tutor*]." Reportedly, Olivia thought that the movie was in "bad taste" and that Matt's scenes would upset her family (presumably not meaning Rona, who was certainly not prudish). The article said that Olivia had asked Matt to pass on doing the movie and that she "says she's definitely not having this unwholesome fellow back."

While the article was undoubtedly exaggerated, some friends and associates of Olivia's say that even then they knew the relationship was strained and that they were already aware of infidelities on Matt's part. ("I definitely knew about that," one of them says with a sardonic chuckle.) But if any split occurred, it was brief; the pair spent the Fourth of July with Travolta and Marilu Henner at Travolta's Santa Barbara ranch during a short break from filming. Later in July, the *Daily Mirror* published a photo of Olivia and Matt together at a movie premiere in Los Angeles, with a brief article that said that "Matt has managed to heal the breach" but that, according to unnamed friends of Olivia's, "Livvy is ready to give him the elbow if he steps out of line again."

Filming on *Two of a Kind* wrapped on July 21, 1983, but the soundtrack album had not been completed yet. Unlike Olivia's previous movies, this one was not a musical, but MCA Records still wanted an album out of it. David Foster produced most of the album, including Olivia's songs, which, including a duet with John Travolta, totaled four. The other six on the album were by Patti Austin, Steve Kipner, Boz Scaggs, Journey, Chicago, and an instrumental by Foster.

Not only did Kipner contribute a song as a recording artist, but having cowritten two of Olivia's recent hits, "Physical" and "Heart Attack," he cowrote another for this album. For each of these songs he wrote with a different collaborator; this time he worked with his friend and former bandmate (and Liverpool native) Peter Beckett. "I had flown over from England to the United States for the first time in 1974," Beckett recalls,

> to join a band with him [Kipner] that would eventually become Skyband. Olivia came over to visit Steve at the apartment we were sharing above Sunset Strip. Over the years I saw her several times, at a party at her house in Malibu, in the studio, a few social events, etc., and she would always ask what I was up to.

After Skyband failed to make it big and disbanded, Beckett formed another group called Player, which signed with RSO Records and hit number one in 1978 with its first single, "Baby Come Back," which Beckett wrote with bandmate J. C. Crowley. By 1983, Player had disbanded. "I was at Kipner's house," Beckett says, "working on some new songs when Roger Davies, Olivia's manager, called and said he was looking for a song for a movie starring Olivia and John Travolta, which was coming out in the fall of '83. Kipner held the phone up to the speakers, and we played a bit of one of the songs we'd been working on."

> Roger loved it and told us to finish ASAP. He sent us the script and clips of the movie so we would know what it was about. The lyrics we wrote were based on the plot of the movie. We recorded it in Kipner's studio, and it went to David Foster for final production. Kipner and I went down to Foster's studio to watch Olivia record it. She sounded great.

The song was "Twist of Fate." It would play over the closing credits of the movie.

Another one of Olivia's recent cowriters of hits—Tom Snow—came up with a song for the soundtrack album too. He wrote "Livin' in Desperate Times" with Barry Alfonso, who he says was "a writer I signed for a while, and he pretty much was responsible for the lyrics…. I think it was more about the tough, sexy girl," in keeping, to some degree at least, with Olivia's "Sandy #2"/post-*Grease* image. Snow went to Sunset Sound in Hollywood when Olivia recorded the song, but he found that he couldn't collaborate with David Foster as he had (and would again) with John Farrar. "David just takes charge and does David's thing, and you just have to sort of sit back. There's no real collaboration."

Olivia also chipped in as a songwriter for the soundtrack. While being interviewed for the November 1983 issue of *Interview* magazine, she said,

> I co-wrote a song with David Foster and Steve Lukather the other night—Steve's with Toto—and we sat down at about two in the morning to write the B-side, but it's turning out so well that it may end up the main track. It's a song John [Travolta] and I are going to do. It's called "Take a Chance on Love."

Olivia's other vocal contribution to the soundtrack, the piano-driven ballad "Shaking You," was written by Foster with Paul Howard Gordon, who cowrote the '80s hits "Friends and Lovers" and "Next Time I Fall," and Tom Keane, whose past collaborators included Peter Allen.

MCA Records released "Twist of Fate" as a single on October 21 and the *Two of a Kind* soundtrack album on November 21; 20th Century Fox released the film on December 16. As with *Xanadu*, the soundtrack album was successful, and the film was not. *New York Times* film critic Janet Maslin wrote,

> Can it really have been *that* difficult to find a passable screen vehicle for John Travolta and Olivia Newton-John? Any old romantic fluff should have sufficed, and yet something as horrible as *Two of a Kind* has been tailor-made for its stars. The results are so disastrous that absolutely no one is shown off to good advantage, with the possible exception of the hairdressers involved.

The film didn't win approval from the public, either, only managing to draw about $23 million at the box office, even though 20th Century Fox spent $6 million promoting it.

Peter Beckett sums it up pretty accurately: "The movie *Two Of A Kind* came out and didn't do that well, but… 'Twist Of Fate' ended up at number five on *Billboard*'s Hot 100. It was Olivia's last big hit. In hindsight, everyone thought the movie should have been called *Twist of Fate*." Even that probably wouldn't have helped the movie much, but, given that the single was climbing the Top 10 when the movie came out, it couldn't have hurt. The duet that Olivia cowrote for her and Travolta to sing, which ended up with the title "Take a Chance," was released on the B-side of "Twist of Fate" and reached No. 3 on *Billboard*'s adult contemporary chart. MCA released "Livin' in Desperate Times" as the follow-up single, but it only made it to No. 31 on the Hot 100.

To add insult to injury, the soundtrack album didn't sell as well as the *Xanadu* album had, which may have been due in part to its lesser number of contributions from Olivia, although the album had a fairly star-studded roster of recording artists. It included Journey's "Ask the Lonely," which became the biggest album-rock airplay hit in the United States in January 1984, even though MCA couldn't release it as a single under the terms of the deal that the label had to make with Journey's label, Columbia Records, to get permission to include it on the soundtrack. Danny Goldberg, who as a music consultant for 20th Century Fox worked with Roger Davies and Olivia on putting the album together, explained the motive of Journey manager Herbie Herbert and Columbia for putting the band on there. "Journey's biggest audience," Goldberg said,

> has always been in America, but the band isn't so well known outside of the country. Being on an Olivia Newton-John soundtrack album will give them an enormous amount of exposure in Europe, Australia and Japan, where Olivia is a big star. That way the next time they put out a Journey album, they'll already have a foothold in those places.

The *Two of a Kind* soundtrack reached No. 26 on the *Billboard* album chart, the poorest showing by any of Olivia's albums (soundtracks and greatest hits collections included) since 1977's *Making a Good Thing Better*. It still managed to sell one million copies in the United States, certainly enough to be profitable, but *Xanadu* had sold double that, as had the *Physical* album and both of her *Greatest Hits* albums. *Two of a Kind* received a similar response from record buyers in Australia, where it charted at No. 33, Canada (No. 30), and Japan (No. 29). It flopped in the United Kingdom, though.

For Olivia's film career, the back-to-back flops of *Xanadu* and *Two of a Kind* proved ruinous. Upon the release of *Two of a Kind*, she told a journalist for *People* magazine that in 1984 she'd be at work on a film to be titled *No Names, No Pack Drills*, which would be set in Australia in the 1940s and "could be a musical." Travolta told *People* that he hoped he and Olivia, having made a non-musical this time, would soon star together in another musical and that he was already on the lookout for a suitable script. "We'll try to do it sooner this time. It's always good to follow a hit with a hit," he said, too optimistically as it turned out.

In fact, Liz Smith, a nationally syndicated entertainment (and gossip) columnist, had reported in April 1983 that Olivia and Travolta might soon be set to star in the film version of the Tim Rice and Andrew Lloyd Webber musical *Evita*. Smith wrote that "Robert Stigwood, who owns the property, is negotiating with the popular co-stars of his big hit, *Grease*, and he definitely wants Olivia as Eva and John as the revolutionary commentator." Bill Oakes recalls, "It was a time when Stigwood had fun throwing out ideas to the press. As far as I remember, nobody took the idea seriously, especially not Rice or Lloyd Webber." Nevertheless, the flop of *Two of a Kind* could not have bolstered support for the idea, although the many delays in getting the film made—it came out in 1996—made it a moot point.

In any event, even Travolta's film career went into a slump with *Two of a Kind*—and unlike Olivia, acting was his sole vocation. He wouldn't have another hit film until *Look Who's Talking* in 1989. Olivia wouldn't even be in another film until 1996, when she took a role in Randal Kleiser's low-budget, limited release *It's My Party*.

She took on a new role of a different sort in 1983, though: retail owner and operator. On October 3, she and Pat Farrar opened Koala Blue at 7366 Melrose Avenue, less than half a mile west of the famed Pink's Hot Dogs stand. Alison Martino, daughter of the legendary crooner Al Martino and the leading authority on the cultural history of LA, described the shop after Olivia's passing: "One of the hottest boutiques located in the trendy section of Melrose Avenue, Koala Blue was one of the first boutiques to kick off on the Melrose scene. Inside it had an Aussie milk bar, replete with an authentic menu. I still remember the candy bars: Polly Waffles, Violet Crumble, Cherry Ripe. It was certainly unique." The *Los Angeles Times* reported that

Koala Blue ("Korner of Australia in Los Angeles") started out as an Aussie milk bar (soda fountain) but was expanded to incorporate fashions of such Australian designers as Stuart Membry, Ken Done and Briony Gyngelle, plus bunches of Aussie merchandise from chocolates and daily newspapers to cute stuffed koala bears. And, of course, the menu of sandwiches, salads and Aussie fast foods you can try at the counter.

Olivia came up with the store's name. "We had a million names," she told writer George Christy.

Down Under, and all this stuff. One day I was driving alone, and, I have this habit… I love to make stories out of license plates on cars about the initials and the numbers—my mum used to do that with me. And suddenly I looked, a license plate near the stop said KOAL, and I thought, goodness, look what it spells out, Korner of Australia L.A. I thought that I was gonna have plenty of time to get the shop together, but it's taken much longer than we thought. The movie, the shop opening and my recording have all come at once, so I try to split myself in all these areas—it's been a crazy month.

The inspiration for the venture, she told Christy, came

last year [1982] when I was on the road with my manager Roger Davies and his wife Nanette. We would talk about home [Australia] a lot and about things we missed, like the candies and things you can't get over here—the milk shakes are different, and the meat pies and things like that. And one day I was thinking it might be fun to open a little place where all the Australians could hang out—where you get the newspapers and candies…. And on my birthday last year I had a little party, and Pat and John [Farrar] were there, and I was telling her about this idea, and she had been thinking about opening a boutique for clothes. No one had done it before. We embarked on this wide-eyed and bushy-tailed, not realizing how much work was involved. We went back to Australia last Christmas, and we looked at the clothes and saw designs with kangaroos and koalas and wallabies; it was the perfect timing for us since these things were very different, very novel. We've got everything Australian. Books, fantastic clothing, jewelry, children's clothes and some artwork.

One month before the store opened, according to *People*, Olivia "flew home to do some buying for the store, visit her family and check on her 80-acre sugarcane and avocado farm in New South Wales, where, she says, 'I'll probably retire.'" Once the store opened, she was not an absentee owner, either, despite her continued status as one of the world's most popular singers. Peter Leinheiser, who had toured with and gotten to know Olivia in 1976 when he was the lead guitarist for her opening act, the Hudson Brothers, walked into her Melrose Avenue store not long after it had opened. As he was looking around the store, he heard a familiar voice say, "Hello, Peter." He looked and there was Olivia. "I felt quite charmed," he recalls.

About a month after the opening of Koala Blue, Olivia's friend Alan Thicke, who had worked on her 1978 and 1980 ABC television specials, paid a visit to the store that was taped and aired on his new (and short-lived) late-night show, *Thicke of the Night*. The visit was presented to viewers as if it were spontaneous; when Thicke arrived, Olivia was "in the Sheila" (Australian slang for the women's restroom). He asked her through the door to guess his identity, with the "hint" of "Who's your favorite American TV personality and helped you have the most American TV success?" She answered Dick Cavett, then Dick Clark, and then Bob Hope.

After she emerged, she gave Thicke a tour of the store, showing him goods for sale such as a stuffed toy koala and Aboriginal art prints as well as Australian candies and the Vegemite food spread that many Americans had heard of in the recent number one hit "Down Under" by the Aussie band Men at Work. She also showed him the milk bar. Much of the merchandise was clothing.

A few weeks later, on December 1, 1983, Olivia and Travolta appeared on *The Tonight Show* to promote the forthcoming release of *Two of a Kind.* Joan Rivers was serving as the substitute host for Johnny Carson, as she often did during that era. (When Rivers tried in 1986 to challenge Carson with her own late-night show on the fledgling Fox network, he never spoke to her again. Rivers, like Thicke, failed to last long against the late-night legend.)

Rivers greeted John and Olivia by saying, "You look great *together*, you know that? Are you an item?" After more questions along those lines, Travolta told her good naturedly, "Of course, it's none of your business what actually happened" between Olivia and himself, to which Olivia responded with an approving fist pump, and Joan laughingly (and sarcastically) replied, "No, nor would I want to pry."

Joan then asked Olivia about Matt Lattanzi. After noting that Olivia looked young for thirty-five, Joan asked her, "How old is *he*?" Before Olivia could answer, Joan said, "He's only twelve!" A bit later in the conversation, after the subject of marriage came up, Joan asked Olivia, "Why don't you get married?… Don't you think it's time?" Olivia seemed a bit reluctant to answer the question but said that for her the time to get married would be when she wanted to start a family. "I've got a few years left," she said. Joan then started teasing her about how many eggs she had left.

By now Olivia was wearing a gold ring that Matt had given her, and she told *People* journalist Carl Arrington that she was indeed aware of her "ticking biological clock." "The time is never right to have a child," she told him. "You just have to do it." Yet Arrington wrote that "she is reluctant to marry, partly out of fear of failure."

As Olivia and Travolta continued to promote *Two of a Kind*, they gave an interview to movie critic Gene Siskel. In the resultant newspaper feature, he wrote of Olivia, "Marriage and babies… are not in the cards now." "I want my marriage to last," she told him.

She also gave Siskel an indication that she wasn't too confident about her new movie and the future of her film career. "If I never get another movie role," she told him, "it's okay. This is all icing on the cake for me. If I get to do my perfect movie, that's great; if not, it's enough already. Basically, I consider myself a singer, and I think I'll be able to record for a while."

13 SOUL KISS

"I used to gravitate toward men who were strong, self-assured and almost arrogant," Olivia told the Hollywood author and journalist Jane Ardmore around the beginning of 1984. "Matt is more relaxed, not in the least driven, and that's great for me. I really do know there's more to life than business."

"I don't really expect success to last. I can certainly look back right now and say I've achieved what I've wanted to. Which leaves me to get on with my personal life, which I'd let slip for a long time. These last few years have been very personal. I feel a lovely freedom."

At this point in the interview, Lee Kramer's name came up. Olivia told Ardmore that she gave Lee a lot of credit for the success she had achieved during his years as her manager, but that she had also learned not to mix business with her personal life to such an extent. Before Lee, Bruce Welch had also been heavily involved in her career, of course, writing songs for her and coproducing and playing on her records.

As was the case in seemingly all of Olivia's interviews around this time, the subject soon turned to marriage. Once again, she expressed ambivalence and reluctance. "I don't need to marry for security," she insisted to Ardmore. "It's not a decision I take lightly…. I have certain fears about marriage." She cited the litany of divorces she had seen in her family: her parents, her sister, her aunts and uncles. "There's hardly a member of my family who hasn't been through it. I guess I've been affected by that. If you've never seen a relationship that lasts forever, then you tend to believe it's not possible."

Olivia also admitted to vacillating on whether she wanted to become a mother. "Currently," she told Ardmore, "the threat of nuclear war seems so close that I have thought it kind of foolish or unfair to bring kids into the world now because we're killing ourselves off with pollution, poisoning our food, threatening each other with nukes." But, she conceded, "a few weeks from now, I'll probably change my mind and say, 'I survived, my generation survived, maybe I should have a child and hope that child will somehow improve the world.'" She then repeated her concerns, however, about what she saw as the necessary prerequisite for having any children. "Marriage, to me, is a lifetime commitment. People change and grow as they grow older, and you want to make sure you change and grow together."

The interviews that Olivia gave to publicize *Two of a Kind* suggested that she was willing to ease up on her career and, perhaps, marry and start a family. She also seemed enthusiastic about Koala Blue. "It's really a labor of love," she told Ardmore. "Eventually I hope to get into designing my own line [of clothing]." In an interview a few weeks later, Pat Farrar affirmed her friend and partner's commitment to their joint venture. "Don't worry," she said. "Olivia has a strong interest in this store. It's much more than just a commercial venture for her. It's something both of us have wanted to do for a long, long time."

The 1984 Summer Olympics came to Los Angeles, from July 28 through August 12, and gave Olivia and Pat further opportunity to celebrate their former home country. On July 17, the two of them hosted a welcome party for the Australian Olympians at Koala Blue, with, reported a columnist for the New York *Daily News*, "a real live koala from the San Diego Zoo and just loads of authentic Australian cuisine including shrimp, flown in for the festivities, meat pies, and pavlovas, the little meringue cups stuffed with fresh fruit and anointed with whipped cream." Drinks included Seaview Australian champagne and Foster's Lager. Olivia and Pat each made welcoming speeches, and the Australian comedian Barry Humphries performed in character as Dame Edna Everage, a role that he had created in 1955 with great success that he eventually duplicated in Great Britain and, to an extent, the United States as well. For the finale, Olivia, the Little River Band, and the English-born Australian rock star Billy Thorpe, whom Olivia and Rona had both known in the 1960s, performed "a smashing rendition of 'Waltzing Matilda.'"

Other Australian celebrities (in addition to the Olympians) on hand for the party included Peter Allen, Helen Reddy, and the actor Bryan Brown and his wife Rachel Ward. Plenty of Hollywood stars attended, too, including Alan Thicke, who was about a year away from finally making it big with the TV series *Growing Pains*, and John Travolta and Marilu Henner. "Matt Lattanzi, Olivia's boyfriend, took pictures of everything (so did all the TV media)," reported the *Daily News*, "and turned his camera over to Cristina DeLorean to photograph him whilst he frolicked with John Travolta." Portions of the party would air on Australia's Ten Network a little over a week later.

By then, Olivia (with Matt) had flown to Sydney, where she taped her segment at the Admiralty House, the official residence of the governor-general of Australia, for the *Olympic Gala* TV special. This "three-hour spectacular combining Hollywood glamour and Olympic superstars of the past," as Hollywood journalist

Vernon Scott described it, was hosted by Jane Fonda and Robert Wagner at the Greek Theatre in Los Angeles. Muhammad Ali undoubtedly ranked as the most famous person to appear on the program, which was shown by ABC in the United States and Channel Nine in Australia. Paul Hogan joined Olivia in wishing the Olympic athletes well, particularly, they good naturedly added, the Australians, and then Olivia sang "I Still Call Australia Home" and "Waltzing Matilda," accompanied by two children's choirs and the Military District Band. An "old school chum" of hers, Peter Faiman of the Nine Network's Special Projects Division, produced and directed her performance.

Olivia and Matt did not return to Los Angeles for the Olympics. She told the *Sydney Morning Herald* that she'd be taking a monthlong vacation "up north" in Australia—specifically, her avocado farm near Coffs Harbour on the mid-north coast of New South Wales, although she understandably made it a point not to divulge the name of the city or any other details that would allow unwelcome visitors to find her. She said that she'd also been looking for clothes for Koala Blue.

In an interview for the Australian *Woman's Day* magazine, Olivia said,

Sure I'd like to live here full-time. But, if I'm realistic, it would be half the year here and half in America. That is starting to happen now. I'm coming back quite a lot. I feel I'm safe here. Maybe it's to do with my childhood. I feel comfortable. I miss the people. The place is beautiful, but places are places—it's really the people who make a place. I have family here and I have friends here.

She added that being gone from Australia for more than six months made her "terribly homesick."

Upon returning to the United States, Olivia kept a fairly low profile for a while. She and Pat held a party for the members of Australia's "Circus Oz" troupe at Koala Blue, which Paul Hogan attended. She appeared on a television special titled *A Salute to Liberace*, which was taped live in Las Vegas in honor of his fortieth anniversary in showbiz. Shirley MacLaine hosted, and other guests included David Bowie and Elton John.

In November 1984, Olivia and Matt made an announcement that those close to them and even the media had been long expecting to hear: they would be getting married at the end of December in Los Angeles. (That date proved a bit later than the actual date, perhaps in an attempt to fool the press.) Olivia's publicist, Paul Bloch of Los Angeles–based Rogers & Cowan, said that the wedding would be private. "Ideally I'd love to get married quietly," Olivia said, "without fuss and without anybody knowing. But I know that will not be the way it will happen. It is very difficult to keep that kind of thing a secret." Olivia did manage to keep one secret. She was pregnant while she and Matt were planning the wedding. But she suffered a miscarriage—the first of several.

Olivia and Matt married on December 15, 1984, at their home in Malibu. "Olivia's entire clan," the New York *Daily News* reported, "flew up from Australia to witness the launching": her parents and her siblings Hugh, Toby, and Sarah. (Rona, who at the time was married to one of Olivia's *Grease* castmates, Jeff Conaway, was of course present but lived nearby—in fact, when living with Conaway proved dangerous during his spells of drug and alcohol abuse, she and her son Emerson would take refuge at Olivia's home.) Nieces and nephews of Olivia's also attended, and Matt's family traveled down from Oregon.

Olivia wore "a white silk taffeta dress trimmed with lace and beads. The groom looked spiffy in a black tux." Nanette Davies (Roger's wife), a fashion designer, had spent six weeks making the bride's dress. The ceremony was followed by "a traditional English dinner of turkey, ham and a three-tiered wedding cake filled with chocolate chips." Seventy guests attended. Brin walked his daughter down the aisle. Not surprisingly, Olivia also included Jackson, the Irish setter that a fan had given her after a concert in the Mississippi city of the same name a decade earlier, in the ceremony. She dressed him in white bows for the occasion, and he stood near her as Judge Jerry Pacht led her and Matt through their vows and pronounced them man and wife.

The newlyweds then went to Europe for their honeymoon. First, they spent time in Paris, where they were photographed walking on the streets without being bothered. Then they traveled by train to what the London *Mirror* described as "the Swiss tinsel town" of Gstaad, a skiing resort. There they were joined by Victoria Principal and her fiancé, the plastic surgeon Harry Glassman. (Olivia and Matt had met Victoria in 1981 while the *Dallas* star was in a relationship with Andy Gibb.) Photos published in newspapers and magazines showed the two couples bundled up and strolling in the snowy terrain. They also encountered Elizabeth Taylor and her latest fiancé, Dennis Stein. According to the *Mirror*, Taylor "hinted that Elton John's New Year arrival might have something to do with playing her favorite tune—'The Wedding March.'" In its typical overblown and snarky tone, the paper reported that "all this proved too much for eternal bachelor John Travolta, who left weeping on the arms of his chums Matt and Olivia (nee Newton-John) Lattanzi."

For Olivia, 1984 had been the first year in which she had put her personal life above her career; she made no records, no films, only a handful of television appearances, and gave no full concerts. She was now intent on having a baby. At the same time, she wasn't ready to walk away from her career as a pop star, either.

After her late-1970s legal faceoff with MCA Records, Olivia was no longer under pressure to keep recording albums at a rapid, or even a steady, pace. Since 1977, she had given MCA two platinum albums in *Totally Hot* and *Physical*, plus two more with each of her greatest hits albums, and she had been a major contributor to two platinum soundtrack albums for the label, *Xanadu* and *Two of a Kind*. She'd also provided MCA with seven Top 10 singles during that time (including the "Xanadu" collaboration with the Electric Light Orchestra), among them the biggest hit of the 1980s with "Physical." (Of course, those hits didn't reflect the entirety of her popularity during that period, as all the *Grease* recordings were released by RSO Records.)

The perpetually mismanaged MCA Records went through yet another shake-up in 1983. Irving Azoff, who had made a name for himself in the record industry in the 1970s as the manager of the Eagles, Steely Dan, REO Speedwagon, and Dan Fogelberg, took over as the president of the label in 1983. Azoff hired Richard Palmese as executive vice president and general manager. Both men held those roles for just about the remainder of Olivia's tenure with the label.

The new regime would have an aloof relationship with Olivia. "Unfortunately," Palmese recalls, "my contact with her was brief. Her manager at that time, Bill Sammeth, worked with us on her behalf." Roger Davies was still Olivia's manager when Azoff and Palmese took over, but by the mid-'80s he was turning his attention elsewhere.

"Olivia got married and pregnant, and Tina [Turner]'s career took off—we did *Private Dancer* [1984] which sold 12 million [worldwide]," Davies recalled in 1993.

> It was good timing. Olivia wasn't working too much, and she got involved in Koala Blue, the clothing shops, which was something I had no expertise in. I think the clothing business is far more sleazy than the music business, and I wasn't involved. Tina had become so popular, it was really demanding on me, and Olivia had really lost the desire to work, and I told her she didn't really need me anymore. It was a really sad parting because I really adore her and she's a great person.

Sammeth, whose clients included Cher and Joan Rivers, had already been working with Olivia as an agent and became her manager after Davies moved on, although Davies would not fully step aside until after the next album was completed.

While Olivia had had at least one Top 10 single per year every year from 1978 through 1984 ("Twist of Fate" remained in the Top 10 until the end of January 1984), during her more than one year out of the recording studio, the pop/rock landscape for female singers began changing rapidly. In addition to Tina Turner's huge comeback as a solo artist in 1984, Madonna (whose "Like a Virgin" single and video made the controversy over "Physical" seem even more laughable) and Cyndi Lauper both emerged as superstars. Whitney Houston was just around the corner; her first hit, "You Give Good Love," reached the Top 5 in the summer of 1985.

Perhaps Olivia sensed that the demographics of her audience were (once again) starting to change. On New Year's Day, 1985, a new cable television music video channel premiered: VH-1, which stood for Video Hits One. MTV Networks Inc.

owned the channel. According to a press report, MTV and VH-1 were "designed to complement each other and not to compete for the same audience." The report described MTV as "aimed at 12-to-34-year-old rock and roll fans" with its "mix of hard rock, heavy metal and new wave." VH-1, in contrast, sought to appeal to "the 25-to-54-year-old [adult] contemporary music listener, including the parents of the kids who sit glued to MTV for hours on end." Olivia agreed to appear, without being paid, in radio and television commercials for VH-1, exclaiming, "My music's on the hot one, the very hot one, VH-1," for the spots. Others who did the same included Kenny Rogers, Melissa Manchester, Smokey Robinson, Julio Iglesias, Herb Alpert, and Stevie Wonder—artists who occupied a different realm of the pop music marketplace than MTV stars such as Duran Duran, Rick Springfield (another member of Los Angeles' "Gum Leaf Mafia" of Aussies), and Michael Jackson, who broke the unspoken color line of MTV's first year and a half.

In early 1985, Olivia and John Farrar went to work in Farrar's Moonee Ponds Studio in Malibu, which was named after the Melbourne suburb where he grew up, to begin recording her first full album since *Physical* four years earlier. They had begun planning the album and selecting material for it in 1984, and they were still working on it when Matt told a reporter at the beginning of June 1985, "Don't be surprised if you see a little Newton-John–Lattanzi around in about a year." But when she and Matt did a brief interview together for the US television program *Entertainment This Week* (a cousin of the better-known *Entertainment Tonight*) that same week, neither of them said a word about her being pregnant, although she indeed was. When she went to London about a month later to appear in a television special, she told the press she was not pregnant. This lie reflected her long-held desire to maintain some semblance of privacy in her personal life, but also the fear that she later said had dogged her throughout the pregnancy that she might suffer another miscarriage.

Olivia stuck with her familiar team for the new album. Farrar not only served as the producer, but as had long been the case, he also played instruments and/or sang backing vocals on most tracks and contributed as a composer, cowriting four songs. Tom Snow, Steve Kipner, and Paul Bliss also contributed as writers, and Snow and Kipner each played synthesizer on a track. A number of past band members and session players returned for this album, too, among them Steve Lukather, Tom Scott, Mike Landau, Carlos Vega, and Abraham Laboriel.

The well-oiled machine that had supported Olivia through so many hits didn't operate as smoothly this time, though. Olivia would later say that the new regime at MCA Records had pushed her to deliver an album that (although she didn't say it, the implication was clear) would push her further in the direction of the sexy image of *Totally Hot* and *Physical*, in the hopes of appealing as much to MTV viewers as VH-1 viewers. She had reinvented herself from the pop-country songstress of "Let Me Be There" and "Please Mr. Please" to the sultry pop-rock singer of "A Little

More Love" and "Physical" in her early thirties, and as she entered her late thirties and was about to become a mother, it may have, in hindsight, made more sense for her to shift into more of the pop–adult contemporary mode into which she had always comfortably fit rather than trying to compete with Madonna. Certainly, the front and back album cover photos shot by Helmut Newton gave the impression that the latter was MCA's intent.

Nevertheless, an album that had the kind of radio-friendly hits that *Totally Hot* and *Physical* did might have achieved a comparable level of success. The annual Gallup Youth Survey of American teenagers' favorite singers, conducted during January and February 1985, ranked Olivia as the eighth most popular female vocalist, indicating that she did indeed still have a lot of credibility with the MTV generation.

Unfortunately, her stable of regular songwriters failed to deliver anything of the caliber of the hits that they had written for her in the past. Tellingly, the album's two singles were both songs that Tina Turner had rejected, which Roger Davies subsequently played for Olivia. Mark Goldenberg, cowriter of the Pointer Sisters' Top 5 hit "Automatic" (1984), wrote "Soul Kiss," which became the album's title track and first single. Katey Sagal sang backing vocals on the track, two years before she hit it big as a star of *Married… with Children*. The second single, "Toughen Up," was written by the Scottish singer-songwriter Graham Lyle and Terry Britten, who had made contributions to previous albums of Olivia's as a songwriter and guitarist. Lyle and Britten had recently written Tina Turner's huge 1984 comeback hit—and first solo hit—"What's Love Got to Do with It."

The *Soul Kiss* album included a song written by Farrar and Snow, "You Were Great, How Was I?" This was the team that had written, as Richard Perry put it, the "quiet" million seller "Make a Move on Me," but MCA didn't deem this new song, despite being recorded as a duet between Olivia and Carl Wilson with Christopher Cross on backing vocals, as worthy of release as a single. In some ways, this song—both with its suggestive title and in its failure to deliver on the talent of those involved—summarized the entire problem with the album.

Still other problems vexed the album. Final preparation and delivery of the finished product to MCA was delayed first by last-minute decisions over which finished songs to include (perhaps a tacit admission that there was no "Magic" or "Physical" among the bunch) and then by difficulties in the mixing process. By the fall of 1985, Olivia was far enough along in her pregnancy that it was visible— that fact plus her understandable desire to put the health of herself and her unborn child above any career considerations meant that, unlike with *Physical*, a complete video album couldn't be made. Instead, she made a mini-video album, with five songs including the two singles. Director David Mallet made sure that Olivia was filmed at angles and positions, and in attire, that concealed her pregnancy. Olivia did the rounds of interviews for the album, but she did not tour—she had made it clear when the Physical Tour ended three years earlier that she was not planning on hitting the road again anytime soon, regardless of any pregnancies—and she didn't make it to *The Tonight Show* or *Solid Gold* or any other television program where she might have performed any songs from the album.

MCA released the "Soul Kiss" single on September 25, 1985, followed by the album on October 15. In an interview with Paul Grein for *Billboard*, which was published in the October 19 issue under the headline "Olivia Explains Her Change of Image," she said, "It's a very young market out there. They don't call it disco anymore, but it never dies, really; it just becomes another name—dance music. That seems to be a very important part of the record industry and how kids hear music and are introduced to it." Olivia also told Grein that she had "self-indulgent dreams" of recording another country album and, as Linda Ronstadt had recently done, an album of pop standards. But, she explained, "I seem to make albums so irregularly that when it came time to do one, it was like, 'Let's get something commercial out here,' and I don't feel anyone really felt it was a viable thing at the time."

Billboard and *Cash Box* both predicted big success for the "Soul Kiss" single and album. *Billboard* described the latter as "all classy techno-pop plus a couple of ballads for her AC [adult contemporary] base." In a review for *Rolling Stone*, which years earlier had almost pulled the plug on Ben Fong-Torres's feature on Olivia before *Grease* made her "relevant" again, Davitt Sigerson wrote that *Soul Kiss* featured "a kinky Helmut Newton cover, a lean John Farrar production and a fun single, the album's title track. Originally (and wisely) passed on by Tina Turner, 'Soul Kiss' is just right for Newton-John. She proves once again that she is the best pure pop singer working today."

Sigerson wasn't entirely sold on the album, though. "Too bad the rest of the material doesn't match up," he wrote.

> There are good songs, but no other bull's-eyes, and a pair of embarrassments. "Queen of the Publication" is a Livvy-as-crack-journalist fantasy that would have worked better as the storyboard to a feminine-deodorant commercial. In "Culture Shock," Newton-John asks her hurt beau if her other beau can move in with them. It's a male pipe dream in which nothing but the pronouns have been changed.

Somewhat surprisingly, *People* magazine, which had given Olivia plenty of good publicity since she first made it big in the United States, gave the album an acerbic review. "Olivia convinced everyone with her 1981 album *Physical* that she was aware of sex. Recent events in her personal life would seem to have sufficiently reaffirmed that awareness. So why this exercise in supersleaze, which runs from the kink of the jacket photograph through the tune 'Culture Shock,' which seems to be a musical tribute to ménages à trois?" The review went on in similar terms.

In the title tune, Olivia wails on about getting down on her knees and sighs passionately. So curious is this preoccupation with the details of mating that it detracts mightily from the musical aspects of the LP... there's no need for all the blatant tarting up. If Olivia's career keeps going this way, just about the only thing she will be able to do next is record an album of duets with Dr. Ruth.

Olivia brushed off the criticism of "Culture Shock." "I know plenty of people," she said, "who have been in that [threesome] situation who'll get a giggle out of it." She joked that the song, which wasn't released as a single, "might get banned in Salt Lake City [a reference to the radio ban of 'Physical'], but I can't imagine anyone else getting upset." "I'm too old to be innocent," she added.

Commercially, *Soul Kiss* met with mixed success, which meant, in other words, a comedown from the long hot streak that she had been riding ever since *Grease*. The title track reached No. 20 on the pop singles charts of both *Billboard* and *Cash Box*. Grein noted in *Billboard* that when "Soul Kiss" became Olivia's twenty-eighth Top 40 hit, it made 1985 "the 13th consecutive year that the singer has cracked the top 40 on the pop singles chart. That record is matched by only one female singer in chart history: Jo Stafford," who had accomplished the feat from 1944 through 1956. "Soul Kiss" also reached No. 20 in Australia, and No. 21 in Canada, but those were the only markets besides the US where it became even that much of a hit.

The *Soul Kiss* album reached No. 29 in *Billboard*, 19 in Australia, 34 in Canada, and only 66 in the United Kingdom (where the single only managed to crack the bottom of the charts at 100). Only in Japan, where fans had been almost unfailingly loyal to Olivia since the mid-1970s, did the album became a bona fide hit, reaching No. 5. The album did sell the half million copies in the United States required for a gold record, but it became Olivia's first American album in eight years not to reach the million-sales (platinum) mark.

Years later, Olivia would confirm what many critics had suggested about *Soul Kiss*. "It was kind of contrived, and I wasn't comfortable with that." Perhaps this was one case where Lee Kramer might have saved her from a misstep. Roger Davies didn't know Olivia personally as well as Kramer had, wasn't as protective of her, and Lattanzi didn't play much of a role in making career decisions for her. "He encourages me," Olivia said of Matt upon the album's release, "supports me and is happy for me to do anything I feel comfortable with"—even if, in this case, she didn't really feel comfortable.

But by January 1986, the album was not the paramount matter on Olivia's mind (if it even had been while she was making it). She'd had a frightening, painful episode just before Christmas of 1985 which her ob-gyn had told her might be a late-term miscarriage. Her baby—which she and Matt chose not to learn the gender of in advance—was due around mid- to late February 1986. But Chloe Rose Lattanzi, named after the perfume that Olivia was wearing when she met Matt, came prematurely on January 17 at 5:17 a.m. (From then on, Olivia would consider seventeen to be her lucky number.) The baby was healthy, but Olivia suffered an unfortunate ill effect from the delivery. She had wanted a totally natural delivery, but at the end of (not so luckily in this case) seventeen hours, she let a doctor give her an epidural. The needle hit her spinal cord, and she was nearly incapacitated for a month. She continued to suffer from headaches, sometimes "pretty severe," for "five long years," she recalled in her memoir.

This unfortunate development would, of course, affect her career, but her career no longer played a dominant role in her life once Chloe was born. "She is just wonderful," Olivia told a journalist shortly after giving birth. "I want to spend every minute with Chloe. She is just wonderful," she repeated. "I can't imagine life without her." Rona saw Chloe immediately, as did Matt's parents. Irene took a flight from Australia to LAX as soon as Olivia went into labor, and she stayed with Olivia, Matt, and Chloe for two months. "She has large, beautiful eyes which at the moment are very dark blue," Irene said of her new granddaughter. "I was terribly thrilled. I was hoping Olivia would have a child before it was too late." Irene, who by this point had become an established professional photographer, took the first photo of Chloe, being held by her broadly smiling parents, that was released to the press.

Irene said that she expected Olivia and Matt to have more children. Olivia said the same shortly thereafter, telling a reporter that she and Matt had already picked the name Jesse if they had a boy. Irene quipped, "I'm sure they won't be taking Chloe on tour." Touring, though, remained the furthest thing from Olivia's mind—the rest of the 1980s would pass without her even planning a tour.

In September 1986, Los Angeles–based reporter Ian Hislop came to Olivia's ranch in Malibu, which was "behind a high wall [and] protected by an array of security devices," to interview her for Australia's Seven Network. "I don't have any great desires to work, which is terrible," she told him.

I suppose my life is a lot quieter, but it's more enjoyable and fulfilling because Chloe has brought a dimension to my life that I didn't know was there. I think until you have a baby you're missing out on an awful lot of life. And now all kinds of things have opened up to me that I wasn't tuned into at all. I shouldn't have waited so long!

"I think now," she reflected, "when I look back on my life, I won't be thinking about my gold records, but about my family. Chloe is my greatest achievement."

14 LOVE AND LET LIVE

" 'm happy and fulfilled being with my baby," Olivia told journalist Carol Nuckols in October 1986. She said that she knew Chloe would grow up fast, and "I don't want to miss anything." "I don't want to work right now," she said in regard to recording and touring. "I've taken [time] off from that."

She proved how much she meant that when she turned down an offer earlier that year to tour with Frank Sinatra. "My daughter was pretty newly born," she recalled in 2019.

I just didn't feel right going on tour. I was in that very early breastfeeding stage. I really wanted to experience going on tour with Sinatra of all people. It would have certainly been so extraordinary. I would have loved to have sung a duet with him. I was very flattered, of course. But my daughter was more important. That's why I didn't do it. And I know I made the right decision.

Olivia did, however, record a duet at that time, "The Best of Me," with David Foster, who wrote the song with Jeremy Lubbock and Richard Marx. "This was two weeks after she'd had her baby," Foster said in an interview shortly after they had made the record.

We rolled a truck up to her house. She's sitting there feeding the baby [at] the microphone, she's singing the song. She's such a great chick, and she's so mellow and helpful. And it came out great, and of course the record company [Foster's label, Atlantic Records] went, "Oh yeah, we'll take that one for the first single [from his album]." So now I said, "Olivia, well now we have to make a video, I mean, do you mind?" "No no, no problem." She came over, brought the baby, Rebecca [Dyer, Foster's first wife] watched the baby, her husband was there watching the baby, and we'd shoot a little, she'd feed a little, and the video's done.

Atlantic released the single internationally, but it found (moderate) success in only two countries, the United States and Foster's native Canada. It reached No. 80 on the Hot 100 and No. 6 on *Billboard*'s adult contemporary chart, and in Canada, No. 17 on the pop singles chart and No. 3 on the adult contemporary chart. It would be Olivia's last single for two years. In August 1986 she participated in the David Foster Celebrity Softball Game in Victoria, British Columbia, which drew a paying crowd of about 5,500 to watch her, Rob Lowe, Tommy Chong, Michael Damian, and the game's namesake, among others, play a game that ended in a 12–12 tie. The event raised $100,000 for children in need of organ transplants.

While still expressing happiness with motherhood and marriage—"I was terrified [of marriage], but now I don't know why I was so frightened," she told a reporter in September 1986—Olivia was also formulating career plans, albeit of a nonmusical nature. She and Pat Farrar had sold Koala Blue franchise rights to two New York businessmen, Edward J. Pastucha and Jon E. DeLuca. Pastucha's daughter, Hallie Latos, recalls that Olivia "interviewed tons and tons of big companies and little companies, and she ended up choosing my dad and Jon DeLuca."

They began opening additional Koala Blue stores in the area between LA and San Diego. In October, Olivia and Pat traveled to Dallas for the opening of another store. Plans for further expansion, nationally and internationally, were underway. By then, though, in an ominous sign for the company's future, DeLuca had hired an attorney to sue Pastucha, Koala Blue Inc., Pat, and Olivia for what he alleged were violations of the California Franchise Investments Act. Olivia became involved in another lawsuit that summer, in Australia, as a plaintiff alongside her longtime Aussie record label, Festival, which sued record stores that had sold imported copies of the *Soul Kiss* album, thus violating Festival's exclusive rights in Oz.

At the same time that she and Pat were focusing on Koala Blue, Olivia was also planning another crack at the silver screen. She told Ian Hislop of "a secret film project" that she and one of her best friends, Nancy Gould Chuda, had sold to Paramount Studios, even as the two of them were still writing the script—a comedy, with a role for Matt as well. Olivia and Nancy had met during the early to mid-1970s, when Nancy's stepfather, Gerald Breslauer, was managing Olivia's US business affairs. By the mid-1980s, the two friends decided they wanted to become mothers at about the same time. As Olivia laughingly recounted in an interview, when she learned she was pregnant with Chloe, "I called her up and I said, 'NOW!'" Chloe and Nancy's daughter, Colette, were born within four weeks of each other and were as close as two small children could be until Colette's tragic death from a rare form of cancer at the age of five.

In mid-September 1986, Olivia and Matt took eight-month-old Chloe to Australia for the first time. The Victorian Football League had invited Olivia to sing at its Grand Final at the Melbourne Cricket Ground. She had turned down previous invitations, always too busy with work commitments in the United States or somewhere else in the world, but the timing was right this time. As Australia's *Woman's Day* magazine put it, "She saw the VFL's offer this year as the perfect opportunity to show off her daughter." Before a live audience of one hundred thousand and an international television audience of seventy million, Olivia sang "Advance Australia Fair" (Australia's national anthem) and "Waltzing Matilda."

The day before her performance, she "celebrated her 38th birthday quietly with friends," according to *Woman's Day*. She, Matt, and Chloe spent about a month in Australia, staying in Ballina in northern New South Wales, where she had purchased a three-bedroom house in the rolling hills of the countryside. "I hope to take Chloe to Australia as often as I can," she told journalist Heather Waby. "I was raised here as a child, and it is a healthy environment for children. I am not so sure about Los Angeles to raise children. Chloe will need to go back to Australia to get a bit of down-to-home treatment now and again."

Once back in the States, Olivia threw herself back into the expansion of Koala Blue, which by the spring of 1987 had added locations in San Francisco, Costa Mesa (Orange County), and Miami. Andy Gibb, who was writing songs with his brothers again and planning to relaunch his dormant recording career, showed up at the Miami opening on April 8, 1987. (He also had come to at least one previous opening, in Westminster, California, the year before.) Olivia, too, had decided by then to get back into the recording studio. For nearly two years, she told the *South Florida Sun-Sentinel*, "I didn't do anything, and I loved it. I never thought I'd come back, actually. I don't know what triggered it. I missed singing." Pat Farrar told the reporter, "I told her she would."

Olivia said she'd be returning to the recording studio in June and also taping another special for HBO, which she said would premiere in November along with the release of her next album. When asked about *Soul Kiss*, with its "racy" album cover and songs that "included one about a menage a trois," Olivia replied, "I think it's good to change, to be adventurous. So now I've been adventurous. Now I feel I'm going back to a little more grown-up approach. The thrust [of the new album] will be a more adult approach."

She added that she would not be touring in support of the album, notwithstanding her admission that traveling with Pat to openings of Koala Blue stores was "sort of like touring, though. We got in [to Miami] at one in the morning and ended up at this 24-hour pizza place." When Olivia, along with Pat, went to the counter to order, the man on the other side didn't recognize her and "growled 'Whaddya want?' and 'Here's your pizza'" at them.

Olivia and Pat spent less than twenty-four hours in Miami, though. Most of the longer Koala Blue–related trips were undertaken by Pat. Hallie Latos, who says she "was hired on as the gal who merchandised and made the stores look nice" because of her experience as a Ralph Lauren merchandising coordinator, took a ten-day trip to Hong Kong with Pat. "[We] went to check out factories there and pick clothing designs and manufacturers and stuff like that. That was kind of neat."

Olivia was actively involved in Koala Blue though. "I remember working with Olivia," Latos recalls. "I remember going to her beautiful ranch in Malibu… this was when she was breast-feeding Chloe. I sat there and talked with her about [Koala Blue]… beautiful memories." "Out of everybody that I worked with," Latos says, "Olivia was definitely the sweetest, most genuine, beautiful, just like she comes across, you know. She *was* that way to work with, she was."

By mid-1987, though, Olivia was returning her attention to her recording career. After the long break, however, some glitches emerged. Roger Davies, who had been more focused on Tina Turner even at the time of *Soul Kiss*, had by now established an office in London. In addition to still working with Tina, he was also working as a creative consultant to Mick Jagger. It was at this point that he and Olivia decided by affable mutual agreement that she needed to find a new manager. Billy Sammeth officially took over. Ken Kragen, best known as Kenny Rogers's manager, also came aboard in a managerial role and would produce Olivia's next HBO special.

Still a bigger change occurred as Olivia began work on her next album. In September 1987, she told a reporter for Australia's *Woman's Day* magazine that John Farrar would be producing it, "as," noted the article, "with her other albums." But it wasn't to be this time. Tom Snow, who had written and recorded with Farrar on Olivia's recent albums as well as on Farrar's own 1980 album, reflects, "John's a very practical, humble man, extremely humble, and I think he saw the writing on the wall, you know, kind of bowed out." While it wasn't necessarily Farrar's fault, *Soul Kiss* had been a disappointment by Olivia's standards at that time, and she had become increasingly reliant upon other songwriters for material.

For the next album, she ended up choosing, with the approval of MCA Records, Davitt Sigerson as the primary, although not sole, producer. Since deeming Olivia to be "the best pure pop singer working today" in his partially favorable review of *Soul Kiss* for *Rolling Stone*, Sigerson had begun producing for the Bangles; in fact, he would be juggling the production of Olivia's album, *The Rumour*, which would be released in August 1988, with the production of the Bangles' *Everything* (including the international number one hit "Eternal Flame"), which was recorded over a twelve-month period and came out two months later.

In addition to turning to a new producer, Olivia also turned to a completely different roster of songwriters for the new album. Missing from the credits were Farrar, Steve Kipner, and Tom Snow. She approached her MCA labelmate Elton John and his lyricist, Bernie Taupin, for a new song. "I asked him would he write one for me, and two weeks later it was written. He went to Bernie Taupin for the lyrics and Elton wrote the melody in four hours. I mean, that takes incredible talent. He played on the track and did the vocal backings with me. We had a great time," she told radio show host Barry Scott. "It was wonderful working with [him]." Elton also produced the song with his band member James Newton Howard, who had played synthesizers on "Xanadu." "The Rumour" became the album's title track and first single, a bouncy, upbeat, fun song but lacking the hooks that permeated "Physical" and "Make a Move on Me" and not giving her the chance to show off her vocal versatility and range like "A Little More Love" and "Magic" did.

Other notable songwriters, albeit less famous and successful than Elton John and Bernie Taupin, also contributed to the album. Alan O'Day, a native of Hollywood, had written two number one hits during the 1970s, Helen Reddy's "Angie Baby" (1974) and his own record "Undercover Angel" (1977). For Olivia he wrote "Love and Let Live," a compassionate and, by the standards of 1988, boldly frank song about the AIDS crisis, which in the United States began in 1981 but went largely ignored by President Ronald Reagan until his friend Rock Hudson became the first celebrity to die from the disease in September 1985. A music critic for Louisiana's *Shreveport Journal* would call the song "the most interesting one" on the album while also "find[ing] it a bit annoying and forced," which may have spoken as much (or more) to his own discomfort with Olivia singing a song about AIDS as any shortcomings in the accomplished writer O'Day's lyrics.

Irwin Levine and Sandy Linzer wrote what became the album's second single, "Can't We Talk It Over in Bed." Levine's cowriting credits included "Tie a Yellow Ribbon Round the Ole Oak Tree," an international smash hit for Tony Orlando and Dawn in 1973. Linzer had cowritten, among other well-known songs, the Four Seasons' hits "Let's Hang On!" and "Working My Way Back to You." Linzer produced "Can't We Talk It Over in Bed" with Hank Medress, a former member of the Tokens of "The Lion Sleeps Tonight" fame.

Another one of the album's songwriters was someone who had not crossed paths with Olivia since they had both been teenagers performing in the jazz clubs of Melbourne: John Capek. Capek had migrated from Australia to Canada in 1973, and among the musicians he worked with in Toronto was the New York–born Canadian singer-songwriter Marc Jordan. Capek and Jordan began writing songs together, and subsequently Capek also wrote with Jordan's wife, the Toronto-born singer-songwriter Amy Sky, who had just begun working with Olivia, singing backing vocals on two of the album's songs.

"I re-met Olivia through Amy Sky in Los Angeles," Capek recalls. "Amy and I were writing together, and she brought Olivia up to the house, to my house in North Hollywood, and that's where we [John, Amy, and Olivia] wrote 'Let's Talk about Tomorrow,'" one of four songs that Olivia cowrote on the US release of *The Rumour*. Capek and Olivia also wrote "It's Always Australia for Me," which would be released on the Australian version of the album.

Capek sensed that something was amiss with his old acquaintance. "I have to say," he reflects, when she came to my house with Amy and the three of us sat down and wrote the song, I just was observing that she didn't seem particularly happy. She seemed pretty hyper. She seemed anxious. She wasn't reflecting her beauty in any way or her personality. And so, you know, obviously there were some troubles that I wasn't aware of. She wasn't what I remembered of her when she was 16, when she'd be calm and professional and beautiful and, you know, all of that. At the time when we wrote together, there seemed some troubles had come along. I have no idea what they were, but she certainly didn't seem calm or happy at the time.

Lenard Allen, a professional backing vocalist who had worked with, among others, Captain and Tennille and Andy Gibb, got a firsthand glimpse of one problem that was vexing Olivia when they both attended Andy's funeral in Los Angeles on March 21, 1988. Andy, who had signed with Island Records in London and seemed poised to make a comeback, had died of myocarditis on March 10, five days after his thirtieth birthday. "At the time," Allen remembers,

she [Olivia] had some crazy people that were ruining her life with death threats. And… something had happened where it was no longer taken as [it was] *kind* of going to happen, it was *going* to happen, and so she had three guys that looked just like secret service with an earpiece and they were standing in the back of the chapel, and one guy was outside.

As Karen Carpenter's passing had been, Andy's death was a blow to Olivia. "I knew him very well," she told Barry Scott a few years later.

It's a tragedy to me that he's no longer here. I hadn't really seen him much for the last few years, because I had a child and he was in Miami a lot. But we had been very close at one point when I made the record[s] with him. He was very talented and very sweet. It's a real loss for everyone.

At Andy's funeral, recalls Allen, "In the pew farther down from me was Olivia Newton-John… and so I sat next to her, and we only knew each other through a couple interactions, but I looked at her, and she looked at me. And I just said, 'This is *sad*.' And she teared up."

Still more was weighing on Olivia as she worked to make her first album in three years. She and Matt had been trying to have a second child. "It sounds corny," Matt later told a journalist, "but Livvy had always envisioned the little farmhouse, the while picket fence, having two children and living a very normal type of life." In the early stages of working on the album, she learned she was pregnant. During the fourth month of the pregnancy, though, she suffered a miscarriage. She kept this knowledge private to her family and close friends at the time. Two years later she revealed it publicly, telling a reporter, "It was devastating. I can handle it now, but it was sudden and unfortunate. I rationalized it, but it took a lot of time." Then, true to her strong and sunny nature, she added, "But I was lucky. I have a daughter, a beautiful child, and if I never have another child, I'm blessed already. I can't complain."

By the spring of 1988, Olivia had completed *The Rumour*. Davitt Sigerson had produced or coproduced all of the album except for the two songs that became singles. John Capek, who played on the two songs he cowrote, was impressed with Sigerson. "He was a very talented producer, I thought. He had a really good read on how to make records," he reflects. "I thought he did a great job." Several veterans of Olivia's past records and tours, including guitarist Michael Landau, bass guitarist Abraham Laboriel, and drummer Carlos Vega, contributed to the album.

Australia celebrated its bicentennial in 1988; it was for this occasion that Olivia and Capek had composed "It's Always Australia for Me." In late January, Olivia made a brief trip down under to perform at a special concert at the Sydney Entertainment Center. With Prince Charles and Princess Diana in attendance, she sang "It's Always Australia for Me" and duetted with Cliff Richard on "Suddenly." Two months later she returned to Australia to tape the special that Ken Kragen was producing for HBO, which would also air on television in Australia.

Brian Grant, who had directed the full-length video album for *Physical*, directed *Olivia Down Under* as well. "I've always wanted to do a special in Australia," Olivia told a reporter. "It seemed like a great time to do it because of the bicentennial." The special was partly a video album for *The Rumour* (with an appearance by Matt in one clip and two-year-old Chloe in another) and partly a guided tour of Australia by Olivia, who asked questions of and chatted with various Australians. "Throughout the special," she explained, "we use all real people. There are no actors. I just asked questions. I got a lot of different answers to the same questions." The special made its debut on HBO on July 30, 1988.

While awaiting the premiere of the HBO special and the release of her new album, Olivia remained active in the operations of Koala Blue. "It really takes a lot of time," she told the *Los Angeles Times* in May 1988. "Pat and I speak every day about the business, and we do all the shopping—we call it research when we go shopping for ideas." They also continued to focus on opening more Koala Blue stores. After the franchising partnership between their two original investors, Edward J. Pastucha and Jon E. DeLuca, fell apart, Olivia and Pat took on a new partner, a Los Angeles businessman named David Sidell.

Olivia and Pat continued to make appearances at the grand opening of new stores. Olivia, a seasoned pro at making public appearances, smiled, posed for photos, and answered questions from (depending on the size of the city) the throngs of reporters who showed up and asked her the same questions over and over. But in one instance, a reporter asked her about the long trip and long day (beginning at 6:30 a.m.) that she put in for the opening of a store at Northbrook Court, an upscale mall in the North Shore suburbs of Chicago, in June 1988. Olivia's answer indicated that these trips weren't really a welcome labor of love for her. "Today was crazy," she said. "My watch is still set on L.A. time. I don't have to do this too often. I'm hurrying home to my daughter. She's two… and she's asking, 'Mommy, where are you?' I'm coming, I'm coming. It's only one day, but it feels like forever."

Some observers, such as *Chicago Tribune* journalist Barbara Mahany, saw the somewhat uncomfortable juxtaposition of Olivia Newton-John the retail owner and Olivia Newton-John the famous pop star. "As dozens of fans and photographers, amateurs and pros," Mahany wrote, "pushed and shoved, eventually backing the star into the corner by the fire exit, one sympathetic soul stepped back and sighed: 'Isn't this dreadful? Wouldn't you hate to be a star?'" Olivia and Pat's business partners would see the juxtaposition themselves; looking back, one of them reflects that Olivia's celebrity status, even though it helped jump-start Koala Blue, also caused "problems" for the enterprise.

Days after the premiere of Olivia's HBO special, MCA released "The Rumour" as a single. *Cash Box* gave the record a strong review: "This is the snappiest tune that Olivia's done in a long stretch, and she rises to the occasion delivering a heartfelt performance…. The record deserves airplay. Listen for Elton [John] chiming in at the end." It received enough airplay on adult contemporary stations to reach No. 33 on the *Billboard* adult contemporary chart, but it entered the Hot 100 at No. 90 and only rose to No. 62. It reached the Top 40 only in Australia (No. 35) and Germany (No. 36).

The album release of *The Rumour* followed about two weeks later on August 15. *Rolling Stone*, which had equivocated on whether to publish Ben Fong-Torres's interview with her a decade earlier until "You're the One That I Want" rocketed up the charts, raved about the album. "It's a bit of a jolt to hear Olivia Newton-John sing about AIDS, single parenthood and a better environment," the review began.

It's as if, now that she's forty and a first-time mother herself, she suddenly cares about the world. Just as surprisingly, she connects with rock producer Davitt Sigerson's unsweetened settings and delivers believable, unstrained conviction, whether she's championing a cause, romping through the title cut (co-written and co-produced by Elton John and James Newton Howard) or exposing a vein or two on David [Baerwald] and David [Ricketts]'s "Walk Through Fire." For fifteen years, Olivia Newton-John has been one of pop music's prettiest faces; now she just wants a little respect, and with *The Rumour* she earns it.

But, perhaps not surprisingly without a hit single to drive sales, the album fared no better with the record-buying public than the single did. It reached only No. 67 on the *Billboard* albums chart, and it became her first album in eleven years to not earn a gold record. The album cracked the Top 40 only in Australia (No. 30) and Japan (No. 31), which for well over a decade had been one of her strongest markets (but also one where there would be no tour or promotional appearances in 1988).

In a subsequent interview with Barry Scott, Olivia suggested a variety of reasons why *The Rumour* didn't strike a more receptive chord with her large fan base. "I don't know why these things happen. Maybe I'd been out of it for a long time. I hadn't had a record out for three years." This indeed might have been a factor. Some of the same newcomer female pop stars who had been crowding the marketplace when *Soul Kiss* was released—Madonna, Whitney Houston, and Cyndi Lauper—were still very much on the scene in the late 1980s, and had been joined by others such as Janet Jackson, Taylor Dayne, and the Bangles.

Furthermore, MCA Records may have had higher priorities by this point. The label was promoting a new roster of female pop stars of its own who had major commercial success in 1988—Belinda Carlisle, Tiffany, Pebbles, and Jody Watley—as well as New Edition and its member Bobby Brown and, of course, Olivia's longtime labelmate Elton John, whose "I Don't Wanna Go On with You Like That" reached No. 2 on the Hot 100 shortly after "The Rumour" was released. Elton had left MCA in 1980 for David Geffen's new label, Geffen Records, which also signed Donna Summer and John Lennon and Yoko Ono that year, but he returned to MCA in 1987 and immediately delivered a Top 10 hit with a live version of "Candle in the Wind."

Without directly saying it, Olivia suggested to Barry Scott that MCA could have done a better job of promoting *The Rumour:* "I [spoke] to fans who didn't even know that album was out, which is really sad to me because I spent a lot of time on it. But without radio play, nobody gets to hear it, unfortunately." Some radio station program directors, however, simply rejected the single. The *Shreveport Journal* reported that "one music director of a local fun radio station was recently heard to say that she didn't want to play the song, 'The Rumour,' because it just wasn't hit material." MCA released "Can't We Talk It Over in Bed" as a second single from the album, and it failed to chart anywhere.

Whatever the reasons for the album's commercial failure, despite the glowing review from *Rolling Stone*, it would mark the end of Olivia's tenure with MCA Records, which had existed for as long as the label itself had up to that point. Shortly after the album's release, Al Teller took over as the chairman/CEO of the label. "I was a fan and would have enjoyed the opportunity to work with her. [But]

The Rumour album," he laments, "was not particularly successful." In July 1989, a press report confirmed the parting of ways between recording artist and label: "After a long stay with MCA, Olivia Newton-John has now signed to Geffen and is planning to release a new single in the next couple of months."

15 NOT GONNA BE THE ONE

"I think I found what's important in life, and I think what's important in life is your family and children," Olivia told a reporter at an event at Chasen's in Beverly Hills at the end of January 1989. "And it took me a long time in my life to get to the point where I had time to find this out. And I found that this is the happiest part of my life, so I want to enjoy it and I want to be there for my daughter."

When the reporter asked her what she had been up to professionally, though, she replied, "I had an album out, but" and then with a self-deprecating smirk and laugh, "it's gone!" The reporter then asked her if she would make another album soon. "I will make an album this year," she answered, "but it will be a very special kind of project that I've wanted to do for a long time."

The special project would be an album consisting primarily of children's lullabies. Olivia told syndicated columnist Marilyn Beck in September 1989, before the album's release, that this had been "a four-year dream" of hers. She told Beck that she had made the album with Chloe in mind, but that it wasn't intended to be an album just for children. "There are a few lullabies, one song I wrote with John Farrar especially for Chloe, and some romantic love songs. I think—I hope—it will appeal to mothers and their children, and to lovers, too."

Her desire to make such an album proved to be one more factor in her split from MCA Records. That label, she told Beck, "wasn't particularly interested in what I wanted to do on this album." Although Olivia had been so committed to making the album that she "was ready to make it on my own," Billy Sammeth suggested that they approach Geffen Records. "Thankfully," Olivia said, "Geffen was [interested]" and signed her.

John Kalodner, a legendary figure in the pop/rock music industry, was the head of A&R at Geffen at the time. "Either her lawyer," he recalls, "or somebody who represented her mentioned to me that she wanted to make this record, and I had the power to say, within reason monetarily, that I wanted to do it. I wanted to work with her." He understood why MCA wasn't interested in the album, but he was undeterred. "I think they just didn't want, you know, it's a lot of effort to put into a lot of these records, and this one kind of had a limited market, but because I thought she was such a fine artist and she had made such great music, I just wanted to do it with her."

Olivia wouldn't start working on her first album for Geffen Records until the summer of 1989. In the meantime, she remained active with Koala Blue, and, perhaps due to the realization that her singing career had lost momentum, she sounded more positive about making public appearances at stores than she had the previous year. "This has been a whole new life for me, really. It's show biz," she told reporter Susan Baer in Fairfax, Virginia, on May 1, 1989, "in a way that you see the malls and hotels instead of the concert halls. But it's not as nerve-racking. It's a lot less stressful and more long-term. Show business is not something you can rely on." The occasion of the brief interview was the grand opening of the twenty-eighth Koala Blue store, the first in the Washington, DC, area.

Olivia also discussed the state of her singing career with Baer. "I had an album out last year. They're playing it now," she said as one of the songs from *The Rumour* played in the background while she and the reporter talked in the new Koala Blue store. "It didn't really have much success."

She seemed to accept that her uncommonly long run at or near the top of the record charts and radio station playlists had reached its end. "It would be wonderful to have that success again, but that was an incredible time," she said, almost as if it had been longer ago than it actually was. "I don't know if you ever have *that* kind of period again in your career. But that's fine. I'm really happy. I feel like I've achieved everything I set out to do—and more. And now this is a whole new phase. You can't be up there on the peak of it all the time. You'd be exhausted." She did, however, enthusiastically tell Baer about the new album she'd be recording for Geffen, referring to it as "a dream I've had for a long time."

With the switch to Davitt Sigerson not having delivered the commercial success that Olivia had hoped for with *The Rumour*, she asked John Farrar to resume his role as producer for the album, for which having a "comeback" hit was clearly not her motivation. The track list included "Twinkle Twinkle Little Star," "Rock-a-Bye Baby," "Over the Rainbow," and the Disney favorite "When You Wish upon a Star." The first two songs on the album, "Jenny Rebecca," an ode to a four-day-old baby written by the American composer Carol Hall, and an old Czechoslovakian-English Christmas carol called "Rocking," were both suggested to Olivia by her father. Olivia turned to the legendary songbook of Burt Bacharach and Hal David for the album's lead single, "Reach Out for Me," which Dionne Warwick had had a Top 20 hit with in 1964.

After recording all of her previous albums either in England or the United States, Olivia recorded most of this album, which would be named *Warm and*

Tender after a song that she wrote with Farrar, in Australia. Most of the songs were recorded at the Melbourne Concert Hall with the Victorian Philharmonic Orchestra, while some others were recorded at a Melbourne studio, Metropolis Audio. Olivia and Farrar, who played on some tracks, also made some of the album at the well-known Ocean Way Recording at 6050 Sunset Boulevard in Hollywood, where the album was mixed. The album cover featured Olivia, Chloe, and Colette Chuda sitting outdoors in front of a tree; Colette gave Olivia a kiss while Chloe stood behind her mother, touching her hair. The liner notes to the album included environmental advice that Olivia wrote, such as recycling tips.

Geffen Records released "Reach Out for Me" as a single on October 20, 1989, followed by the *Warm and Tender* album four days later. (In Australia, Festival Records continued to release Olivia's records.) *Cash Box* and *Billboard* both reviewed the album in the issues dated November 11, 1989. *Cash Box* had reviewed Olivia's previous two albums, *Soul Kiss* and *The Rumour*, favorably, but expressed ambivalence about this one. "Motherhood," the review began, "has really had quite an effect on everyone's favorite *Xanadu* roller babe. No longer does she yodel about hopeless devotion or high school graduations. This is Olivia: the Mother, crooning every childhood ditty that you can recall and even a few that you can't." The rest of the review continued in this cynical tone: "The entire album is dreamy, ethereal sleepy-time music, so effective, in fact, that I had a hard time staying awake for side two" (a somewhat dated term to use by then given that compact discs were accounting for most album sales in the United States at the time). "I don't see a lot of commercial possibilities here," the review concluded, "but it seems as if Olivia is after a more loving-expression kind of thing rather than her former hungry-for-pop success. Hey, if Linda Ronstadt can do it, so can Sandra Dee."

Billboard reviewed *Warm and Tender* more favorably, opining that Olivia's

label debut [for Geffen] finds the Aussie lass gratefully shedding her contrived sexpot image and donning the serene veneer of motherhood. Beautifully orchestrated set of lullabies could warm the heart of the toughest AC programmer…. This is the perfect environment for Newton-John's smooth and silky voice, and may very well be the springboard for her return into the pop spotlight.

That prediction proved too optimistic. The album took several weeks to even reach the *Billboard* chart, and it only reached No. 124 (and only 151 on *Cash Box*). It reached No. 109 in Australia. Only in Japan, where Olivia retained a strong following despite not having toured there in over a decade, did the album remotely approach hit status, reaching No. 43. "Reach Out for Me" didn't crack the *Billboard*

Hot 100, although it reached No. 32 on the adult contemporary chart. Geffen subsequently released "When You Wish upon a Star" as a single, but it failed to make any impact on radio or at retail.

Short of getting back onto the concert stage, Olivia made reasonable efforts to promote the album. She did an interview on *Live! With Regis and Kathie Lee*, and she sang "Reach Out for Me" on *The Tonight Show*, an episode in which Jay Leno was filling in for Johnny Carson, and on *The Arsenio Hall Show*. She also made a half-hour special for VH-1, in which she discussed not only the making of the *Warm and Tender* album, but also issues near and dear to her heart, such as motherhood, the environment, and animals. A visit to her Malibu ranch showed her grooming her horse, Judge, and also featured an appearance by the now fifteen-year-old Irish setter Jackson. The special also included a visit to the Koala Blue store on Melrose. It concluded by showing footage from the filming of the video for "Reach Out for Me," and then with this message from Olivia shown as words on the screen: "This program is dedicated to the children of the world and to the people who are striving to make our planet a better place for them to live."

The United Nations had just named Olivia as a Goodwill Ambassador for the Environment, a role that she would serve in for four years, and the VH-1 special also included footage from a trip that she had recently made to the Amazon rain forest in Brazil. In every interview she did to promote her new album, she also discussed her concerns for the world's environment. She told California journalist Dave Nordstrand, "I used to think I could go to a remote farm in Australia and be safe. But the wind blows, the smog and pollution catches up with the world. We all end up in the same boat."

The visit to Brazil would be featured more fully in another television program that aired in November 1989, an episode of the Fox newsmagazine program *The Reporters*. This episode consisted of reports from five celebrities—Olivia, Carole King, Robert Wagner, Christopher Reeve, and Christie Brinkley—on matters of environmental concern. Olivia not only appeared on the program for free, but she also paid the expenses of her and Matt's trip to Brazil. Her report examined the "slash-and-burn" operations that were threatening the Amazon rain forest. She also participated, along with many other well-known recording artists, in making a charity single called "Spirit of the Forest," which was released by Virgin Records in June 1989 to raise money to help save the rain forests. She also appeared in the video for the record.

Ironically, at about this very time, Olivia faced a lawsuit in which she and Matt were being sued by environmentalists. Olivia and Matt had bought beachfront property in Malibu's Paradise Cove and hired a contractor to build a $2 million home. In December 1989, according to the *Los Angeles Times*, "environmentalists complained that tons of dirt and sand were illegally piled on the beach during construction of a sea wall on the property, and that a permit to complete the work had expired." They also charged that trees and plants had been ripped out and that beach cliffs had been destroyed. The Seacliff Estates Homeowners Association filed suit in Santa Monica Superior Court in April 1990, asking a judge to halt construction of the home.

Olivia soon showed once again that she was not the meek Sandra Dee that some people seemed to believe. "Dirt and garbage have never been dumped on the beach or in the ocean," she said in a statement that was given to the press. "This lawsuit represents an environmental tragedy because trees died for the paper that was used to spread false allegations against me."

In fact, according to the *Los Angeles Times*, she had hired architect Jim Chuda (the husband of her close friend Nancy Chuda) "to see that the home was environmentally conscious in its design and construction, using nontoxic building materials as well as air filtering and water purification systems." Nevertheless, the lawsuit continued to make the newspapers. One neighbor suggested that Olivia was a phony "public environmentalist" who was building the beachfront house "for decoration or to impress [her] friends." Once again, Olivia replied in kind when asked about the lawsuit by reporter Frank Sanello later that year. "I don't want to give that thing the time of day," she told him. "The next-door neighbors thought they could get some cheap publicity out of me because I'm in the public eye. The whole thing is going to fade away, and that's all I'm going to say about it." She was right, although the nuisance of the lawsuit did delay the completion of the house, which dragged on until 1993.

More significant lawsuits were on the horizon, however, for Koala Blue. In 1989, the chain of stores was booming, with sixty-two locations (all but thirteen of which were owned by franchisees) in five countries. But the United States, and many other western nations, entered a recession in 1990. One casualty of this recession would be the presidency of George H. W. Bush, even though the recession had technically ended by the time Bill Clinton defeated him in the election of 1992. Olivia had performed for President Bush and First Lady Barbara Bush at a charity Christmas concert in 1989. Rona accompanied her, and, "after the performance, Rona and Olivia were escorted by US Secret Service agents to a cocktail reception at the White House with the First Family," wrote journalist Michele Manelis. "They were greeted by President Bush and given a private tour." Olivia, Rona, and their mother attended a state dinner at the White House in October 1991.

The same recession that contributed to the failure of President Bush's reelection bid also played a role in the demise of Koala Blue. The rapid expansion of the chain was already causing problems before the recession started, and in 1990 Olivia and Pat parted ways with David Sidell and brought in two new partners. Gloria Teague, who had apparel industry executive experience with Cherokee, Guess Inc., and Code Bleu, became Koala Blue's chief operating officer, and Dan Zuckerman, a corporate transactional lawyer, became its vice president. Zuckerman recalls that Olivia and Pat brought in Teague and himself to "resuscitate Koala Blue."

Teague sounded optimistic in a statement to the press in September 1990. "We're just starting to write the business plan and meet with a few people," she said, "but we think we already have some good partners." But on March 5, 1991, newspapers reported that Koala Blue had filed for Chapter 11 bankruptcy protection, a type of bankruptcy that allows a debtor to reorganize its debts and continue the operation of its business. In the bankruptcy filing, the company listed $6 million in liabilities and $3.9 million in assets. "We own twelve stores in America and we may close as many as eleven of them [meaning all but the original Melrose Avenue store]," Zuckerman told a journalist. With the bankruptcy, he added, "we can sweep away the dead wood and start again. People weren't paying their bills. But everything has a silver lining: Livvy and Pat have wanted to go into department stores for a long time, and this is our opportunity to refocus our direction and press ahead for a bright future."

Who were the "people [who] weren't paying their bills"? Many of the franchisees, Zuckerman now explains. "They fell for the business concept," he says, "on the basis of being involved with Olivia and her name, and the Koala Blue name, but in many or even most cases they were not properly capitalized and/or didn't have the business experience, and so it was just a big house of cards." By the time of the bankruptcy filing, Zuckerman recalls,

> There were problems getting merchandise to these store owners…. Olivia and Pat were trying to keep control over the brand name and what could be sold in these stores. But there were problems supplying them with merchandise, so in order to survive, they [the franchisees] turned to selling things that weren't authorized, and so that sort of just exacerbated the whole situation. And once you start sliding down that ramp, it's hard to get off.

By the summer of 1991, Olivia was getting the worst publicity of her life as Koala Blue continued to spiral downward. *People* magazine published a story under the headline "Losing Their Shirts with Olivia." A franchisee named Laurie McCray told *People* that she had sunk $1 million into two Koala Blue stores in San Diego. "I started out two years ago with $360,000, two cars and money for my daughter's college," she said. "Now I have nothing. My father cosigned my loans and is about to have a heart attack over this. Olivia's big thing is 'Save the Earth,' 'Save all the little animals.' I just wish she'd start worrying about some of the people who are being destroyed."

A franchisee of three Koala Blue stores on Long Island, a twenty-five-year retail veteran who had by this point closed two of them, told *People*, "[Olivia and her partners] were supposed to have the expertise, but this group of people had the highest level of incompetence—beyond our wildest imagination." When asked for a comment, Olivia declined. One year later she would say, "We [she and Pat] worked really hard, put everything into it, did our best and we failed."

On August 4, 1991, a notice appeared in the *Los Angeles Times*, under the bold-type heading, "FOR SALE: KOALA BLUE NAME AND LOGOS." The notice stated that the sale would occur by auction at the US Bankruptcy Court on North Figueroa Street in downtown Los Angeles seventeen days later with an opening bid of $355,500. In early 1992, Koala Blue was liquidated. Olivia and Pat ended up reviving the name and logo in 2002 for a short-lived line of Australian wines.

The liquidation of Koala Blue met with swift repercussions. Franchise holders in Minneapolis and Chicago filed suit against Olivia and Pat, seeking millions in damages. A Los Angeles judge dismissed the lawsuit in October 1993, barely after the tenth anniversary of the opening of the original Koala Blue store on Melrose Avenue. Olivia's friend Liona Boyd recalls Olivia telling her how the collapse of the whole enterprise "stressed her out a lot."

The downfall of Koala Blue was far from the only calamity that Olivia faced in 1991. In Australia she became embroiled in controversy when she supported a proposed twelve-home community village near her Ballina home in New South Wales, which was to include land to be set aside as an "environmental protection zone" and for "permaculture agriculture," which is defined as "an ecological and sustainable farming system that integrates various elements, mimicking natural ecosystems." Local residents near the proposed community banded together in opposition to the proposal, however, citing a long list of concerns that included the likelihood of increased traffic, the undermining of the area's rural character, sewage runoff into local creeks, and, according to one press report, the likelihood that the community would become "a potential haven for drug addicts, dole bludgers and religious fanatics."[1]

All of these problems paled in significance, however, compared to the death of Colette Chuda, Jim and Nancy's daughter and Chloe's best friend, on April 21, 1991, a few weeks after her fifth birthday. Colette passed away about one year after being diagnosed with Wilms' tumor, a rare kidney cancer that primarily affects children. Her doctors could not tell her parents why Colette was stricken, so Jim and Nancy set out to find an answer themselves. "When Colette died," Nancy recalled, "there was no proof that anything in the environment could have affected her in the womb until we discovered a study that had been done in Brazil with parents who had been exposed to pesticides, and their children later developed Wilms' tumor."

Nancy would recall something that had happened when she was three months pregnant that she and Jim believe caused Colette to develop Wilms' tumor. They were living in an apartment building in Hollywood that was fumigated during their residence. They left for the day but returned a day later. Toxic residue still lingered in their apartment. "I walked back into that apartment," Nancy would recall, "and breathed that air. I touched whatever particles were left behind. Those chemicals affected Colette's development."

In 1992, Jim and Nancy Chuda established the Colette Chuda Environmental Fund and an organization called the Children's Health Environmental Coalition (now called Healthy Child Healthy World) with the goal of reducing children's exposure to toxins. Olivia helped them launch these efforts and would remain involved with them for the rest of her life. She would often attend or sing at functions and fundraisers for Healthy Child Healthy World.

As Olivia recalled in her memoir, she was backstage in Spain, about to perform on a television special, when Matt called to tell her that Colette had passed away. She didn't want to take the stage, but ever the professional, she knew the show must go on and she sang. Olivia and Matt had by this point decided to adopt a brother or sister for Chloe, and Olivia had a suitcase full of toys and children's clothes, which she was going to take to Romania for the child. After learning of Colette's death, she wrote, "I never made it to Romania." In an interview later in the year, she described 1991 as the "worst year of my life."

By the time 1992 began, Olivia had decided that it was time to make a full return to her singing career, which she had left largely dormant for the past two years. The collapse of Koala Blue, she admitted in an interview, made her decide to "go back to focusing on what I know best." She was still under contract with Geffen Records, and while the label had signed her with the understanding that *Warm and Tender*, a special project to her with limited commercial appeal, would be her first Geffen album, the focus would now shift to having a "comeback" hit. John Kalodner, who had played an important role in reviving Cher's recording career during the late 1980s, would take the helm in trying to do the same for Olivia.

Kalodner came up with the idea of releasing a single compact disc greatest hits album, as opposed to the volume 1 and volume 2 greatest hits albums that MCA had released in 1977 and 1982, with the addition of four new recordings. (Geffen Records would give MCA an override royalty for using the past hits for which the latter still owned the rights.) "I picked those four songs," he recalls, "with her [also] involved in the song selection." The four new tracks would lead off the album, *Back to Basics: The Essential Collection 1971–1992*.

"I just A&R'd them [the four new songs] for her to try to see if we could have another Top 40 hit," Kalodner says. "I think she needed to have some great songs, which I tried to get to the best of my ability, because her great producer, John Farrar, really had run his gamut of incredible songs… I think he was kind of out of hit songs at that time."

Another of Olivia's favorite songwriters, Steve Kipner, wrote one of the new songs, "I Need Love," with John Lewis Parker. About eight years earlier, Kipner and Parker had written Chicago's smash hit "Hard Habit to Break." Olivia liked the message of "I Need Love," which she saw as sort of an update of "Physical" in the era of AIDS. When discussing the song with a writer for *Billboard*, she said, "We need to rethink relationships. It's not wise to jump into bed with people indiscriminately. In fact, it's downright suicidal." A friend of Olivia's, hairdresser Armando Cosio, who had styled her hair for the "Physical" video, had gotten sick with AIDS and died while Olivia was pregnant with Chloe. Epidemiologists did not have a clear understanding at that time of how AIDS is spread, and Olivia's doctors told her it wouldn't be safe for her to visit Cosio. In 1992, when she appeared in an AIDS awareness television special, *A New Light*, she said she regretted not having visited him before his death, and that she had loved him very much. Her friend Peter Allen, cowriter of "I Honestly Love You," also died of AIDS-related complications on June 18, 1992. Olivia called him frequently during his final months.

Another of the four new songs came from a songwriter who was working with Kipner at the time. Seth Swirsky had emerged as a major pop/rock songwriter in the late 1980s by cowriting Taylor Dayne's first two hits, "Tell It to My Heart" and "Prove Your Love." He began writing with Kipner after signing with EMI Music Publishing and moving to Los Angeles in 1990. About a year or two later, he wrote a Bee Gees-esque song called "Not Gonna Be the One" and played it for Kipner, who said to him, "I've gotta get this to Olivia."

"I think that he had told me," Swirsky recalls, "that she had listened to it a bunch of times on her cassette player in her car, and she had gotten it from someone else as well, so a couple of places were hitting her with it. I think John Kalodner at Geffen also took the song... I remember having a few meetings with John about the song."

For Swirsky, having Olivia record his song "was a *tremendous* thing... I grew up loving her." "I got a phone call," he says, "from John Farrar, who was producing it, and he said, 'Come by my house. I want you to hear where we're at with it.' And I was obviously very honored." Swirsky went to Farrar's house in Benedict Canyon (Beverly Hills) to hear the record.

> I think they recorded it in his house, because he had a fabulous studio there. And he played it, and I *loved* it. I just love what she did with the tune. And I know she had a good time doing it, too, because John told me they did an old-fashioned recording in a sense, between the two of them, stacking vocals. She loved to stack all those harmony vocals.

John Kalodner had brought Cher songs written by Diane Warren (most notably "If I Could Turn Back Time") for her late 1980s comeback, and he asked her for a song for Olivia. Warren contributed "Deeper than a River," a ballad that Olivia sang with a breathy vocal on the verses. Kalodner also suggested that Olivia record "I Want to Be Wanted," a ballad that Brenda Lee had a number one hit with in 1960. "Oh gosh," Kalodner says of Olivia's version, "it was so great. She just did such a great job. It's a *great* recording."

Not only did each of the four songs come from different writers, but Olivia recorded each of them with different producers. Diane Warren and Guy Roche, who had served as the producers of "If I Could Turn Back Time," produced "Deeper than a River." Kalodner asked Peter Asher, who had produced numerous hit cover versions of oldies for Linda Ronstadt, to produce "I Want to Be Wanted." "I called him to do it," Kalodner recalls. "He was a great producer, and he really wanted to work with her. I was working with him with Cher at the time, so it was a natural thing for us to do to try to get a hit for [Olivia]." For "I Need Love," which would be the first single, Kalodner picked producer Giorgio Moroder, whose long list of hits included No. 1's for Donna Summer, Blondie, Irene Cara, and Berlin, to take the helm. "Another real superstar in my opinion," Kalodner says. "That's why I put them together."

For Kalodner, who worked with, among others, not only Cher but also Aerosmith, Foreigner, Santana, Journey, Chicago, REO Speedwagon, and the Black Crowes, working with Olivia was a highlight that he remembers fondly. "She was just really about her music, and she was really good about taking directions and suggestions, and it was just a joy to work with her," he says. He knew that getting a big hit for Olivia in 1992 might be a long shot. "Radio was totally different [than it had been during her heyday]… I knew it was going to be difficult… it was just a different time, which happens to all artists. I just gave it my best shot because I thought she was such a superior person and a great artist."

Kalodner recalls Olivia as being very professional and dedicated to her work, but he also says that "she definitely was not desperate" to come up with a new hit, and she wasn't going

to change herself into something she didn't want to be. She already had proved that she was a superstar. She just wanted to make the music she wanted to make and did the best she could, and, like I said, you have to have a song. No matter who the artist or A&R person is, you have to have some luck and some timing. So that was the problem.

Geffen Records released *Back to Basics: The Essential Collection 1971–1992* on June 9, 1992. In Australia, Olivia's longtime label Festival Records released it, and Mercury Records released it in Great Britain. Several details about the release suggest that Geffen didn't treat it as a high priority. The cover photo of Olivia was reversed, showing her turned toward the right when she was turned toward the left in the original photo, and so her facial features were on the wrong sides of her face on the cover. Furthermore, while the album contained variations in the selection of past hits from one market to another—for example, "Deeper than the Night" was on the US version but not the Japanese version, whereas the latter included "If Not for You," which was not on the US release—using the years 1971–1992 in the title was inaccurate for the US release, which included no tracks from earlier than 1974. (Limiting the number of "oldies" on the American version to thirteen meant that some of her big US hits, such as "Let Me Be There" and "Make a Move on Me," got left off.)

"Geffen Records was behind her," Kalodner insists,

> but, I mean, given where Geffen was at then with Nirvana and Aerosmith and all this stuff… they were trying for AC [adult contemporary] radio, obviously [with Olivia's new recordings], but I'm not sure how much effort got put into anything else. And because, obviously, she couldn't do a lot of things such as TV shows, which everyone would want her for, that was the thing that we never got to take advantage of.

Olivia couldn't make more than a handful of television and radio show appearances to promote the new album and the "I Need Love" single that Geffen released in mid-June, nor embark on a planned eight-week US tour that was to begin in August, because of shocking news that appeared in newspapers around the world on July 14, 1992. Her longtime security chief Gavin de Becker issued a statement on her behalf announcing that she had been diagnosed with breast cancer. "I am making this information public myself," Olivia said in the statement, "to save 'enquiring minds' 95 cents" (a reference to the *National Enquirer* tabloid).

The weeks leading up to the diagnosis had been difficult ones for Olivia. In late June she and Rona had traveled to Australia to visit their father, who was terminally ill with liver cancer. The family had not expected him to die immediately, but Brinley Newton-John passed away on July 3, 1992—his son Hugh's fifty-third birthday—at the age of seventy-eight. "It's sad," said Rona's ex-husband Brian Goldsmith, "because she [Olivia] only left the day before he died." In her memoir, though, Olivia would write that when she said good-bye to her father, she sensed that he would not live long enough for her to ever see him again. Rona was at the same time worried about Olivia. "I had been worried about her for about six months," she would recall, "because she hadn't looked well."

After returning to Los Angeles, Olivia, Matt, and John and Pat Farrar went to the San Juan Islands in the state of Washington to spend the Fourth of July weekend with friends who had a vacation home there. While Olivia and Matt and the Farrars were en route at an airport in Seattle, Matt received a page from Olivia's longtime personal assistant Dana Sharpe. When Matt spoke to Sharpe from the San Juan Islands, he learned of Brinley's passing, which he told Olivia of immediately, and that the doctor whom she had seen for a lump in her breast wanted to see her on Monday, July 6. Matt waited until they returned home on Sunday to tell her that. "I've always been grateful to Matt for that," she later said. "I was in such pain over my father, and Matt knew it was enough for me to deal with."

The news that she had breast cancer was, of course, also devastating for her. "I was in the room when she found out she had it," Billy Sammeth remembered, "and Olivia was absolutely on the floor, like she had lost her soul…. She was in pieces."

As further evidence of her unflagging professionalism, Olivia's announcement that she had cancer also addressed her planned tour, which she had been scheduled to kick off on August 6 at Caesers Palace in Las Vegas. "I regret the inconvenience to the thousands of fans who have bought tickets for my upcoming shows, and I look forward to rescheduling soon." That wasn't to be, however, and the comeback that she had spent months working for, between recording the four new tracks and rehearsing for the tour, essentially died on the vine. The *Back to Basics* album only reached No. 121 on the *Billboard* album chart, and "I Need Love" barely cracked the Hot 100 (No. 96). The album did better in some foreign markets, including Australia, New Zealand, and Great Britain. As the only Olivia Newton-John greatest hits album in print in the United States at the time, it ultimately reached the half-a-million-copies sales mark needed for a gold record six years after its release. "Deeper than a River" cracked the Top 20 on the adult contemporary charts in both the United States and Canada.

For John Kalodner, however, the relative lack of commercial success of his efforts with Olivia is practically a moot point. He remains happy and proud that he got to work with her. "She was one of the easiest, most pleasant artists I ever worked with. It was so great to work with her regardless of the result. Being in the studio with her and having meetings with her, there were never, ever any problems." Her legacy, he says, was "being a great person as well as a superstar artist."

16 NOT GONNA GIVE IN TO IT

"Congratulations. Now you will grow," Jim Chuda told Olivia when he learned of her cancer diagnosis. "It stuck in my head and years later, I think he's probably correct," she reflected in 2015. "Until you go through something difficult you don't realize how much you will grow…. When you are faced with something scary, you have to reach down into your core and find out who you are."

In late July 1992, Olivia underwent a mastectomy on her right breast, followed by chemotherapy for six months and reconstructive breast surgery. "At that point [when she learned of the diagnosis] I confronted death with fear, but deep down, even though I knew something was wrong, I knew that I'd be alright," she said during the summer of 1993. "I think I prayed to every possible spiritual thing I've ever come across. I just want everyone to know I'm fine."

"She is so optimistic," said Matt Lattanzi in 1993, "that I can only be optimistic too." Her ordeal became an ordeal for him as well. "I can't tell you how much this has weighed on me," he told London journalist Fiona McIntosh. "I've had my moments of weakness. I feared for her in my heart. I got depressed for her."

"Until something like this happens to you," he continued,

you don't know how low you can go. You don't know how scared you can get. At first, you ask yourself, "Why her?" But you have to look at how you can benefit from it. With cancer, a lot of it has to do with your attitude and outlook for the future. Livvy and I have built a strong foundation together over the past twelve years. This was a large earthquake, but it didn't shake us.

Billy Sammeth, who was still Olivia's manager at the time, felt that Chloe was utmost in her mind as she went through surgery and chemotherapy. "Olivia became a warrior," he later said, "and she was fighting this disease for Chloe. This was all about, 'I am not going to leave this earth not having the time I want with my daughter.'"

Olivia and Matt tried to conceal her cancer diagnosis from six-year-old Chloe. "The only reason I didn't tell her," Olivia said years later, "was that her best friend had died of cancer the year before. That's what cancer meant to her. So, I didn't want to terrify her." Still, Olivia knew that Chloe could sense that her parents were suddenly under a new level of stress. "Children pick up on energy in the house; she knew something was up and didn't know what it was."

Ironically, Olivia and Matt managed to conceal her diagnosis from Chloe when they were still living in Malibu, only to have her learn of it in an unexpected way in 1993 while they were residing at the family farm in Byron Bay in Australia. A classmate of Chloe's at her school told her. When Chloe and Olivia appeared together on Australia's *60 Minutes* in 2019, Chloe recalled how she confronted her mother when she returned home that day. "I was upset with her because I wanted to take care of her. I said, 'Why didn't you tell me? I could have taken care of you.'"

"Not talking about it," Chloe remembered, "made it more powerful, because it created a much bigger monster than it really was…. I think explaining it to me would have given me more of a sense of control. I feel for my mom, though, because, God, imagine having to tell your daughter; she didn't want me to have to stress." Years later, Olivia would wonder whether having concealed her illness from her daughter had been the right decision, musing that her well-intentioned deceit became the root of, as she put it, the "trust issues" that Chloe would later evince.

Olivia and Matt decided to move to Australia in 1993, even as their new Malibu beach house was finally being completed. (Olivia also still owned her older Malibu house, and it was badly damaged in the Malibu fire of late October–early November 1993, which occurred while they were in Australia.) Matt auditioned for and accepted a role in *Paradise Beach*, a soap opera that would air on television in Australia for about thirteen months.

Olivia told a reporter in July 1993 that, having returned to the country that she considered home, she was living "the most normal life I've ever known. Now my day is simple: yoga, school, gym, housework, washing, mummy time, dinner, and bed. I haven't retired, but, if I sing again, it will be because I want to." When the interviewer, who was writing an article commemorating the fifteenth anniversary of *Grease*, asked Olivia if she wanted to take a role in another movie, she replied, "I don't know that I want the pressure of films again."

Olivia was, however, writing. She coauthored a children's book, *A Pig Tale*, an "eco-conscious tale" that received a favorable review from *Publisher's Weekly*. "The money from this book is going to the foundation we've formed to research the link between childhood cancer and the environment," Olivia explained.

When discussing the book, she revealed that she was writing songs. "I've been inspired to write music… songs about all the experience I've been through. I hope they'll help other women." At the same time, she wasn't ready to commit to recording them. "If I do an album," she said, "it will be only songs I love, and it will happen in an easy, gentle way. No heavy schedule." She also amended her previous comment about films, saying that she'd love the opportunity to act again if she could do it in Australia. (In what turned out to be a bizarre coincidence, she made these comments to an Australian journalist named Pat McDermott, a name, although not the same person, that would figure prominently in her life after her first marriage ended.)

In fact, Olivia already had begun recording some of her newly written songs when McDermott interviewed her. Utilizing Byron Bay's Music Farm Studios, where well-known Australian artists such as Kylie Minogue and Midnight Oil had recorded, Olivia cut an entire album between June 1993 and April 1994. She was the sole composer of all twelve songs, and she produced the album with Murray Burns, formerly of the New Zealand new wave band Mi-Sex, and Colin Bayley, who had, among other credits, played with Mi-Sex and Men at Work.

Burns, who lived only a few miles from Byron Bay in Byron Shire, had met Olivia by chance and talked with her. She phoned him a few months later and asked him to coproduce and play instruments on the album, as would Bayley. "It was a magical time for her," Burns would recall, "as she had never been able to record [her own] songs—she always had been coerced into doing other people's songs. She didn't play an instrument, but she had perfect pitch—she could sing melodies beautifully."

Burns came to appreciate Olivia's kindness as well as her talent. "She taught me a lot about humility," he told an Australian journalist shortly after her passing. "She would cook food for us and when we stayed with her in Los Angeles she treated us like family."

Olivia paid for the recording of the album herself so that she could exercise the artistic freedom that Burns mentioned. Furthermore, except for her long-standing affiliation with Festival Records in Australia, she no longer had a record label. For years MCA had put forward the money for the recording of her albums, although those costs would then be charged against her royalties. Festival released the album, *Gaia: One Woman's Journey*, on July 26, 1994. ("Gaia," pronounced "GUY-ya," is a Greek word that means "mother earth.") The album became a Top 10 hit in Australia—her first since *Physical*—and the single "No Matter What You Do" cracked the Top 40. Many of the songs on the album bore clearly personal titles that spoke to her recent ordeals, such as "Not Gonna Give In To It" and "Why Me," and in the notes for the album, she explained the inspiration for each song.

She dedicated "Why Me" to her father, who she noted had "died with dignity of cancer on the day that I was diagnosed and he never complained for a moment." She elaborated on her father and his passing in an interview shortly after the release of *Gaia.*

My father was an incredible man and left a big hole because he was larger than life. He was intelligent and well-read and funny and handsome. He was a lot of things, and, uh, quite a taskmaster. So, if you earned a "well done" from him, you really knew that you'd done well. Because he was very critical about things being good, he always wanted things to be good.

Despite the success of *Gaia* in Australia, in other countries Billy Sammeth had to search for labels to release it. A small British label called D Sharp released the album in the United Kingdom in early 1995 and it reached No. 33 on the albums chart. In the United States, however, *Gaia* didn't get released until 2002, when Hip-O Records issued it.

For Olivia, however, whether or not the album became a hit was not the point. "I never had the confidence before to write my own album," she told an interviewer shortly after its release.

I'd written a song here and there, but I never really thought I had enough to say, or what would I write about, and all this kind of stuff. I didn't feel brave enough to show myself. And I think this is the first time. I think once you've gone through something like breast cancer, you're not really afraid of anything anymore. So, therefore I'm not afraid to show my feelings, which I was before. I really learnt a lot from making this album. It was a growth experience.

There would be no tour, though. But she did star in her second American Christmas TV movie in four years in 1994, *A Christmas Romance*, which included Chloe in the cast as well. Olivia also began making an Australian television series, from 1994 to 1996, called *Wild Life*. (In the United States, the series would eventually air on the Discovery Channel with the title *Human Nature*.) In one episode, she would free bald eagles into the wild; in another, she fed white tigers.

Olivia also met some interesting and equally well-known people while making the series. Michelle Day, who was the stills photographer during the second season, was present when Olivia met the American astronaut Buzz Aldrin and the former Soviet president Mikhail Gorbachev. "We bumped into Buzz and his then wife Lois," Day recalls, "at a hotel in Monaco. He invited us to have tea with him, so we just popped right down. I remember him talking about aliens a lot, which we giggled about later." The meeting with Gorbachev, in his office in Moscow, was also over tea. "She was in awe of him, I think the whole crew was," Day remembers. "It was such an honor to meet such an incredible man."

In October 1994, Olivia told a reporter for Australia's *TV Week* that she planned to sell her two houses in Malibu and move (with Matt and Chloe) to Australia full time. In addition to the TV series, she was becoming more involved in environmental causes in the country where she had spent most of her childhood. In 1992 she had met Australian environmental activist Jon Dee. Four years later, they started National Tree Day in Australia. They later founded the organization One Tree Per Child, which would be responsible for planting well over 130 million trees (and counting) in more than eighty countries. "We also," Dee notes, "helped to expose the logging of old-growth forest and the deliberate poisoning of wildlife in Tasmania."

But on the heels of the reports that Olivia and her family would be leaving California for Australia, the Australian press dropped a bombshell at the beginning of 1995, claiming that Olivia and Matt would be divorcing. The family was back in Malibu when the news broke, and the couple phoned Australia's *New Weekly* magazine to "set the record straight." Reporter Jenny Brown wrote that they were angry and upset about their daughter "hearing the rumors and coming home from school in tears."

"We've been hurt by this once too often," Matt told Brown.

I just don't know how these stories get around; they always seem to start in Australia and then they travel the world. We heard from someone here that rumors were flying again. In the past, we've let them go. This time we want you to help us put the record straight. Livvy and I are fine, we're together and we're tired of this bullshit.

Then Olivia spoke up. "We're definitely living together, there's no doubt about it! We've just moved into the house that Matt built for us here in Malibu and it's wonderful…. I just can't imagine how such stories get started. We are still very much together, and it will take more than lies to destroy our love for each other."

Barely three months later, though, on April 24, 1995, Olivia and Matt jointly released a short statement: "[We] regretfully announce an amicable separation." *People* magazine subsequently reported that the split came after "several months of recent couples therapy." The magazine quoted Olivia's niece, Tottie Goldsmith, as saying that during her illness, Matt had been "so supportive of her," but adding that "the people she chooses to mix with now are very spiritual. She needs to find her equal." *People* predicted that the split would be permanent, quoting an unnamed friend of Olivia's who said, "Sometimes there is no putting Humpty Dumpty together again."

The article also reported that Matt had said that marriage is "work," and "if you feel it's not worth the trouble…" Even in reporting the marriage's demise, though, the unnamed correspondent for *People* couldn't risk making the same kind of crack that tabloids had made about the couple's union when it had first become public knowledge: "At 31 [when the relationship had begun], Newton-John was well into adulthood, [but] Lattanzi, at 20, was barely old enough to order a drink."

In an interview clip shown in *The E! True Hollywood Story* in 2006, Matt recalled that Olivia "didn't want to end the relationship. She wanted to give it another chance. And I couldn't fit into her lifestyle at that point. I had changed. It was painful, but," he said insistently while wagging an index finger, "I knew the best thing I could do for her was to leave."

About four years before her passing, Olivia told interviewer Mia Freedman,

Because I was older [than Matt], I think I always had a, maybe a slight knowing that it may not last forever because he was going to get to his manhood and, you know, it's kind of normal that he might want to explore life or [that] it may not work. I didn't want that to happen, but I think in the back of my mind, maybe there was a knowingness. So, we made a promise to each other that, if anything happened between us, that we wouldn't let our daughter become the tool in the middle of our divorce like we'd watched other people use their kids as the bartering tool and make the kids suffer. So, we said, "No, whatever happens, she has access to you as much as she wants, and we'll try and be civil with each other because it's not fair on the kids."

Of course, Olivia's own childhood greatly affected her determination in this matter. "I'd been through a divorce—he hadn't—but my parents were divorced," she explained to Freedman, "and I really, you know, sometimes—and that's another thing, our divorce was around the same time as my parents' divorce [meaning that she and Chloe were nearly the same ages when their parents divorced]—so sometimes you unknowingly repeat patterns in your family."

In another interview nearly two dozen years after the divorce, she told the London *Daily Mail*,

I think our marriage would have eventually come to an end, but it happened sooner because of the cancer, which was a good thing. It was very painful, but we were never at odds with each other. We have tried to remain friendly because we have a child, and we made a pact that she was the most important thing in our lives and that we would never fight over her. What happened between us was between us, and we wouldn't allow it to affect her.

"Divorce," she added, "is never all right. Everybody wants the happy ending and the white picket fence, particularly me. My own parents divorced when I was ten and, maybe because of that, I kept putting marriage off. When I did get married, I wanted it to last forever, but that wasn't to be."

In the aftermath of the divorce, tabloids from Australia to Great Britain to the United States went into a frenzy when they learned the identity of Matt's new girlfriend. He had met Cindy Jessup, about twelve years his junior, at a cycling club in Lismore (about 25 to 30 miles from Byron Bay) in October 1993. At the time she had a boyfriend, but she and Matt continued to encounter each other in 1994. Cindy decided that, in June of that year, she would make a bicycle ride from Sydney to Perth (nearly 2,500 miles) to raise money for breast cancer research. Olivia sponsored the ride, and she got Holden Special Vehicles to provide a Commodore ute (a sporty, V8 pickup truck) in which her nephew Emerson, who at nineteen had begun his motor racing career, accompanied Cindy. Cindy came to the Byron Bay farm, posed for photos with Olivia and Matt and Emerson, and she would babysit Chloe.

According to the *Daily Mail*, "Newton-John began to have suspicions about the relationship between Jessup and Lattanzi—and reportedly confronted him in an agonizing showdown. The row led to Lattanzi moving in with Jessup and divorcing the singer." Lattanzi and Jessup married in Malibu in 1999, and eight years later they divorced.

According to both Lattanzi and Jessup, though, the reports of them having an affair while Lattanzi was still married to Olivia were fabricated. An unnamed friend of Olivia's confirmed this to a reporter at the wedding, which Olivia and Chloe attended: "It looks bad, because Cindy would often babysit his daughter and she was a friend of his and Olivia's—but in those days there was no romance."

As her marriage dissolved, Olivia found a measure of comfort by throwing herself into a project with two old friends with whom she'd worked a fair amount in one case (Cliff Richard) and a great deal in the other (John Farrar). Cliff had conceived of a stage musical to be called *Heathcliff*. The musical would be about the character of that name from the classic mid-nineteenth-century novel *Wuthering Heights* by Emily Brontë. Sir Tim Rice wrote the lyrics for the musical, and Farrar wrote the music.

The musical would premiere in Birmingham, England, in October 1996. While Olivia, contrary to some early press reports, did not take a role in the stage production, she did sing with Cliff on the album that he made and released a year in advance of the musical. Singing in the role of Cathy from the Brontë novel, Olivia recorded five duets with Cliff for the album, *Songs from Heathcliff*. EMI released the album, which was produced by Farrar, in Great Britain, and it reached No. 15 on the album chart. The label released one of Cliff and Olivia's duets, "Had to Be," a romantic, midtempo pop ballad, as a single; it reached No. 22 on the UK pop singles chart. Cliff and Olivia made a video for the single. He wore a suit with a black jacket and pants, and she wore an elaborate black dress and, at first, a veil. They also sang the song before an audience that included Queen Elizabeth II at a Royal Variety Performance in London.

For Olivia, the project proved reinvigorating. "It's fantastic to work with Cliff again," she told Australian journalist Pippa Leary.

> He's like my mentor. When I started out in England at 17, Pat Carroll and I did backing vocals for him on stage. Then Cliff asked me to do a duet, and after that I started doing songs and comedy sketches with him on his television show. So, he launched my career in the very, very beginning because our voices worked so well together.

"I know the part of Cathy is a real departure for me," she added, "but I love the challenge. It's also great for Cliff, because Heathcliff is the opposite of his personality but it's rewarding sometimes to play against yourself." Olivia also explained that, although she had never worked with Sir Tim Rice before, she and he were old friends. "Actually, in the Seventies Tim, Sir Andrew Lloyd Webber and I all went to see Elvis in Las Vegas. Andy was telling me recently that the three of us had our photos taken and made into a pin, which Tim has kept. Now my producer, John Farrar, and Tim are working together. It's the closing of a circle for me." Of working with Cliff, Farrar, and Rice, she said, "It's been a very fruitful coming together."

Olivia then reunited with another friend with whom she had not worked in years (nearly twenty in this case). *Grease* director Randal Kleiser had written, and would be directing and coproducing, a film titled *It's My Party*. Kleiser based the script on the true story of the death, in 1992, of his former lover Harry Stein, who had been a successful architect and designer. When Stein contracted AIDS and subsequently became terminally ill, he held a farewell party to say good-bye to those close to him before taking his own life in a dignified manner.

Although Olivia had recently expressed ambivalence about making any more films, she readily agreed when Kleiser asked her to join the cast, which featured Eric Roberts in the lead role. "I've lost friends to AIDS… so it struck a chord with me," she said. "The character of Nick [the one based on Stein] epitomizes probably thousands of men and women in the world who have AIDS and want to be allowed to die with dignity." She also contributed one of her songs from *Gaia: One Woman's Journey* (still unknown then to Americans except for a small number of imported copies), the moving "Don't Cut Me Down," to the film's soundtrack.

A low-budget film—Olivia and others worked for scale (the minimum union rate)—*It's My Party* had a limited release upon its March 22, 1996, debut in theaters, and it would only earn a bit over $600,000 at the box office. The film premiered, however, at the prestigious Sundance Film Festival in January 1996, which Olivia attended. On their television show *At the Movies*, Siskel and Ebert each gave the film a favorable review, with the latter describing it as "sometimes very funny, but mostly… gentle and sad." Despite its limited commercial impact, *It's My Party* would later be released on DVD and Blu-ray.

At around the same time that the Sundance Festival was being held, the press—particularly in Australia—started publishing articles claiming that Olivia and Matt had reconciled. Australia's *Woman's Day* reported that Matt, still living in Australia at the time, had returned to Olivia's house in Malibu for Christmas. The magazine quoted an unnamed but "close" friend of Olivia's as saying, "You could have knocked me over with a feather when Olivia called me just before Christmas and said, 'Well, Matt and I are back together, and we have never been happier!' She was gushing like a schoolgirl as she confided to me that Matt had moved back into their beach house."

About a month after the publication of that article, however, Olivia phoned another Australian magazine, *New Idea*, to set the record straight. She said that the Christmas reunion had not been the reconciliation that it was reported to be and had only been an effort to give Chloe a family Christmas. "Matt and I are separated, and we are still very good friends," she insisted. She also told the reporter that they had no plans for a divorce, but in fact the marriage would officially end in December 1996.

By then she had met and begun dating Patrick McDermott, a forty-year-old Korean-American cameraman and cinematographer. They met in Los Angeles; she was shooting a commercial for which he was a cameraman and lighting technician. In her memoir, Olivia wrote that her mother, a photographer herself, spotted Patrick before she did, telling her, "I'd like to take his photograph. That man has a beautiful face." Patrick himself had been divorced recently, and he had a four-year-old son. Patrick was athletic and, like Olivia, he loved the outdoors and hiking. He was also a photographer, and he would shoot one of the photos for Olivia's next album, *Back with a Heart*.

In contrast to Matt Lattanzi, who'd had a poster of Olivia on his bedroom wall years before they met, Patrick said of Olivia, "I never had a crush on her or enjoyed her music. But when I got to speak with her and make true eye contact for the first time, we were locked as if we had known each other for years in past lives." Soon he and Olivia would be eating candlelight suppers, cooked by him, on the beach in Malibu. The pair would have an on-and-off romantic relationship for the next nine years.

Always one to try to keep her private life private, Olivia kept her relationship with Patrick under wraps for a time (as she had done with Lattanzi). For his part, by some accounts, McDermott was not particularly fond of Hollywood and didn't like the spotlight that sometimes came with being Olivia's partner. It would take the tabloids about two years to catch on. On October 11, 1998, the London *Sunday Mirror* broke the story under the headline "He's the One That She Wants: Olivia Finds New Love with Cameraman Patrick." The two accompanying photographs showed them walking hand in hand and embracing during a public outing in Malibu.

But even as her new relationship with Patrick boded well for her personal life, Olivia confronted another health scare at the end of 1996. "I had a really sore throat and a lump for a while," she told a reporter in 1998. She went to a doctor, and X-rays revealed that she had a growth behind her larynx, nonmalignant, which had apparently been there for her entire life but which she had never noticed before.

"It made me think," she told the reporter. "I believe the body sends you messages, and I thought, 'I'm so lucky to have this voice; what if I lost it?'" In attempting to get over her sore throat and the irritating lump, she said, "I did all kinds of therapy," including six weeks of daily acupuncture treatments. "Nothing worked. But the minute I started singing, the lump went away."

At the same time (late 1996), Olivia got a welcome and unexpected sign that the US pop music market might be ready for her again. In 1990, to help promote a home video release of *Grease*, Polydor Records (which had absorbed the catalog of the by-then defunct RSO label) had commissioned two British record producers, Phil Harding and Ian Curnow, to weave "You're the One That I Want," "Greased Lightnin'," and "Summer Nights" into a single titled "The Grease Megamix." Polydor didn't release it in the United States, but it reached the Top 10 in no less than nine countries, including No. 1 in Australia and Spain. (It came close in Great Britain, reaching No. 3.) The record remained unreleased in the United States for six years.

That changed in October 1996, when Polydor included it on a various-artists compilation CD of disco classics called *Pure Disco*. The label released "The Grease Megamix" to radio as a promotional single for the album. Since the single wasn't released to retail, it was, under the *Billboard* rules of the day, ineligible for the Hot 100. But on the *Radio and Records* Contemporary Hit Radio/Pop Top 50, which solely measured radio airplay, "The Grease Megamix" reached No. 12. The release to radio did its intended job of promoting the *Pure Disco* album, which against all predictions sold over one million copies. The popularity of "The Grease Megamix" also spurred something of a revival in sales of the *Grease* soundtrack album.

Of "The Grease Megamix," Jon Zellner, program director at Kansas City's Top 40 station Mix 93.3, said, "It's one of our most requested songs. It's a multigenerational thing. It's generating a whole new audience; the older listeners know the original, and the younger listeners have never heard it."

Less than one year after the release of *Pure Disco*, Olivia would be on a stage in Australia before sixty-two thousand people on hand for a rugby match, singing "You're the One That I Want" with New Zealand rock singer Jon Stevens as part of a somewhat premature twentieth-anniversary celebration of *Grease*. "I always get nervous before performances," she told a reporter before she took the stage. "But I'd better get used to it."

17 BACK WITH A HEART

"Nashville's newest country star wannabe is pop queen Olivia Newton-John," began an article in the Nashville *Tennessean* on October 31, 1997. "Sounds wacky, no?" Writers for the *Tennessean* had made some harsh comments about her in the mid-1970s, and the beginning of this article by columnist Brad Schmitt suggested that perhaps nothing had changed.

But then Schmitt answered his own question: "Well, no. You might recall that Olivia got her start in country, earning CMA's Female Vocalist of the Year prize in 1974." Schmitt went on to report that Olivia had told him that "she feels out of touch with the pop world. So—and I know you've heard this dozens of times with other artists—Olivia's going back to her country roots." She had just signed with MCA Nashville Records, a natural choice given her long affiliation with MCA, and, as Schmitt noted, "arguably the most powerful of the country music labels."

Given that she hadn't had a pop hit (aside from "The Grease Megamix" the year before) in a dozen years, as well as the fact that she had said more than once during the 1980s that she wanted to make another country album, this seemed like a logical step as she tried again to revive her recording career in the United States. MCA Nashville seemed like the right label as well. "I started going to Nashville and meeting people, and I really liked [MCA Nashville president] Tony Brown," she told *Billboard* in April 1998. "I met everybody, and everyone was wonderful, but also I'd been with MCA a long time, and they have my catalog. So, it makes sense for me to be there." Brown thought so, too. "It just seemed natural for us to give it a shot," he reflects.

Olivia's long history with MCA wasn't the only connection that brought her to MCA Nashville. By this point, Billy Sammeth was no longer managing her; he was focused on another client, Cher, who was about to make a major comeback (yet again) with "Believe," which would be released in late 1998 and would be ranked by *Billboard* as the number one hit of the year for 1999. Olivia, who would write a sweet note to Sammeth in the liner notes of her new album, moved on to the Fitzgerald Hartley Company (Larry Fitzgerald and Mark Hartley), which was based in both Los Angeles and Nashville. Fitzgerald and Hartley's client roster included Vince Gill, who, Tony Brown recalls, "I signed and turned into a superstar." Furthermore, Olivia's longtime attorney, John Mason, was also Brown's attorney. "So, all the people with her," Brown says, "we were all friends, and we worked together and we had success together." His expectation when he signed Olivia was that "we [would] go in there and just blow the roof off it with [her]."

"When we signed her," Brown recalls,

the strategy was, we had these meetings, and we didn't sign someone like her just on a whim... because it was a pretty decent-sized deal, and to cut records, you know, we probably spent, every record I cut back then, cost around three or four hundred grand. So, it wasn't like we were gambling for the hell of it. We really thought about it, and it just made *total* sense that she would fit.

Early signs portended well for the album finding the kind of success that Brown expected. Gary Burr, who produced and, with Olivia, wrote two songs on her album for MCA Nashville, including the title track "Back with a Heart," was at a concert in Nashville that Olivia performed at just before she signed her new recording contract. "It was a very country line-up; she walked out on stage and that place exploded," he told journalist Alan Cackett in 1998. "It was as if they had been waiting, saying, 'Where have you been?' She got the only standing ovation of the night. I think she's going to be totally embraced by the country audience."

On November 17, 1997, Olivia performed as one of several acts on the bill at a charity concert for Operation Smile at Nashville's Opry House. She sang "Please Mr. Please" and "I Honestly Love You." Then, after a change of clothes, she and Vince Gill sang "You're the One That I Want" together, and the audience went crazy. "It took everybody by surprise," recalls Chris Farren, who was working with Olivia on her new album at the time. "I just remember that moment... her in those black leather pants and that outfit... looking every bit as good as she did when she made the movie. It was a great moment."

Burr and Farren were among the established writers that Olivia collaborated with for *Back with a Heart*. Having finally stepped forward as her own songwriter with the *Gaia* album, she was determined to keep writing, but she wanted to write commercial material this time. Upon the album's release, she would tell journalist Tamara Saviano, "I wrote an album a few years ago—it wasn't released in the United States—about my experiences with breast cancer and about environmental issues, things like that. I discovered," she told Saviano with a laugh, "people really didn't want to hear that stuff."

Olivia had made a concerted effort to further develop her songwriting skills since the release of *Gaia*. In 1995 she had attended a well-known annual songwriters' retreat hosted by Miles Copeland in his castle in southern France, where, among other compositions, she wrote a song with her fellow Aussies Keith Urban and Andrew Farriss of INXS, which never saw the light of day. "It was about three months after my mom passed away of cancer," Farriss recalled in 2021. "It was interesting... because, you know, I think Olivia herself had been through a difficult experience with her own health concerns, and my mother had passed away, and so we got on quite well talking about various things... she's a lovely lady and awesome talent."

Olivia would cowrite seven of the eleven songs that made it onto *Back with a Heart*. John Farrar wrote two songs for it, and "Big Al" Anderson of NRBQ and Robert Ellis Orrall wrote "I Don't Wanna Say Goodnight." The last song on the album would be a remake of "I Honestly Love You."

Burr was one of the first writers that Olivia worked with for the album. She had met him in 1996, when she once again participated in Copeland's songwriters' retreat. In 1997, "She started coming to town [Nashville] and we started to write more consistently," Burr told Alan Cackett. "We wrote some songs that she said she really wanted to have on the album, and she said, 'I want you to produce the ones that we wrote.'"

"You know, you meet a lot of artists that say, 'I'm writing' or 'I'm gonna write' or 'I want to write,' and basically they're just there to tell you what they would or wouldn't say," Burr said.

But Olivia does it all for writing. She walked in and just said, "Okay, here are my ideas: this, this, this... " and she kept going through all these ideas. Finally, she had this idea for a verse and I said, "That's the one I want to work with, that sounds great." She was singing to the verse, and we took it from there and ended up with the up-tempo "Back with a Heart." She's really good... a great writer.

"I was really thrilled to get to work with her," Burr told Cackett.

I was familiar enough with her music so that everything that she and I have written together very much captures the flavor of what she used to do back then. She's not trying hip-hop, it's real compatible with what you would expect. But this is not just someone coming along trying to recreate something. She's not trying to rebuild a fire, she's going to start a whole new one.

MCA Nashville helped Olivia find additional talented cowriters and producers. Chris Farren, who had signed a songwriting contract with MCA in 1983, was one of them. Farren worked in Los Angeles, but he says, "I had spent a lot of time in Nashville. I had just produced a record called 'Strawberry Wine' by Deana Carter [a number one country hit in 1996]... so I had a big country song being a guy from

LA." When someone at MCA Nashville invited him to work with Olivia, "I gladly accepted," he recalls.

Farren first met Olivia at her house in Malibu. "We sat down [in the living room]," he says,

> and started writing the song, and then she got up and made me a sandwich. It was just *so normal*. It was like, it was abnormal in one respect and so normal in the other respect, just working with this woman who was, you know, an icon, and she's making me a turkey sandwich… there was just something kind of surreal about that, but also unbelievably cool about it.

Farren holds another clear memory of working with Olivia at her home. One day she said to him, "Hey, let's go take a walk on the beach. Let's clear our heads." "I think," Farren remembers, "we'd hit a bit of a [writing] block or something."

He was soon struck once again by a feeling of surrealness.

> We're walking along the beach, and, all of a sudden, I kind of had a glimpse of myself from above going, "Wait a minute. I'm walking down the beach in Malibu side-by-side with Olivia Newton-John. If my high school girlfriend— my high school girlfriend who dumped me—could see me now."… Just even as friends, walking down the beach in Malibu with Olivia Newton-John was pretty heady stuff for me at that time.

Olivia also made several visits to Farren's home in suburban Los Angeles to work on new songs with him. "She drove herself," he recalls, "and she parked in the driveway, and she walked up, and she talked to my kids, and talked to my wife, and had lunch at our table, and, you know, it wasn't like she had handlers and people there or had to take phone calls. She was there, and she was completely present." Farren and his wife had a baby at the time, a daughter, and on one visit, Olivia brought a gift for her. "She was so thoughtful," he says. "She was incredibly gracious and honest and real. I think that was part of her appeal, was that she *was* that girl next door… incredibly cute and real and honest and simple, and that's really who she was."

Farren and Olivia wrote two songs together that she recorded, which he produced. "Don't Say That" would be included on *Back with a Heart*, while the other song, "What's Forever For," was left off but would later be released as a bonus track on a Japanese CD release of the album. "Don't Say That" was, according to Farren, "a true collaboration. I don't remember how that song even came about… it might have started with a groove or something…. I think the title may have been hers."

"We wrote in Malibu, we recorded [and] tracked in Nashville," where Farren got a firsthand glimpse of Olivia's fame and popularity. "Everywhere we went,

I mean, we'd go to lunch in Nashville, people would turn their heads." Upon returning to California, they recorded vocals and overdubs at Farren's studio in Woodland Hills.

Olivia used six producers on the album, although each of the eleven tracks only had one. Label president Tony Brown produced two songs, "Love Is a Gift" and "Attention," both of which were recorded (except for overdubs) at Nashville's Ocean Way Recording Studios, so named because the original Ocean Way studio was in Santa Monica. As had Chris Christian over two decades earlier, Brown brought in Nashville's "A-team session players," who were "all, like, beside themselves to be playing on this record," he recalls laughingly. "It was like a fan fest in the studio for her with the players. They all were just like all over themselves being able to work with her."

Brown and Don Cook, another of the producers who worked on *Back with a Heart*, also produced, together, a recording that Olivia made in 1997 with another newly signed MCA Nashville act, the Raybon Brothers. The song was called "Falling," but it was not the song of that title that John Farrar had written in 1980. The Raybon Brothers, Marty and Tim, were starstruck, too. "To be in the studio with her, and to know that she's coming there to be on your record… it was a strange feeling, really mind boggling," Marty later said. The Raybon Brothers and Olivia made a video for the record, and MCA Nashville released it to country radio stations, but it didn't make much impact.

Even Tony Brown, who had spent two years touring as a member of Elvis Presley's TCB Band and had recorded with him, found himself somewhat starstruck to be working with Olivia. "There was a part of me," he admits, "that was a *little* intimidated." Olivia, he says, was the first "full-blown pop star" that he had ever produced. "I must tell you, it was frightening," he recalls laughingly. "Even though she was sweet, it was frightening."

The album included at least two producers who weren't starstruck to be working with Olivia. John Farrar produced the two songs that he wrote for the album, and Olivia brought in David Foster to produce and do the arrangement for a new version of "I Honestly Love You." It was the only song on the album that was not recorded in Nashville; they cut it at Chartmaker Studios in Malibu. Foster also played keyboards on the recording, and Kenneth "Babyface" Edmonds sang background vocals. "David Foster was responsible" for that, Olivia said in a *People* magazine AOL chat in May 1998. "He ran into Babyface at a party and asked him would he like to do it and luckily for me he agreed. I love the fresh sound that he put in the song. So, if you're reading this Babyface, thank you a million times over."

It was Olivia's idea to tackle the song again. "With all these remakes going around," Olivia told a reporter when the album was released, "I was scared to death someone would get to it before me. It's just a great song." MCA Nashville thought it would be a hit. "My favorite song on that record," says Tony Brown, "was the one that [she and] Babyface recut…. I thought that was the coolest version of that song ever cut, personally." Dane Bryant, who had worked with Olivia in 1995 and would later work quite often with her onstage and in the recording studio, concurs: "[It was] great… I really dug that version."

The recording of *Back with a Heart*, which had begun in October 1997, ended in February 1998. MCA Nashville slated the album for a spring release. As soon as Olivia finished recording the album, she went on tour for the first time in sixteen years, joining Cliff Richard, at his invitation, on a seven-week tour of Australia to celebrate his forty years as a recording artist.

The pair made a press appearance together in Melbourne. When a reporter urged Cliff, whose status as a confirmed bachelor remained a matter of much press speculation, to spill the beans on matters of "love and intrigue," he turned to Olivia and said, "I'm in love with her and she's intrigued." Olivia, according to a reporter, responded with "squeals of laughter." "I feel really comfortable with Cliff, and he makes me feel confident," she then said. "Our voices blend well, and I feel safe with Cliff because he's my friend."

Olivia returned to California in March in time for another high-profile event. *Grease* coproducer Allan Carr had been lobbying Paramount for a long time to rerelease the movie for its twentieth anniversary. When *Entertainment Weekly* ran a feature on the enduring popularity of the original stage version of *Grease* in 1996, "I bought 20 copies," Carr told the magazine in 1998. "[I] sent them to the executives, then marched into [Paramount president] Sherry Lansing's office and said, 'We're sitting on a gold mine.'" The success of the twentieth-anniversary rerelease of *Star Wars* in 1997 further swayed Paramount to grant Carr his wish.

Once Paramount made up its mind, it launched a full-scale promotional effort. The studio booked Mann's (aka Grauman's) Chinese Theatre, site of the original *Grease* premiere party, for the premiere of the rerelease on March 25, 1998. Just as the original premiere party had been made into a television special, so was this one (for VH-1). Olivia and many other stars of the film—except, notably, John Travolta—were on hand. The promotional efforts paid off handsomely, but more than anything else, the success of the rerelease demonstrated the enduring popularity of the film: during its first weekend (March 27–29), it earned $13 million at the box office. The only film that did better that weekend was *Titanic*, which had won eleven Academy Awards on March 23. It was all something of a last hurrah for Allan Carr, who died of liver cancer at age sixty-two on June 29, 1999.

The success of and flurry of publicity surrounding the rerelease of *Grease* seemed to bode well for the release of *Back with a Heart* less than two months later (on May 12). Olivia had no trouble at all lining up a bevy of press appearances, from magazines to television to the aforementioned AOL Chat, then quite the hot and cutting-edge form of promotional media, for *People* magazine. A syndicated newspaper article on the album's release ran under the headline "Rereleased Film Revives Singer's Career."

"Six months ago," the article began, "'70s sensation country/pop singer Olivia Newton-John… was off the '90s radar screen…. But with the rerelease of 1978's *Grease* in March, Newton-John's still-smiling face was suddenly all over newspapers, magazines and TV." The article also noted that "at almost 50, she has even found herself among Hollywood's hottest hunks and heartthrobs in *People* magazine's latest '50 Most Beautiful People' issue." "I thought there was some kind of mistake at first," Olivia said with a grin. "But I am very flattered, if a little embarrassed."

Upon the album's release, Olivia embarked on her most vigorous promotional campaign (short of actually touring) for any album since *Physical*. She appeared on former Grand Ole Opry announcer Ralph Emery's TNN show *On the Record* for a lengthy interview. "I don't relate to pop music anymore," she told Emery. "And the camaraderie in Nashville is something that I've always loved, something that made me feel welcome." This was a generous statement on her part, given the mixed reception she had received there two dozen years earlier.

She did the rounds of newspaper and magazine interviews as well. She told *Miami Herald* journalist Howard Cohen, who interviewed her numerous times over the years,

> I think country today is what pop was ten years ago, and some of the stuff I was doing back then is kind of happening now. I feel comfortable with that, and I love the songs that are coming out of Nashville. It's about the singer and the song. With this album, I was trying to make a good mainstream record. *Gaia* was a very personal record, and no one wanted to release it here. You learn something from that.

What Cohen remembers most clearly about that telephone interview over a quarter of a century later, however, is an interruption when Olivia "briefly paused to attend to a question her daughter had posed to her…. I recall liking that mothering side of her." Olivia told Cohen that whenever she was at home, she tried to never miss picking up Chloe at school. "It's an amazing thing to be a parent," she told Cohen, "and I waited until I was a lot older to become one. Things like picking them up is important to children. If you ask them half an hour later what happened during the day, they forget. If I'm not working, I like to do it."

She also visited radio stations with Tony Brown, but, as he recalls, this proved disappointing in terms of promoting *Back with a Heart*, which of course was the purpose of the visits. "The funny thing about it was, every program director… was dying to have their picture taken with Olivia," he recalls laughingly, "but they wouldn't play the single [the new version of 'I Honestly Love You'] in heavy rotation. They would all come out and try to get their picture, with their family, their kids, with Olivia, and then they wouldn't play the record."

Chris Farren could see that Olivia's comeback attempt was going to be challenging. He thought that the label knew it, too, and that that was why so many different producers were utilized on the album. "I think that was intentional," he says.

> I think it was like trying to see how they could have… a [hit] country record with a, for lack of a better word, middle-aged pop star. I think it was kind of a unique challenge in a certain way. You know, it was like her fame was a huge asset, but, in another way, it was maybe a hurdle.

Farren thinks that the purpose of pairing Olivia with so many producers and songwriters was to see

> if somebody could find a song or write a song or produce a song that could be the vehicle to help promote the record. And I'm not sure that we did. But… I think it was, it wasn't a great record, but I also think it was kind of a tall order to think that she was going to go [back] on country radio at that point, you know? It was worth a try, that's for sure.

The album wasn't a flop, but neither was it the hit that Olivia had been hoping for and that Tony Brown had been expecting. It reached No. 9 on the *Billboard* country albums chart, but only No. 59 on the Top 200 (pop) albums chart. It met with a similar reception from the public in Australia, where it reached No. 66. It didn't chart at all in the United Kingdom.

"I think," Tony Brown reflects, "we were expecting it could be a platinum album, 'cause everybody back in those days, every country act was having a gold or platinum album. *Everybody!* And I think we just expected that was a platinum one for sure." As it turned out, though, it wouldn't even reach gold status (five hundred thousand copies sold).

At least part of the problem was the lack of a hit single that was usually required to propel an album to gold or platinum sales. The remake of "I Honestly Love You," even with the cachet of Babyface being involved, stalled at No. 67 on the Hot 100. It reached No. 18 on the airplay-based adult contemporary chart, but it missed the *Billboard* Hot Country Singles and Tracks chart altogether. (It did reach No. 16 on the *Billboard* Top Country Singles Sales chart, but by that time many hit singles were being released only to radio, not to retail.) A cystic fibrosis charity single called "One Heart at a Time," which Olivia recorded as part of a supergroup that also included Garth Brooks, Billy Dean, Faith Hill, Neal McCoy,

Michael McDonald, the song's composer Victoria Shaw,[1] and Bryan White, did about as well as her own single, reaching No. 56 on the Hot 100 and No. 69 on the country singles chart. MCA Nashville later released a track from *Back with a Heart*, "Precious Love," to country radio, but it didn't crack the country singles chart.

Brown reflects upon *Back with a Heart* now with second thoughts and regrets. "I must say, during those sessions, I was still like, my career was just finally starting to come together, and I was a little intimidated, I must admit, in the studio. As I listen to this record, I think back going," he laughs, "'Damn, I wish I could be me doing that *now*,' you know. I would do it so much differently. I would have approached it differently… I could have done a much better job. I would have stepped up to the plate a little more than I did." He mentioned three times in a forty-minute interview that he wishes he could have a "redo" in the making of *Back with a Heart*.

He blames himself and others at the label more than he blames Olivia. "Not that I think we failed," he says. "I just think that we didn't do things right like we could have." Olivia, he recalls,

was totally involved in what she wanted, and she spoke up… she was such a team player. She would do anything we'd ask her to do. I've worked with a lot of superstars, and some can be a bit difficult. She was *totally* a team player, and I think we played [it] too safe. We should have went for it.

"I don't think it's a bad album," he says.

I just don't think the magic… the only magic on that album, *real* magic, is "I Honestly Love You." And I think "Love Is a Gift" has a little bit of that in there. But the rest of the album doesn't. And there should have been at least three or four songs that had the magic of "I Honestly Love You."

The one way in which Brown will concede that he thinks Olivia could have done more to make a better album involves her role in cowriting most of the songs. "I think," he admits,

had I been further down the road in my career, I would have insisted we do publishing company visits and have her cowrite with other writers or either just have all the best writers in Nashville give us songs. Because she could have gotten the best of the best. Everybody in town would have *died* to have an Olivia Newton-John cut.

"I think," he continues,

what we did was we sort of catered to her, the fact that she wrote songs, and she had some songs that were pretty good, but they weren't, in hindsight, they weren't good enough, actually.... I think this deal landed on our desk, and we decided to play ball with *her* so quickly, and please her, and not offend her by saying, "Will you do outside songs?" that we rushed into cutting this album. What we should have done, we should have spent like six or eight months, just beating [the] streets for songs, you know? Putting her into cowrites with great writers and also getting just outside songs, and I think it would have been a great album.

Brown puts some of the blame on himself as the label president. "I think we were a little thrown off by her superstar status. But, you know, with Larry Fitzgerald and Mark Hartley, I should have gone over there and had a 'come to Jesus' meeting with them," he laughs. Brown also suggests that Fitzgerald and Hartley could have been more helpful to Olivia when it came to *Back with a Heart*. "They had their eyes," he says, "really on Vince [Gill]. I think they just thought that because Olivia was Olivia, it would happen just naturally, and it didn't, and that's where we all made a mistake. We had work to do, and we didn't quite do the work we needed to do to make Olivia a great record."

Reviews of the album generally agreed, another factor that didn't help its sales. For example, *Arizona Republic* music critic Randy Cordova praised the new version of "I Honestly Love You," but, "unfortunately," he wrote, "nothing else on the Nashville-recorded disc rivals that song for sheer memorability. The production is contemporary country, with pedal steel guitar and strings laid alongside synths and keyboards. The songs are never less than pleasant but rarely more than that."

Brown concedes that "in order to compete with Shania [a fan herself who would later show up at at least one of Olivia's concerts] and Faith Hill and Reba," she needed better material.

I mean, there was so much more there that we didn't take advantage of, and I think it was out of respect for her, which worked against us as opposed to working for her and for us together.... I just wanted to please her. My God, I loved her records, and I loved her as a person, and I did not want to disrespect her in any way, and it worked against me, I think.

Despite some regrets, however, Brown still has positive memories of working with Olivia. He takes pride in the fact that "Love Is a Gift," which he produced, won a Daytime Emmy Award for outstanding original song in 1999 after being played on the soap opera *As the World Turns*. That, Brown happily notes, "had to make her feel like, 'I've still got it,' you know?"

Moreover, he says, "I will never regret the opportunity that I had to get to know her. What a wonderful person she was, and what a great singer she was. She used to sit at a piano and sing, and it was *great*, just great." Working with her, he reflects, "was quite an experience… she was just really a good person… she was totally accessible."

He also recalls Olivia, even though she wanted the album to be a big hit, not seeming particularly fazed when it wasn't and when MCA Nashville subsequently dropped her from the label rather than letting her try again.

Through all that, she never ever, it never seemed to really frustrate her or make her upset. She was just totally the coolest, most professional, and nicest superstar I've ever worked with. She could have gotten, like, kind of really upset about that, but she didn't. She went along with the flow, and when it didn't work, she just moved on.

This wasn't surprising. The promotional interviews that she gave for *Back with a Heart* seemed to indicate that while she was happy to be reviving her career, it never again would be the most important thing in her life. When she was asked in May 1998 if she had ever known Linda McCartney, who had died of breast cancer a month prior, she replied, "Unfortunately, no. I never met her though I really wanted to after I heard that she was ill. I was very sad when I heard of her loss. She reminds me of how lucky I am to be here." In another interview that month, she revealed that she had turned down a role in a television sitcom because it would have meant spending too much time away from her daughter. "The hardest thing about being a mom," she explained, "is knowing that she is going to grow up and leave home. I enjoy her company so. Also, knowing all the dangers out there, there are so many frightening things. You have to arm them with knowledge you don't want them to have yet."

Furthermore, the various concerts that she did in 1997–1998, including the tour of Australia with Cliff Richard, proved that even if she couldn't sell records like she used to, she still had plenty of fans who were thrilled to see her perform in person. One such display of her enduring appeal as a live performer came at a sold-out "Z-Day" concert at Radio City Music Hall (for New York City's Top 40 station WHTZ-FM/Z-100) on May 31, 1998. It was, like many of her live performances at this time, a charity concert, with the proceeds going to PAX, a newly formed nonprofit organization that was dedicated to preventing gun violence. The star-studded bill included some top hit makers of the day, among them Matchbox Twenty, Third Eye Blind, Gloria Estefan, K-Ci and JoJo, and Paula Cole. A report in *Billboard* singled out two "favorite moments" for the crowd: NYSNC's portion of the show and "a duet between Mariah Carey and Olivia Newton-John on 'Hopelessly Devoted to You.'"

18 DARE TO DREAM

"It was a fantastic party," Olivia told a reporter of the party for her fiftieth birthday, which she reached on September 26, 1998. "We had it at the home of two of my oldest friends, Pat and John Farrar. I've known them since I was fifteen, and we had Koala Blue together." Neither Olivia's mother nor her siblings in Australia could make it to California for the party, but Rona was there, as were (in addition to the Farrars) old Australian friends such as Steve Kipner and Billy Thorpe. "I think it's important to be with the people you are closest to on an occasion like that," she said.

I suppose because life is all about the people you know and the good times you've shared with them. It was a wonderful reminder to look around the room and see all of the people I love and care for, and to realize that I had a special memory with each one of them. And having them all there definitely helped me go through the transition of turning 50.

The party also marked the public coming out of Patrick McDermott as, in the words of Australia's *Woman's Day* magazine, "her new man." "We've managed to keep it quiet for two years," Olivia said laughingly.

Because so little of my life is private, I intend to try to keep this as private as I can. My relationship with Patrick is great. It's a lovely thing. We've been friends for two years now. We met while we were filming a commercial together and he was a gaffer. It's just nice to be able to share experiences with someone. We have a lovely time together—we like to play tennis and hike and do all those sorts of things.

Barely a month after turning fifty, Olivia was in Australia starting a twenty-nine-concert, nearly eight-week tour as a co-headliner with John Farnham (like Olivia, a British-born Australian singer) and Anthony Warlow, a theatrical singer who starred in Oz productions of famed musicals such as *Phantom of the Opera* and *My Fair Lady*. The performers were backed by a forty-piece orchestra and Farnham's eight-member band. "Billed as *The Main Event*," the Melbourne *Age* explained, "this was designed to be a home-grown version of the 1991 [actually, 1989] Australian concert series by Frank Sinatra, Liza Minnelli, and Sammy Davis Junior (without egos and tantrums)." The newspaper reported that the first show by Olivia, Farnham, and Warlow did not sell out but that "more than 65,000 people have bought tickets to the six Melbourne concerts."

The concerts allowed the three performers to sing together as well as separately. A very favorable review in the *Sydney Morning Herald* (November 18, 1998) explained, "The first half [of the two-and-a-half-hour show] is made up of short solo sets," which in Olivia's case included some of her hits and "a couple of tracks" from *Back with a Heart,*

and the second features the trio in all possible permutations. They pick the eyes out of their individual back catalogs but use the looseness of the occasion to reinterpret their roles and their images, venturing into new and old territory for no reason other than the joy of it.... It is this willingness of the threesome to have a go, to move out of their usual frames, that makes the evening a delight.

During the Main Event Tour, Olivia worked not only with John Farnham's band but also with his musical director, Chong Lim. A native of Malaysia, Lim emigrated to Melbourne in 1977, at the age of nineteen. After earning a mechanical engineering degree at the University of Melbourne, he began a career in the music business. He began working for Farnham in 1994. Lim recalls that when the Main Event Tour began, Olivia "had a lot of mental blockages about performing live" but that she visibly relaxed as the tour progressed. "She felt very comfortable with us [Farnham's band] as a team, and after the tour, Mark Hartley and she decided they should put a tour together for her in America. So, they approached me, and that was the start of my association with Olivia," one that would last for most of the remainder of her career. "She became a great personal friend. She was that kind of person, a very caring, beautiful person."

Joe Creighton, who was the bass guitarist in Farnham's band, recalls her saying to Farnham, "I just love your band. I love the way that you lean back on them and the support that they give you. I really wish I had that." Farnham told her, "Why don't you just use these guys [for her American tour] because I don't use them all the time. We only tour once a year, and it's only for about two or three months."

"Could I?" Olivia replied. "Would you mind if I did that?"

"Not at all, and they'd love it." Mark Hartley worked out the business arrangements with the band. By the end of the year (1998)—beginning, in fact, on New Year's Eve—Olivia was performing at the Hilton Convention Center in Las Vegas, the beginning of a brief "greatest hits" tour that worked its way through western and midwestern US cities over the next two to three weeks.

Chong Lim remembers Olivia being nervous on her opening night at the Hilton. "She was almost fearful," he says,

> and I think part of it was a stalker who [had been] stalking her. When we did our first concert, first night in Vegas, she was so nervous that she literally hid in the wardrobe, and she was really worried that he would turn up at the concert. But he didn't. And I think that was part of the mental blockage, you know, all that stuff.

Not long after that, though, recalls Joe Creighton, "We had to get security one time for one of the casinos. We had a bit of a stalker fan who was seen on her floor… probably harmless… but it was just like, it had been creepy."

Lim also thinks that Olivia's devotion to Chloe played a role in her seeming "very reticent" to tour.

> She wanted to be a good mother to Chloe and didn't tour. But… a performer is always a performer. When she did "The Main Event," she found that, her calling, again. And the first concert in Vegas, all of us were kind of nervous to see whether, how it would go, and it was triumphant. The first concert was triumphant.

"And after that," he continues, "*all* the concerts were really great… literally a standing ovation every night, very responsive crowds, and she got the bug and got her confidence back, and so she went on touring a lot."

"She was very humble," Lim reflects. "[She] worried about whether people would come to the [opening Las Vegas] concert, whether she could put it all together again, and, indeed, it made her very happy." Joe Creighton also recalls Olivia having been "pretty underconfident" about touring again when she set out on the Main Event Tour, and that "it took her a little while to really strengthen her voice again and get used to it, and just to really get back in form."

Creighton, too, saw how quickly Olivia began to enjoy performing for live audiences again and how much she appreciated her fans. "I just think it really warmed her just how, the reception that she got, how everyone really wanted to see her, how much she was loved and adored by all her fans. I think she'd forgotten that." The fans, Creighton saw, certainly had not forgotten her. "They were back in *force*, and they were there for her. It was incredible. It was a great experience for me as well." He would tour with Olivia in Europe and Asia as well as Australia, the United States, and Canada. He would also don a black leather jacket and sing "You're the One That I Want" with her during concerts.

"I really had no intention of returning," Olivia told a reporter around this time. "But mentally and emotionally, I'm strong, more ready than I ever have been before…. I feel good about the music I'm doing now."

Longtime Minneapolis *Star Tribune* music critic Jon Bream reviewed her sold-out concert at the Mystic Lake Casino Celebrity Palace Theater in Prior Lake, Minnesota, on January 14, 1999. Although he disliked some of the newer songs she performed ("Not Gonna Give In To It" and "Don't Cut Me Down," while praising "Love Is a Gift"), he was impressed with the show overall. "She performed," he wrote, "with a striking confidence that never came across when she played the big arenas back in the 1970s and early '80s. The 2,200 casino goers seemed very pleased." Bream noted that Olivia mentioned during the show that her first US tour (several tours, actually) had been done with musicians from Minneapolis, although her reunion with most of the musicians who had constituted thisOneness would have to await a future Minnesota tour stop.

Olivia's comeback did not mean, however, that she was backpedaling on her various forms of activism and helping others, particularly women diagnosed with breast cancer. On March 6, 1999, at a ceremony in Santa Monica, the American Red Cross presented her with its Humanitarian Award. Her friend David Foster presented her with the award, which the *Los Angeles Times* reported was given to her "for her commitment to causes such as the Children's Health Environmental Coalition, [the] Revlon/UCLA Breast Cancer Foundation, Operation Smile, the Make-a-Wish Foundation, the Starlight Foundation and the Susan G. Komen Breast Cancer Foundation." Olivia then sang "I Honestly Love You" and "Over the Rainbow," accompanied only by Foster playing piano.

During the summer of 1999, Olivia embarked on a longer US tour, kicking off on July 16 with a three-night engagement at the Desert Inn in Las Vegas and ending on September 4 at the Riverside Theater in Milwaukee. By now she was starting to have to hire some American musicians to join her, as not all of John Farnham's band members remained available to her. The first American addition to her band was guitarist Andy Timmons from Texas, who recalls Olivia as "a near and dear person to my heart." He would tour with her from 1999 until 2015, and he would play on her final recording, a duet of "Jolene" with Dolly Parton. Before joining Olivia's band, Timmons had already played with another country-pop star, LeAnn Rimes.

For Timmons, Olivia would be more than just a friend who "was very easy to love."

"She saved my life," he says, "and I told her this many times."

When he and Olivia were first getting to know each other, she told him how she had gone to three doctors in 1992 before one diagnosed her with breast cancer. She had been suspicious of the first two, she told him, who had not found it, because she had known she was ill. "If you ever feel like anything's wrong with yourself," Olivia told him, "just go to the doctor and get it checked out. Don't wait. Just go!"

In 2013, Timmons says, "I looked in the mirror and I could tell something was wrong around my eyes, and I was having some pain in an area of my body. And so, I just, I heard her voice and so I just went to the doctor. I didn't wait."

Three days later,

I was in surgery, and it was cancer. The doctor said that it was a very aggressive form of this particular cancer, and had I not come in it would have been a very different outcome. So, you know, I'm glad I had her around many years to thank her for being that catalyst. I really, truly believe she saved my life by sharing that experience.

He also took inspiration from her "fighter attitude… that resilience, and that buoyancy of just pushing through and keeping going," which he believes extended her life beyond how long someone with a less strong mentality would have survived. In later years, after Olivia's Cancer Wellness & Research Centre opened, she would offer more direct help to another one of her guitarists, Stuart Fraser, who underwent treatment for lung cancer there before his death in 2019, and to Dane Bryant's son, who survived and recovered from a bout with cancer.

Soon after Timmons joined Olivia's band, he and Mark Hartley gradually began putting together a new band for her. "When they made me the musical director," Timmons says,

I got to pull in some of my people, and he pulled in some of his people that he knew from his touring bands from Nashville and what not, and it was a really caring, loving group of people. And I know that had a lot to do with her wanting to continue [touring] because she said to me once, "I'm really enjoying this. I never truly enjoyed it on this level." Because she always had so much pressure on herself. You know, she really was a perfectionist, and that can be torturous for an artist, and it takes some of the joy away when you're too busy agonizing over things that weren't perfect.

Chris Farren witnessed this when he, his wife, and some friends went to one of Olivia's concerts in Las Vegas in the early 2000s. He and his small party visited her backstage after the show. Even though she was "as gracious to us as ever," he recalls, she seemed a bit anxious.

"Oh my God," Olivia said to Farren. "I wasn't so good tonight, was I?"

"No, no," Farren replied. "You were great."

"No no, come on, Chris, you can tell me. I know I wasn't!"

Farren continued to try to reassure her. "Olivia, it was great, it was great!"

"Now what about on that one song?" she insisted.

By now Farren felt that "she was almost begging me for a critique."

So he relented. "Well," he told her, "you know, you missed a couple of notes on that one song, but I don't think anybody noticed. It was fine!"

"I kind of fluffed it off," Farren recalls. Olivia seemed relieved.

After Chris and his group left, a male friend of his, a "huge Olivia Newton-John fan" from Australia, said to him in disbelief, "I can't fucking believe you just told Olivia Newton-John that she sang shitty!" Farren laughs at the recollection, insisting that he said no such thing and that Olivia was being too harsh on herself.

Chong Lim recalls similar conversations after her concerts. "She used to say, 'Chongie, I wasn't really good tonight.' I said, 'Olivia, *please*. You were *incredible*!' Of course, she was very self-critical and self-analytical. And she was a perfectionist."

Andy Timmons has a thought about at least one source of Olivia's perfectionism and all the pressure she put on herself. "I think some of that came from her father from something she said to me," he recalls. "Maybe he was that way, you know, maybe he put that pressure on those around him."

Just like many of the musicians and backup singers who had toured with Olivia during the mid- to late 1970s and on the Physical Tour in 1982, Timmons recalls that she and her entourage were "all family" onstage and off. "There was a lot of social time. If there was a night off, she was always putting things together for us to do, between her and her assistant, Martha Real. We'd go to comedy clubs, we'd go for dinner, we'd go dancing," he laughs.

One night Olivia and the band had a night off in Phoenix and she phoned him. "Andy, do you fancy going to see Elvis Costello?" Timmons, a big Elvis Costello fan, gladly agreed. The band Phantom Planet, whose members included Sam Farrar, John and Pat's son, was Costello's opening act.

"So, we all went," Timmons recalls, "[and] we went backstage after the show. We're talking to Elvis, and Elvis had just been in Australia. And he says to Olivia, 'Oh, you know, when we were in Australia, I did "Hopelessly Devoted to You." I almost did it tonight. I should've done it!'"

Another American musician who joined Olivia's band not long after Timmons was bass guitarist Alison Prestwood, who also recalls a family-like atmosphere while touring with her. "We would always be welcome to talk to her. Certainly, before the show, we'd have nice little powwows. She was very sweet, charming, and we would do the Namaste prayer."

"I was always welcome," Prestwood says,

> to approach her for anything. And the times on the bus were very comfortable. She wasn't one of those stars that had to just separate or segregate herself from everybody else. She was very *easy* to get along with, and fun, and there's a picture of us at a truck stop. She and I are, you can't see either of our faces, but we're doing downward dog, doing yoga in the grass,

Laughing, she continues, "With bathrobes on... it was crazy!"

"I got engaged while I was on tour with her, and I remember we were on the tour bus going through Manhattan and looking at bridal magazines together. That was fun. She actually ended up coming to my wedding, too, in November of 2000, which made all of my relatives completely freak out," Prestwood recalls laughingly. "It was great having her there... everybody, my family, was pretty respectful. And I remember her dancing with my cousin's kids at the reception."

The family-like atmosphere that still prevailed on Olivia's tours also still extended to a sense of protectiveness toward her by those in her entourage. When asked if security concerns were an issue on her tours with Olivia, Prestwood replies,

> Oh, I remember that. I *do* remember that. I don't remember details, but absolutely, Dan Waters [Olivia's tour manager] was having to be on alert for all that all the time. Wackos, you know, wackos... some that I think they knew would show up so often that they knew their names and dealt with them. Yeah, you know, she did have to deal with that. I remember some of that. It wasn't, I think it was pretty well under control, or at least they knew how to control the people, so I don't remember it being like a fearful environment. I just remember it being *almost* funny, like, "Oh great, so-and-so is here," and it would be irritating. But I don't think there was a lot of fear by the time I was there, because they were pretty strong watching out for that stuff.

But Stephen Duros, who was Olivia's lighting director in 2003–2004, remembers being on her tour bus one night after a show as Olivia sat with a laptop and replied to messages that fans had submitted on her website. Duros had seen "some really intense fans" that night. As Olivia typed away, Duros looked at her and said, "I gotta be honest, sometimes your fans kind of scare me a little bit." She looked up at him and said, "Ohh, some of them scare me too." "And she was really serious," Duros says. "She had a really serious look on her face."

When Olivia was out among the public while on tour, recalls Andy Timmons, "people approached her. We were all extremely protective of her, of course, and we all watched her like a hawk, even though we didn't say that to her. We always had her back… we went out a lot, all kinds of social events."

Drummer Dan Wojciechowski, whom Andy Timmons brought into the band, concurs.

> She surrounded herself with a lot of band people. We were always with her and walking around with her a lot of times, and either Martha [Real] or Steve [Real, Martha's husband and Olivia's vocal coach] would be with her. So there was always someone kind of keeping an eye [on her] and someone kind of being there, along with maybe a bodyguard or whatever.

Olivia's return to touring didn't douse her relationship with Patrick McDermott. The US tabloid *The Globe*, in its December 21, 1999, issue, ran a brief article with the headline "Olivia Newton-John Gets Physical!—with hunky beau." Included were photographs of the pair embracing and kissing as they walked to a Chinese restaurant in Malibu, along with a breathless report from "an eyewitness" who reported that "Olivia and Patrick are obviously crazy about one another. They hold hands, kiss and hug every chance they get."

Patrick spent enough time with Olivia while she was on tour that her band members got to know him. "He'd come out to a couple of shows," Wojciechowski recalls, "and [he was] pretty cool. I mean, he was a pretty nice guy. And they seemed like they had gotten along pretty well."

"He was a really, really sweet man," Andy Timmons says of McDermott, "and a guitar player… we were definitely buds, you know, when he was around. [He was] a really, really good guy."

Patrick didn't always travel with Olivia, particularly when she went to Australia; after all, he had a job and a son in Los Angeles. The Australian journalists Neil McMahon (who became a friend of Olivia's) and Gerard Wright noted in 2005 that Olivia and Patrick did "not [have] a traditional relationship, something friends are at pains to point out. Newton-John travels constantly, they say, either performing live or meeting the other demands of life as what one calls 'a global business.'" One friend of hers told the journalists, on the condition of anonymity, "Olivia tours six months of the year so they aren't in constant contact like a lot of other couples."

Patrick did not come along when Olivia and Chloe flew to Australia in September 2000 for the Olympic Games in Sydney. There Olivia would once again take the stage with her old friend John Farnham, singing "Dare to Dream" during the opening ceremonies. In her memoir, she wrote of how during their dress rehearsal, she asked him to hold her hand as they walked downstairs to the stage, since she felt a bit unsteady in her high heels. He did "until a pretty girl spoke to him," at which point he let go of Olivia's hand and she tripped and fell. One could almost hear her laughing on the page as she wrote, "I later heard him telling fans and onlookers in his thick Aussie accent sprinkled with laughter, 'I dropped the blonde like a bag of sparkly shit.'" "Oh, God love him!" she wrote.

During the actual performance, Olivia and John both had technical problems with their earpieces, but, being seasoned pros, they nevertheless managed to pull it off without a hitch before an audience of one hundred thousand (plus four billion television viewers around the world). They also had recorded the song beforehand; it would be released within days on the album *The Games of the XXVII Olympiad 2000: Music from the Opening Ceremony*. Chong Lim was one of the producers of the recording. "They were both *so* dedicated," he says of Olivia and John. "Every time we did a take, she'd say, 'One more,' and John would say, 'One more.'… They started out at midday at the studio, Metropolis Studios in Melbourne, and we finished at about 1 a.m."

Lim still remembers it as a highlight of his career. "They were striving for perfection," he marvels. He was "awestruck" at "listening to these two incredible singers collaborate."

While she brought many new musicians into her circle, most of whom became her friends, Olivia also particularly enjoyed working with old friends with whom she felt comfortable. These included Cliff Richard and John Farnham as duet partners, and in films, Randal Kleiser and Del Shores. Shores, a native of Winters, Texas, who was described by the *Los Angeles Times* as "a master of the Texas comedy," first rose to prominence as a writer and director of plays. A fan of Olivia's since her first big US hit, "Let Me Be There," he first saw her in concert at Texas Southmost College in Brownsville on February 25, 1975. Ten years later he met Olivia, as he recalled in a posting on Instagram on the first anniversary of her passing, "at the McCadden Place Theatre [in Los Angeles]… when she saw my first play *Cheatin'* with my friend, her sister, Rona."

In 1996, Shores's fourth play, *Sordid Lives*, opened in Los Angeles. A dark comedy of sorts, it "reflects," wrote Don Shirley in the *Los Angeles Times*, "Shores' coming out as a gay man [but] only indirectly." It met with both commercial and critical success, and in 1999 he wrote and directed a film version of the play. Olivia had told him, upon seeing the play with Rona, that if he ever did so, she wanted to play the role of Bitsy Mae, described by one writer as "a gum-chewing, tattooed, foul-mouthed, leather-clad, lesbian ex-con biker who has an affair with a Texas granny." When she phoned to sing "Happy Birthday" to him in December 1998, he told her that he would be making the film, and she offered to take the part.

Like Kleiser's *It's My Party*, Shores's film was a low-budget, limited-release production, albeit with a fine cast that in addition to Olivia also included Beau Bridges, Delta Burke, and Leslie Jordan. In 2008, Olivia reprised her role for television in the twelve-episode *Sordid Lives: The Series*. Her performance in the movie and series became one more reason why Salon.com would later declare, "Before it was cool or safe, Olivia Newton-John was a queer icon and ally."

In 2000, Olivia recorded her first album since *Back with a Heart*, a holiday album with Vince Gill titled *'Tis the Season*. Each of them sang some songs as solo performances, and they duetted on "(There's No Place Like) Home for the Holidays" and "Away in a Manger." Olivia chose "Ave Maria" as one of her solos, which Karen Carpenter had sung for the Carpenters' 1978 album *Christmas Portrait*. In a novel twist of marketing, Hallmark Cards released *'Tis the Season*, and it was sold exclusively in Hallmark stores for $6.95 on compact disc or $3.95 on cassette with any Hallmark purchase.

Having dipped her toe into the touring waters in 1998–1999, once the new millennium began Olivia increased her concert schedule to its greatest frequency since 1982. In 2000 she toured the United States from March to May; the next to last show, on May 20 at the Civic Arts Center in Thousand Oaks, California, was a reunion of sorts. John and Pat Farrar were there, as were Olivia's mother, who had flown in from Australia; Rona and Emerson, by then a twenty-five-year-old racing car driver; and Steve Kipner. Cliff Richard came too, and he joined her onstage to sing "Suddenly" with her. In October, Olivia and the Farrars went to London to participate in a cruise for Cliff's sixtieth birthday. "We [she and Pat] were both so excited," Olivia told a reporter. "Cliff picked us up from Heathrow a few days before the start of the trip and we had a lovely couple of days. We all went to see the show *Mamma Mia*, which was fun." She also toured Asia that year and sang three songs at a Christmas Eve show in Melbourne, Australia.

In 2001, Olivia and Chloe filmed a television movie in Gold Coast, Queensland, Australia, called *The Wilde Girls*, written and directed by Del Shores. Olivia confined her touring to the United States that year. (Chloe, who was fifteen then, joined her at some shows that summer, and they duetted on a song from the movie.) Olivia's itinerary would take her to New York City just after the terrorist attacks of September 11. "We were out on the road when that happened," Dan Wojciechowski recalls. "And there was a private show that we were supposed to do in New York. And we all talked about it."

"Should we do it, should I do it?" Olivia asked. "I think maybe I should, and maybe people need it."

"And *man*," Wojciechowski says, "I'll never forget how, did they *ever*! Like, just her positive energy. She had everybody in that theater in the palm of her hand, and everybody felt what she felt. It was unbelievable how she could lift people up that way at a time of super deep distress… the power of spirit and music that she had. Incredible." Olivia also joined Brooke Shields and Lee Greenwood and his wife, Kim, in touring Ground Zero at the World Trade Center site and meeting first responders.

Wojciechowski recalls his post–September 11 experience with Olivia as one of the most memorable of his roughly seven or eight years of touring with her. Another, happier event that remains vivid in his mind occurred one year later, on September 24, 2002, at the Paramount lot in Hollywood. Even though Olivia was on tour—she had performed in Atlanta on September 20 and Clearwater, Florida, on the 21st—she flew to Los Angeles with her band, on a private jet, to appear at a DVD release party for *Grease*.

She had agreed to sing at the party, but only after she arrived in LA did she learn that John Travolta would join her. Andy Timmons recalls her phoning him. She told him that Travolta had agreed to sing with her at the event, "but he's really nervous about it." Olivia asked Timmons to come to her hotel room with Wojciechowski and run through the songs with her and John. Timmons phoned his wife, "the biggest *Grease* fan," and told her, "Honey, buy a plane ticket to LA. I'll tell you later what's going on."

What followed was a small gathering consisting of Timmons, his wife, Wojciechowski, Olivia, and Travolta. Andy brought an acoustic guitar, and Dan brought blasticks, which he played on a sofa arm. They started playing the intro to "You're the One That I Want," and then Travolta began singing, "I've got chills, they're multiplyin'." "It sounded exactly, *exactly* like the record," Timmons recalls. They also rehearsed "Summer Nights." "What happened in that hotel room was a different level of magic. It was *so special*… a really incredible memory." Wojciechowski also sensed the electricity of that private, almost impromptu rehearsal: "That was incredible… [I] will never forget it!"

Warren Ham, who played saxophone, flute, and harmonica and sang backup for Olivia from 2001 until 2017 (and as her duet partner on "You're the One That I Want" except on the rare occasions when Travolta was present), says that "the early 2000s were great years" for her. "I think she had a lot of fun, felt good.… We had a ball. All I remember is the good times we had." He recalls Olivia taking members of her band and entourage to the Guggenheim Museum in New York City, to baseball games, to football (soccer) games in Australia, and to karaoke bars "all the time when we were in Japan." "She was always very generous," he reflects. "Such a sweet lady."

Even as Olivia maintained her renewed focus on her career, recording an album of duets with various artists in 2002 called *(2)*, which became a hit in Australia, she became increasingly devoted to charitable and environmental causes. She had, notes her friend Michelle Day, an "enormous capacity to give, and she knew where help was needed." Olivia dedicated the duets album to her mother, Irene, and when she was approached by the CEO of a hospital in Melbourne who requested that she let them use her name on a new cancer center, she asked Irene what she thought. "In life," Irene replied, "if you can help somebody, then you should do it."

This project and the creation of the Gaia Retreat & Spa, a wellness retreat near Byron Bay, would both become long-term projects for Olivia. Her mother would not live to see the fulfillment of either. Olivia was on tour, in Las Vegas, when Rona called her from Australia and told her that she should come now if she wanted to see their eighty-nine-year-old mother before she passed away. Olivia and Chloe took a flight to Melbourne and got to spend the final week of Irene's life with her. She died on August 29, 2003.

Olivia later said in an interview, "I had always said to her [Irene], 'Please give me a sign after you've gone that you're okay.'" Irene had told Olivia that just after her own mother died, a portrait of her fell off a wall, which she took to be a positive sign from her mother. When Olivia was sitting in a room alone with Irene within an hour of her passing, she asked her for such a sign now. Suddenly Rona called out Olivia's name from another room. When Olivia walked into the hallway, she saw that a large candle encased in thick glass, which she had brought from the United States and placed onto a table below a picture of Irene, had exploded and fallen into pieces on the floor.

"So that was my sign," Olivia told interviewer Andrew Denton. "It was a pretty powerful one. She was a pretty powerful lady."

19 STRONGER THAN BEFORE

"When my mother was pretty ill," Olivia told Australian journalist Brenda Cunningham-Lewis by phone from Malibu in the summer of 2004,

she was very excited about me getting involved in creating a cancer center in Melbourne. I felt kind of weird about it—but I knew it would keep me coming back to Australia and I wanted to do something for her as well. Who knows, maybe, with extra money toward research, it might mean we'll be the ones who discover a cure.

"I remember," Chong Lim says,

her starting the journey of raising money [for the cancer center]. I thought, "My God, how is she going to raise this money?" And she would auction off herself singing "I Honestly Love You" at [a] rich person's house. I've done so many of those concerts with her, me on piano and her singing and having dinner with the people… she could get about, I don't know, a five-figure sum. And we'd do a lot of those. And that's how she started… from those humble beginnings she slowly raised hundreds of millions of dollars for the hospital. And every time she came [to Australia] she would have meetings with the prime minister, or the premier of Victoria or something, and raise more and more funds. She was a remarkable person, you know? One of a kind… she used her fame for good… for pure, unadulterated good.

Olivia also spoke about her relationship with Patrick McDermott to Cunningham-Lewis and addressed whether they would be getting married. "We have a lovely relationship," she said. "But yes, I like my independence, and it is still too soon to talk marriage."

Olivia spent much of the first half of 2005 recording her album *Stronger Than Before*, which took its name from a song that she had written with Annie Roboff and Beth Chapman. Chong Lim, who produced that and most of the other tracks on the album, describes it as one of the "kind of *healing* songs" that she often wrote during this period. Chloe wrote the lyrics to one song on the album, "Can I Trust Your Arms," for which Olivia wrote the music. The album represented, in part, a charitable endeavor; in the United States it would be sold exclusively at Hallmark Gold Crown stores for two months, and for every compact disc sold, two dollars would be donated to the Susan G. Komen Breast Cancer Foundation.

Olivia finished recording the album in June, and it would be released on August 29, 2005. She would be in Australia when Patrick McDermott's name started making headlines around much of the world, for just about the worst reason that she or anyone else who loved him could have possibly imagined. Olivia, accompanied by Chloe, had gone "home [to Melbourne] for a holiday, with a little business on the side: National Tree Day, an event she co-founded with Planet Ark's Jon Dee and one of several causes dear to her heart," according to a report in the Melbourne *Age* newspaper. She also would be on hand for a birthday party for her friend Ann Peacock at the Crown Casino.

Olivia was still in Melbourne when she learned the news, which the *Los Angeles Times* would summarize with the headline "Man Missing since Fishing Trip Is Sought: Performer Olivia Newton-John's close friend has been missing since July 1, when he was to return from an overnight excursion." The article went on to report that Patrick McDermott had boarded the fishing vessel *Freedom* at a port in San Pedro (Los Angeles) on June 30, and that his family "began to grow worried when he failed to attend a July 6 event," at which point "they contacted authorities. On July 11, family and authorities learned that he had left a bag of personal belongings and his silver Hyundai behind at the 22nd Street Marina."

Frank Liversedge, the marina's landing manager, said that he believed that Patrick "did not disappear at sea and probably made it to shore, but left his possessions for unknown reasons." "I know he got to the top of that ramp," Liversedge said as the pointed to the dock gangplank. "I've been here 45 years as a boat captain and vessel master. I have never lost a fisherman."

As press reports began suggesting that Patrick had been depressed and heavily in debt, Olivia contacted Gavin de Becker. He sent a couple of his private investigators to Mexico, armed with a list of places there that Olivia remembered Patrick having talked about. They came up empty.

Olivia asked de Becker if she should make a television appearance and plea for anyone who might have any information about Patrick's whereabouts to come forward, but de Becker advised against it. Later, on August 22, 2005, she issued a public statement: "I am hopeful that my treasured friend is safe and well and I am grateful to the officials who are working so hard to find Patrick, whom I love very much. I ask anybody with information that could help to please, please come forward." In November 2005, an investigation by the US Coast Guard concluded that Patrick McDermott had "most likely" drowned.

Olivia's choice of words—calling Patrick her "treasured friend"—seemed odd in the face of the many press reports, and even things she had told reporters, about their relationship. What the press didn't know, however, and what Olivia didn't reveal until she wrote her memoir, was that she and Patrick had always had an "on-again, off-again" relationship, and at the time of his disappearance, they had recently agreed that they were "off-again," although she hadn't made any final decision to break up with him. Chong Lim recalls that Olivia had told him of some "problems" in her and Patrick's relationship.

Olivia then found herself in the uncomfortable position of having to grant interviews, her intent for which was to promote her new album, while the story of Patrick's disappearance was very much in the news. Even though Olivia's representative, Michael Caprio, requested that interviewers not ask her about Patrick, they almost all did. Andy Timmons still bristles thinking about "how the media turned it [Patrick's disappearance] into entertainment. It was really infuriating in a lot of ways, and I really, really felt bad for her. But again... talk about people handling things with grace, I mean, I'd never seen somebody go through that but still come through it with dignity."

Olivia finally agreed to address the subject for CNN's *Showbiz Tonight* in October 2005. "It's a really painful topic. And it's still under investigation. And I'm just—I love him very much, and as you can imagine, this is an incredibly hard thing to go through," she said. "I was just kind of frozen. And you know, life, you have to move forward a little bit. It was one of the reasons that I decided to sing again. I didn't think I was going to sing again, and I had to move forward." Dance instructor Joe Giamalva remembers Olivia coming to his tap-dance classes at Malibu Fitness not long after Patrick went missing, as she had done before as well. "I think it was a getaway for her. It was an hour she could get away and, you know, take her mind off of all that *shit*."

A year to the month after the *Showbiz Tonight* interview, CNN's Larry King surprised her by bringing up the subject of Patrick's disappearance yet again. She told King that she remained in contact with Patrick's family. "I've become very close to his ex-wife, Yvette [Nipar], who's a wonderful person, and we've become good friends, and I see his son, and he's thriving. He's doing really well," she told King. Nipar later wrote, "I'll never forget her calling me from the green room right after this, knowing how protective I was of my son's name constantly being 'put out there.' She had no idea Larry was going to ask this."

Press stories would continue to circulate for years about Patrick supposedly being found alive in Mexico, but none of them ever came with anything resembling proof. "I think there will always be a question mark," Olivia told a journalist in 2009. "I don't think I will ever really be at peace with it." According to Olivia's friend Liona Boyd, "She thought he'd been killed. She thought he drowned. She didn't believe all the rumors about the sightings in Mexico. She said, 'No, I don't believe that.'"

By the time Patrick disappeared, Olivia already had met the man who would become her second husband, John Easterling. Exactly when they had first met is unclear; an article in *Closer* magazine in 2024, for which journalist Fortune Benatar interviewed Easterling, states that he and Olivia had met for lunch "on a blind date around 1995." (Other sources put the date two years earlier; Jim and Nancy Chuda, who facilitated the introduction, had met Easterling in 1992.) "I was a little suspect of meeting a Hollywood diva," Easterling said, "but she had such a great sense of humor and was a really warm, personable human being. She was not what I was expecting." Olivia took an interest in his work with the cultivation and development of Amazonian plants for medicinal purposes (he had cofounded the Amazon Herb Company in 1990, four years before Jeff Bezos launched his internet retail behemoth), and she and John would cross paths occasionally at charity events in the years that followed.

In 2004, Olivia invited John to a benefit concert she would be singing at in Miami. "It was a small, intimate theater," he told *Closer*, "and I heard these Peruvian flutes playing. She walked out onstage and sang 'Pearls on a Chain,'" a song that she wrote with Amy Sky and would record on her next album, "and people around me were so moved they started crying. That's when I recognized who she is—she's a healer! Her song and voice are mediums of her healing gift." "All I could think," he said in another interview, "was that I wanted to introduce her to other healers who work in the Amazon."

Liona Boyd was with Olivia for the occasion. "That was funny," she recalls, "because I was looking for a boyfriend, and she said, 'Oh, here, he's the perfect guy for you, Liona! He's really nice.' He came with this big dog."

Liona demurred. "No, Olivia, I think he's more for you." Olivia laughed and said, "Oh, no, no, no."

Olivia wasn't seeing Easterling when McDermott disappeared, nor during the immediate aftermath. She threw herself into writing songs and recording *Grace and Gratitude*, which, she wrote in the booklet that accompanied the compact disc, had been "inspired by my love for Patrick." Released in August 2006, the album represented more of an artistic endeavor than a commercial one, although once again some of its proceeds would go to cancer charities. "The New Age CD," wrote Howard Cohen in the *Miami Herald*, "features chants from Tibet and Japan, Judaic and Islamic prayers, a Latin benediction from Catholic Mass and The Prayer of St. Francis serving as interludes. Affirmative ballads like 'Pearls on a Chain,' 'Love Is Letting Go of Fear' and 'Learn to Love Yourself' are designed to unlock the Chakra energy that blocks or misdirects healing within the body." She collaborated with Deepak Chopra on his DVD *The Seven Spiritual Laws of Success*, which was released in 2007.

Olivia had long striven to keep her private life private, but in 2007 she would stand by Chloe in public and step into the public eye with Easterling as her new romantic partner. Cohen, who had noted the "motherly side" of Olivia when he interviewed her in 1998, spoke to her for the *Miami Herald* again in November 2006. "Chloe," she told him, "is the most precious thing to me and you have to be here and cope and show her like my mother [had done for Olivia]. Most people discover strength when faced with adversity and you don't know what you have until you cope with it. When you want to give in, you struggle through." Chloe was going through her own struggles at the time, and she later suggested one possible cause to *People* magazine. "I remember being 16 and having the house to myself for months at a time," she said when she was twenty-two. "I had this feeling in me like, 'Okay, you're not a priority [to her mother]—so just deal with it.'"

The tabloid media, which had more or less forgotten about McDermott's disappearance, began running stories about Chloe after she and Olivia were photographed in April 2007 outside of a Whole Foods store in Los Angeles. "Skinny Chloe's Brave Battle," chirped Australia's *Woman's Day* in a brief article that featured the photos. The article reported that they had been taken after Chloe and Olivia had left a UCLA medical clinic that specialized in eating disorders.

Chloe and Olivia confronted the pictures and rumors directly by doing a twelve-minute interview together for *Entertainment Tonight*, which aired in two parts later that month. Chloe candidly admitted that she had suffered from anorexia for two years but said that she had "come out of it now." Olivia told interviewer Mary Hart, "I'll continue to say how proud I am of her to have the courage to sit here and talk to you about this. I think she's amazing. And the fact that she wanted to talk about it rather than be talked about. And I just have a lot of admiration for her." When Hart mentioned Karen Carpenter, Olivia admitted that her friend's demise, which she had seen up close, had made her all the more concerned about Chloe's battle with the eating disorder.

Karen, it seems, was never far from Olivia's thoughts. Neil McMahon was at Olivia's house in Malibu when the passing of Heath Ledger, on January 22, 2008, hit the news. He recalls that Olivia began talking about Karen and Andy Gibb. "When Heath died," he says, "that's what came into her memory, when Andy died and when Karen Carpenter died." Olivia's twenty-first-century band members recall going with her to karaoke bars where she would sing Carpenters songs, and how she would sometimes reminisce about Karen and tell them stories about her friendship with her. Shortly before the Covid-19 pandemic forced Olivia into isolation, she spoke at length about Karen for the documentary *Karen Carpenter: Starving for Perfection*.[1]

In June 2007, Olivia and the Chudas, Jim and Nancy, traveled to Peru together. They would be met at the airport in Lima by John Easterling, who would introduce them to local healers and show them the plantation on which he grew healing plants. Olivia became sick within two days of arriving. John canceled plans to travel to another village. "I couldn't abandon her in the jungle," he told *Closer* in 2024. "That was the day we started having deep conversations…. It was nothing that either one of us expected, but we were bonded from that day on." On July 10, they attended the premiere of the theatrical production of *Xanadu* together in New York City. "Olivia's got a new man," proclaimed the Australian edition of *In Touch* magazine.

The headline was true. In her memoir, Olivia wrote that when she was with John in Peru, she had a premonition that they would be back there one year later to be married. He proposed to her on Valentine's Day, 2008, while they were attending a conference in Arizona. (Since they were playing charades, though, with him getting her to say "Will you marry me?" in response to his clues, Olivia jokingly wrote that he would always say that she was the one who proposed.) They returned to Peru and married in a private ceremony on June 21, 2008, and then nine days later they held another private ceremony ("to make it legal," Olivia wrote in her memoir) at John's home in Jupiter Island, Florida. Even friends didn't know about it until the newlyweds sprang the news at a Fourth of July barbecue at their home in Malibu.

"I have never seen two people more in love," remarks Liona Boyd. "I mean, it was almost over the top, they were just *crazy* about each other. And she was just so happy to have this wonderful man in her life."

Olivia's band members, who spent a great deal of time with her when she was touring or doing casino engagements, speak glowingly of Easterling as well: "An incredible human being," says Dane Bryant. "We all just *loved* having him around because we knew that when he was there, that everything's okay. He's that kind of guy that just when he shows up, it's just, you can exhale and breathe a sigh of relief…. John just had that energy about him, and he still does to this day."

Between the dates of their engagement and their marriage, Olivia undertook a three-week walk of the Great Wall of China in April, an approximately 150-mile trek, to raise money for building her cancer center in Melbourne. She also recorded an album of duets, *A Celebration in Song*, to further bolster her fundraising efforts. Her duet partners included, among others, Cliff Richard, Barry Gibb, and Richard Marx. About two hundred people would join her for all or some of the walk, including Cliff Richard, Didi Conn, Dannii Minogue, Leeza Gibbons, Joan Rivers, and, of course, John Easterling.

Neil McMahon, who walked the entire distance with Olivia, recalls that Easterling, because of a terminal illness in his family, had to leave very suddenly in the middle of this walk… which was very upsetting for [Olivia]. She couldn't leave because of the commitment to this project. And she just kept going on… no matter how she felt—she got sick like we all did—she would just get up every day, get up and walk out and put one foot in front of the other. She'd have to be on camera every day.

The physical conditions that they endured, McMahon recalls, were "really, extremely difficult… it wasn't glamorous at all… it was really rough. And she just kept doing it. Never, never complained. It was an extraordinary experience."

Olivia also rescued a cat, which she would name Magic, on the journey. "She found it drowning in a crate," McMahon says. "It was like a newborn kitten, and she sort of raised it… she loved animals so much." McMahon would be reminded time and again of her love for animals in subsequent years. When his dog, Miss Maudie, perished in a house fire in 2020 that also resulted in McMahon being hospitalized, she sent him a gift hamper and a video message. "I'm so heartbroken to hear about Maudie," she told him. "I cried, too. I'm sorry, I'm so sorry. And you were very brave."

After they got married, Olivia became involved in John's Amazon Herb Company to some extent, while also maintaining her career. Steven Kuhn, a personal business advisor who has worked with, among others, Mick Jagger and Andrea Bocelli, met Olivia and John in West Palm Beach in 2009 through a mutual friend of his named Luke, who was already working with them. Kuhn began working with John and Olivia to promote the Amazon Herb Company.

Kuhn worked with them from 2009 until 2012. During that time, he traveled extensively with them; among the countries they visited were Hungary, Austria, Belgium, Great Britain, Poland, and the Czech Republic. They would make presentations about the herbs the company sold. Kuhn found that Olivia, not surprisingly, was a major asset. "It was easy to sell the product," he recalls with a chuckle, "when you say, 'Olivia's coming to present it,' you know?"

Apparently, Olivia had grown as a businesswoman as a result of the difficult experience with Koala Blue. "She had more business sense than John by a million miles," Kuhn says laughingly. "She was the business person, believe me. She was the one… she was the business person, a hundred percent. She was a tough woman. She was very tough."

As an example, Kuhn recalls an incident that occurred when they were in Poland. "There were some guys in the front row talking [during a presentation], it was like the mayor or something, and she was like, 'If you guys want to talk, you can go out in the back and talk while I'm talking.'" Kuhn was impressed. "I was like, '*Damn!*'"

"She was relentless," Kuhn reflects, "in getting what she wanted, in achieving the goals she wanted to achieve. *Relentless!* One of the most relentless people I ever met. Loving, caring, but no joke, you know what I mean? Like, no one walked on her, no one told her what to do. She decided everything.... [John] did whatever she said," he laughs.

Olivia, Kuhn recalls, "never mixed the business with the music" on these trips. "So, she wouldn't sing, she wouldn't talk about her career... she only talked about the herbs, because she truly believed in them." When Kuhn set up a business-related interview for her in Budapest, the interviewer asked her about the disappearance of Patrick McDermott. "I asked you not to ask me those questions," she replied. "I'm going to get up and leave now unless you stop."

Even though Olivia's attitude at these presentations was, Kuhn says, "You're here to look at the products, not me," she realized that people would "happily pay just to come see her and get her autograph... there was always a photo session afterward. Everyone was lined up to get photographs." "It was quite a journey," he says of his three years of working with Olivia and John. When Kuhn considered running for a US Senate seat in Illinois, which he ultimately decided not to do, "I needed referrals from people who would speak up for me, so I asked her to write me a recommendation letter and she did. It was amazing. She was always helping [people], *always*."

Working with her husband and Kuhn on the growth of the Amazon Herb Company did not stop Olivia from continuing to tour, record, and act. She toured mostly in North America during this period but also in Japan, Chile, Australia, China, Indonesia, Sri Lanka, the Philippines, Malaysia, Singapore, and Thailand. In 2013 she toured the United Kingdom, including a show at London's Royal Albert Hall—the only time in seven years that drummer Mark Beckett thought she seemed nervous and worried about whether she'd be accepted, but of course she rose to the occasion and "was brilliant." She played a supporting role in an Australian comedy film, *A Few Best Men* (2011), and recorded a new song for the soundtrack, "Weightless," written by John Farrar and one of John and Pat's sons, Max Farrar.

In 2012, Olivia reunited with John Travolta to record *This Christmas*, which became her best-selling album since *Back with a Heart*. She continued to have big fans among each new generation of female singer-songwriters. "In 2012, Sara Bareilles was visiting me in Chicago, and over dinner Sara mentioned her idol was Olivia," recalled Richard Marx, a friend of Olivia's since the 1980s.

I discreetly texted Livvy, who answered me within minutes, saying, "So weird! I was going to call you tomorrow. I'm coming to Chicago and hoped we could have dinner." The next night we surprised Sara at the restaurant, and when Olivia walked in, Sara was so overcome she ran into the coat closet, crying. That's who Olivia was. Sweet, kind, loving, and open.

Olivia also published a cookbook, *Livwise: Easy Recipes for a Healthy, Happy Life*, in 2012, and in June of that year, the Olivia Newton-John Cancer Wellness & Research Centre opened about ten miles outside of Melbourne. "The government of Australia supports the center," Olivia told a reporter, "but I helped raise $200 million to build it, and we're still raising money because the government supports the building but not all the programs. Patients have the choice of being treated at the wellness center or the hospital. The whole purpose was to create a place of hope."

During these first several years of their marriage, Olivia and John spent more time in Florida, where he had been living, than in California. In June 2009 they bought a waterfront home at 104 Lighthouse Drive in the town of Jupiter Inlet Colony for $4.1 million. Olivia, Liona Boyd recalls, made many friends there who weren't celebrities, "just everyday people that she took into her little circle." "I have fond memories," Boyd says, "of going down with her to feed the manatees. She loved to go down there and give them lettuce."

Boyd, who recorded her composition "Canadian Summer Dreams" with Olivia as a duet in 2013, had one minor disagreement with her friend that she laughs about. "She was convinced there were no mosquitoes [in Jupiter Inlet Colony]…. I said, 'Olivia, I'm covered in mosquito bites.'"

"Oh, no, no," Olivia replied, "there's no mosquitoes here!"

"She was a denier," Boyd reflects. "That was part of her charm."

In August 2013, while Olivia and John were out of town, a contractor who was remodeling the Juniper Inlet Colony house for them shot himself to death in the living room. "And, of course," Boyd says, "then she felt there was such bad energy in there." Olivia and John sold the house and bought a "little condo" nearby. They "had a lot of trouble" selling their house after what happened there, but someone finally bought it in November 2015 for $5 million.

They didn't use the condo as their main residence for long, though. "She decided," Boyd says, "to make her base in California and not be in Florida so much… she wanted to be with Chloe. Chloe was having some problems. She was a good mother."

While the suicide in her house was unsettling, it was far from the biggest source of grief for Olivia in 2013. That occurred three months earlier. "My beautiful sister Rona sadly passed on May 24th in Los Angeles. It was May 25th in Australia—which was our mother Irene's birthday," Olivia wrote on Facebook.

Rona died of a very aggressive brain tumor and mercifully suffered no pain. She was surrounded by the love of her four children—Fiona, Brett, Tottie and Emerson, and her wonderful friends [and Olivia herself]. I will miss her forever—my beautiful, smart, talented, funny, brave sister Rona. In lieu of flowers the family would appreciate donations to the ONJCWC where a brain tumor wellness program will be started in her name. Thank you all for your kind words of love and support.

Although it wasn't public knowledge at the time, Olivia faced a second bout with cancer in 2013 herself. Just before Rona died, Olivia was involved in a minor collision while driving to visit her. "The seatbelt hit me really hard," she recalled five years later, "and a lump came up." She figured she had just been bruised, as did her doctor, but "time went on and it turned out to be more than that." After further testing, she learned that she once again had breast cancer. "I thought, 'It's my life,' and I just decided to keep it to myself." She was successfully treated with conventional chemotherapy medications as well as, with the aid of her husband, natural plant therapies to support her immune system. She postponed a scheduled Las Vegas engagement at the Flamingo and worked with Rona's son Brett Goldsmith on putting together a seven-song EP (extended play) release called *Hotel Sessions*. Brett produced the tracks, which were recorded in various hotels in Melbourne between 2002 and 2011. *Hotel Sessions* was "dedicated to our sister and mother Rona Newton-John."

After Rona's death, Olivia told Liona Boyd, "I just don't want to do concerts anymore. I'm just so devastated, I want to quit and do something else with my life."

"You've got so much to give to the world," Boyd told her. "You *mustn't* quit." "I kind of encouraged her," Boyd recalls, "to get back on the stage… she was a born performer."

Olivia returned to the stage with an engagement at the Flamingo's Donny & Marie Showroom in April 2014. Before she began, she did an interview with Vegas journalist Valerie Miller, in which, among other topics, she reflected on the "huge" changes that had taken place in the city since she had first performed there forty years earlier. "When I first came to Vegas, there were dirt roads, and few casinos, and gambling, and lots of drinking. But there wasn't all this nice food or good shopping… now you have everything." Olivia would perform frequently at the Flamingo through December 2016.

Olivia, Liona Boyd says, "loved all those Las Vegas dates, because people would come from all over to hear her, and she was happy about doing that… she loved dancing and singing." It wasn't easy for her, though. "I know she suffered a lot," Boyd recalls. "She said her feet were always killing her. She had neuropathy."

During a break from her Flamingo engagements in April 2015, Olivia toured Australia with John Farnham. It may well have been during this visit to the country she called home that she met the young politician and activist Neil Pharaoh, who says he met her "around 2015-ish." Pharaoh worked with her from then on in advocating for causes that they both believed in. "Whether it be support for the LGBTIQ+ community, of commitment to medicinal cannabis before it became 'mainstream'—Newton-John showed time and time again that she was on the right side of history, by doing what she knew as the right thing, even if it wasn't popular, or even legal at the time," he wrote shortly after her death.

Olivia also found the time and energy to join with her friends and previous collaborators Amy Sky and Beth Nielsen Chapman in making a new album during the summer of 2015, which would be called *Liv On*. "What inspired the *Liv On* record," according to Dane Bryant, who was the musical director of Olivia's Las Vegas show and played piano and keyboards and did string arrangements on the album, "was losing her sister to cancer… that was definitely what sparked the whole *Liv On* project. And then it wasn't shortly after that she lost her brother." *Liv On* wouldn't be released until October 2016. "It had a delayed release for reasons of which I'm not certain," Bryant says. In February 2017, *Liv On* reached No. 1 on the country album chart in the United Kingdom.

"We cut that [album]," Bryant recalls, "while we were in Las Vegas doing the shows… and during that time she was going through pain, you know, an unspoken pain that none of us really knew about until after the fact."

20 LIV ON

"Those were tough times, 2016, 2017, even when we did some of the *Liv On* shows," Dane Bryant recalls. "There were times when I literally had to almost carry her, and she was in such pain once the cancer had, you know, metastasized itself in her sacrum." "It was," Bryant pauses before continuing, "the pain she endured was beyond description."

"What she did," Bryant says, "was she surrounded herself with support. In my opinion, the reason she was able to do these shows, from the singing point of view, was her vocal coach," Steve Real (pronounced "REE-al"). Olivia's personal assistant, Martha Real, also gave her "great support," as did her band members. "It was very family oriented," drummer Mark Beckett says. "Everybody looked out for each other… it was just a great family of everybody taking care of each other." "It was," Bryant reflects, "such an honor to be a part of that."

The *Liv On* tour, which also featured her collaborators on the album of the same name, Beth Nielsen Chapman and Amy Sky, took Olivia to London and Glasgow in January 2017. Liona Boyd saw Olivia when the tour came to Toronto, and there were also shows in California. The set list included songs from the album as well as some other favorites. Olivia sang "I Honestly Love You," and Beth Nielsen Chapman sang "This Kiss," the 1998 Faith Hill hit which she cowrote. "The connection between them [Olivia, Beth, and Amy] was quite palpable onstage," wrote a reviewer of the Glasgow concert, "and all three tackled the challenges of coping with the loss of a loved one, the importance of end-of-life care, and the subsequent process of healing the grief."

By the middle of May 2017, however, Olivia had to put off any further shows. A statement to the press attributed the postponements to "a bad issue with Olivia's sciatica." A subsequent statement on May 30 announced that she had been diagnosed with breast cancer "that has metastasized to the sacrum in her lower back." "We knew something was going on with all the pain she was having,"

John Easterling told journalists. "As it turns out, you've got a tumor growing there pressing on a nerve bundle against the pelvis bone." Warren Ham remembers noticing that "she was having some back pain when we were doing our dance routine [in concerts]… but she didn't ever mention it or complain about it. She wasn't that type to ever complain about her situation. She always had a real positive attitude."

In the announcement of her diagnosis, Olivia said, "I am feeling good and enjoying total support from my family and friends, along with a team of wellness and medical practitioners. I'm totally confident that my new journey will have a positive success story."

Olivia resumed touring in late August, performing at US theaters and casino showrooms. By the spring of 2018, however, she was done touring, although she performed in concert in Philadelphia in early September and in Melbourne about a week later. She remained in Melbourne for her birthday (September 26), although not exactly where she would have hoped. "I was in a lot of pain, and I ended up being a patient on my 70th birthday in my hospital," she told *Closer Weekly* in October 2019. In a typical display of her courageous and positive outlook and indomitable spirit, she added,

Which was really amazing. I mean, it sounds strange to say, but it was really a gift because I got to experience what I helped create. The staff was incredible, and the place was beautiful and so this makes it even more inspirational for me to raise more money. So, we can do more research and see an end to cancer in my lifetime, which is my dream.

She remained at the Olivia Newton-John Cancer Wellness & Research Centre, she told the *Hollywood Reporter* in March 2019, "for a month," during which time she found herself "not being able to do anything—I'm walking on my own now but I'm still not strong enough to do a lot of things—it all makes you really grateful just being able to walk." She gave this particular interview to promote her memoir, *Don't Stop Believin'*, which she had had the time to write since she was no longer able to tour or perform in residency in Las Vegas. (Mark Beckett recalls that before her cancer diagnosis in May 2017, "There was a rumor that we were going to go to the Venetian, go there for a residency… it never happened, obviously.")

By this time, reporters knew that Olivia had long tried to keep much of her personal life out of the public eye, so journalist Lexy Perez asked her why she had finally chosen to write an autobiography. Her answer was telling.

I heard that they were going to do a TV movie about me in Australia, and I wasn't thrilled about it. I didn't really want to get involved, but I didn't know what they were going to say. So, I thought, well, maybe I better write my own version. This is a good opportunity to write my version in case they write things that are totally false. That's what got me going.

She acknowledged, however, that the biopic, titled *Hopelessly Devoted to You*, which aired just before her book was published, "wasn't that bad and the lovely girl [Delta Goodrem] who's a dear friend of mine played me and she did a lovely job…. I was happy she was doing it…. But it wasn't like I woke up one day going, 'Oh I better write a book.'" The television biopic, Olivia told Perez, was "what instigated it, and it turned out to be a good thing."

About two months after the publication of her memoir, Olivia's older brother, Hugh, died at the age of seventy-nine. She announced his passing on Instagram, posting a collage of photos of him and writing, "My dear, sweet, gentle, clever, brother Hugh passed away May 7, 2019, in Melbourne, Australia after many years of decline. I love him so and will miss him terribly."

Two months after she lost her brother, Olivia and John traveled to Galicia, Spain, for a family reunion at the home of her half-sister Sarah Newton-John and her longtime partner Heath Savage, an Australian woman whom Sarah had introduced to Olivia about fifteen years earlier. "She welcomed me immediately," Savage recalled in an essay for *Business Insider* in June 2024, "and we developed a respect for each other…. I quickly discovered that she was a down-to-earth, intelligent, funny lady—with a naughty sense of humor."

Savage noted that when the family dined at a café in the local village square during the July 2019 reunion, onlookers were starstruck at Olivia's presence and took photos, but also "were polite and respectful of our privacy." She added that Olivia "relished spending time" with her and Sarah. "She enjoyed hanging out in our garden in Spain or dropping over to our little apartment in Sydney for a quiet supper around the kitchen table. She often came armed with a bottle of Grey Goose vodka." Savage wrote that when she and Sarah married in May 2024, they thought of Olivia and wished she were there to celebrate with them.

Olivia's half-brother Toby and his family came to Spain from Sydney for the family reunion. To Olivia, the fact that Sarah and Toby were Brinley's but not Irene's children made them no less her siblings. "She was the kindest, most sensitive and loving sister you can imagine," Sarah told a journalist just after Olivia passed away. "She always refused to be called 'half-sister.' For her, 'her sister' always flowed."

"We spent three unforgettable days," Sarah said of the reunion.

Several locals have told me that Olivia fell in love with their land. She was so impressed that she asked me to find her a property to live part of the year here. Sometime later she told me that she probably wouldn't be traveling that much, so she scrapped the idea. At no time did she refer to her state of health. She didn't like to talk about her illness. She was the most impressive person that I have ever met.

At around the same time, Olivia began preparing to auction some of her career memorabilia and other belongings, adding her autograph to many of them, through Julien's Auctions in Los Angeles. The first auction would be held in November 2019, and much of the proceeds would go to the Olivia Newton-John Cancer Wellness & Research Centre. Olivia said that she was keeping some of her career mementos, such as her four Grammy Awards, "because they are the height of my success and the most important one I can receive for singing and the music, so I can give them to my daughter." But she did give Julien's her iconic black leather jacket from *Grease* to auction, and it sold for $243,000. These auctions of her belongings would continue, even after her passing, and in 2020 she auctioned off some Zoom calls as well.

She would not be without the *Grease* jacket for long. "This gentleman who wishes to remain anonymous—although I'd love to shout his name out to thank him, but he wants to remain anonymous—bought the jacket at the auction. Gosh, a couple of months later," she told interviewer Alison Martino as footage of the moment played, "and there's this gentleman standing next to me, and he's holding a box, and he said, 'I think this rightfully belongs with you,' and inside was my leather jacket from *Grease* and he gave it back to me, which was the most incredible act of kindness I've ever experienced." Olivia would then send the jacket to her cancer center in Australia to be displayed, and in December 2024 it was once again auctioned to benefit the center, this time for $476,250.

Although Olivia could no longer undertake concert engagements by 2019, she found another way to appear before live audiences. For years, she and John Travolta had been receiving offers to appear at "Meet 'n' *Grease*" sing-along events, which would feature a showing of the movie (lyrics to its songs ran along the bottom as they played) and then a question-and-answer session with the two principal stars. These events had already occurred without them; their *Grease* castmate Didi Conn had hosted the first, in July 2010, at the Hollywood Bowl before a sold-out house of seventeen thousand. Olivia and Travolta had both turned down that offer and all subsequent ones. After nine years, though, Travolta changed his mind, and at that point Olivia did as well. Randal Kleiser would be directing the shows, and several of the original T-Birds also joined the act. At Kleiser's invitation, *Grease* casting director Joel Thurm also joined them.

They did three of these shows, at midsize amphitheaters of around 5,000 to 7,500 seats, all in Florida: at West Palm Beach on December 13, 2019; Tampa on December 14; and Jacksonville on December 15. The *Florida Today* newspaper reported on November 1 that a presale had already started, "with minimum prices from $200 each on up. And they're going fast."

In his memoir, Thurm wrote that the shows "went over very well." Olivia thought so, too; she told interviewer Steven Mackenzie, "We had a blast, John and I. I'd never seen the singalong version with the lyrics, and I've never seen the audience join in. It was just hilarious and fun. And to meet the fans beforehand, all dressed up as different characters from the film. To think that 40-something years later, they still love it is quite amazing." Everyone involved talked about taking the show on tour, with the proviso that they not schedule shows more than three nights in a row. Thurm figured that "we would all be spending the summer of 2020 on the road. A little speed bump called COVID-19 ended all expectations."

Although Olivia's last two albums, *Liv On* and *Friends for Christmas* with John Farnham (a number one hit in Australia), were released in 2016, she had continued to do some recording since then. Shortly before Covid-19 reached the United States in March 2020, Olivia and John Easterling traveled to Nashville; Barry Gibb was recording an album of duets called *Greenfields: The Gibb Brothers Songbook, Vol. 1*, and he invited Olivia to record a song with him. "That was the last time Olivia was in Nashville," recalls Dane Bryant. "She and John came, and we spent a little bit of time together, so that was very nice."

This wasn't the first time that Barry and Olivia had recorded together. In 1984, shortly after Barry had signed with MCA Records as a solo artist, Olivia duetted with him on "Face to Face," which was included on his album *Now Voyager*. In 2008, Barry and Olivia recorded a song that he had written with his sons Ashley and Stephen, "The Heart Knows," for *A Celebration in Song*, Olivia's fundraising album for the Olivia Newton-John Cancer Wellness & Research Centre. Olivia and Barry also sang together at a number of charity concerts in Miami, Nashville, Sydney, and Melbourne between 2009 and 2015. "They were pretty close," says Olivia's longtime band member and friend Joe Creighton of the two British/Australian stars who knew each other for more than fifty years. "They were pretty close."

Upon the release of *Greenfields* in January 2021, Gibb told Howard Cohen, "Olivia, she hadn't been well for a while, and she was so happy to be in a studio and singing. That was something else… and I'd grown up with that girl." The song that Olivia and Barry both chose to record together was "Rest Your Love on Me," as a tribute to Barry's long ago lost youngest brother and Olivia's friend. "She'd done it before with Andy," Barry told the London *Sun*, "which was wonderful, so there was a lot of nostalgia involved. She really brought a good vibe, and I think she's coming out on top. It's amazing how tough she's been." Of her performance in the studio, Gibb said that Olivia had nailed it "instantly."

In February 2020, Olivia traveled to Sydney to perform at Fire Fight Australia, a star-studded concert held to raise money for rebuilding and recovery efforts following a particularly rough summer of bushfires in the country that in many ways she still thought of as home. "I'm pretty much retired, but when I heard they were doing this, I had to be part of it," she told an Australian journalist. "It's so important, and I feel privileged that I'm able to help in some way. Australians are tough. We have a wonderful sense of spirit and humor, and those things will get us through." On February 16, she performed four songs with John Farnham, and another with Farnham, Australian singer-songwriter Mitch Tambo, and Brian May of Queen. It would be her last time on a concert stage. Olivia also took the opportunity to spend time with and lend moral support to Chloe, who was then appearing on the Australian version of *Dancing with the Stars* as a means of raising money for the Olivia Newton-John Cancer Wellness & Research Centre and the Australia Zoo.

One month later, the Covid-19 pandemic forced Olivia, whose health was already compromised, into seclusion. In November 2020, Alison Martino asked her how she'd been doing during the lockdown. "Actually, I feel guilty saying this," she replied, "but I've actually enjoyed it because it's been an opportunity to be in one place. And I feel terribly for people who are stuck in cities and apartment buildings. I'm in the country [at her ranch in Santa Ynez, California] and I'm with people I love and I'm very fortunate, really lucky."

By this time Chloe was living primarily in Oregon, to which her father had returned, with her fiancé, James Driskill; Olivia told *People* magazine in February 2021 that she was looking forward to participating in their "small wedding" later that year. (After her mother's passing, Chloe posted footage from the ceremony on Instagram; Olivia can be seen standing between her and Driskill while exclaiming, "Marriage, finally. My beautiful daughter and handsome son-in-law. I'm so proud of you.") During the pandemic, though, Chloe spent most of her time living with her mother and John Easterling at their ranch. Olivia told another reporter in February that "one of the gifts of this pandemic has been being able to spend time with Chloe because neither of us have been able to go anywhere or do anything. She came here for a couple of months and is back now for some time."

At the time of that interview, Olivia and Chloe had just released their second recording together. Their first had been a reworking of "Magic" called "You Have to Believe." Made in 2015 with the Los Angeles–based DJ/producer/remixer Dave Audé, the record reached No. 1 on *Billboard*'s Dance Club Songs chart. It was the first time that a mother-and-daughter duo had ever reached the top spot on that chart, which was published weekly from 1976 until 2020. Dave Cobb, who had produced the Barry Gibb duets album that Olivia sang on, produced the second Olivia and Chloe duet, a gentle, hopeful piano-and-string-laden ballad called "Window in the Wall." Dane Bryant served as the record's arranger. Olivia told *People* magazine, "There is always something special about singing with my daughter. She not only has a gorgeous voice, she's an amazing musician with tremendous instincts as a singer."

Even though she tried to remain active and cheerful, Olivia's health continued to deteriorate. She told reporters that she was using cannabis, which her husband was growing at their ranch, and she pointed out that it was a better alternative than opioids, which she had taken in the past. "I was nervous of it in the beginning," she said of medicinal cannabis use. "But I could see the benefits once I started using it. It helps with anxiety, it helps with sleep, it helps with pain." She had been lobbying the Australian government for a couple of years to make cannabis legal for medicinal use, and Neil McMahon recalls "what a big advocate she was for medical marijuana before she ever went public with it. She wanted to go public with that quite a long time before she did. She was ahead of her time in that sense."

According to her nephew Emerson Newton-John, Olivia was indeed dealing with a lot of pain by this point. "The last two or three years were very painful for Olivia," he told Michele Manelis in 2024, "but she was very strong about it." He also told Manelis of a visit that he paid to Olivia at her ranch in 2021. They were sitting together outside, with no one else around, and she put her head on his shoulder and started sobbing. "It was sad," Emerson said. "I realized at that moment, 'She's ready.'"

Nevertheless, Olivia and Emerson resumed celebrating their shared birthday together in September 2021, something they had done many times before but hadn't been able to do in 2020 because of the pandemic. Emerson posted a photo on Instagram of Olivia and himself with birthday balloons on what turned out to be her final birthday, and then after he accidentally deleted it, he reposted it "by the request of the world's best aunty." He also posted a video of "possibly my favorite guy ever, Steve Real," singing "a birthday serenade" to him and Olivia, while each of them held a birthday cake baked by Martha Real, who, Emerson wrote, "may be the best baker this side of the Atlantic."

In October 2020, as reported in *Variety*, Olivia had "struck a partnership with Primary Wave Music Publishing that includes the catalog of masters and publishing assets owned by the singer." The first fruits of that deal came one year later with Primary Wave's release of the fortieth-anniversary deluxe edition of her *Physical* album as a 2-CD/1-DVD set. A vinyl release, on 180-gram vinyl in various colors, followed in spring 2022, along with a limited-edition pressing of 2,500 picture discs of the album for Record Store Day.

But as these well-done and well-received reissues of her catalog began, Olivia still wanted to continue recording. Her last record would be a duet of "Jolene" with the song's composer and original recording artist, Dolly Parton. "It'd been in the making for fifteen years," recalls Dane Bryant, who produced the duet. "Michael Caprio [Olivia's longtime publicist and friend] had been trying to make this happen for so long, and thank goodness, he was able to pull it off." Bryant himself played a crucial role by reaching out to Dolly shortly before the record was made. Dolly, he says, "was so onboard about it."

"Livvy," Bryant recalls, "really wanted to be there in the studio [in Nashville] with Dolly," but "with her health [declining]" and Covid-19 making a fall resurgence, she couldn't make the trip. Instead, she recorded her vocals (and was filmed doing so for the song's video) in a studio in Santa Barbara. "And there was definitely concern," Bryant says, "that she would even possibly break a rib or something singing because, you know, the cancer had spread far into her body, and that's when your bones are very fragile. But, once again, she troopered through it and warriored through it, really, and sang an incredible part."

"It was soon after Olivia recorded her final vocal in California that we recorded Dolly's vocal track in October of 2021," Bryant says. When he played Olivia's vocals for Dolly, she told him that Olivia had sung it so well that she was concerned about how she could fit in and add anything to the record. But, she told Bryant, "I'm not going to leave here until you're happy." "She worked so very hard and diligently," Bryant says of Dolly.

[She] went into this character, man, and just worked for two hours, and after that, Olivia wanted to hear it over the phone, and she wanted to have a conversation with Dolly after we were done… and so everybody [else] left, and I was in the room and I called Olivia and put her on speaker phone, and I started to walk out of the room because I knew it was going to be an emotional conversation. And Dolly didn't want me to leave the room.

"And so I stayed in there," Bryant recalls,

and, let me tell you, *that* was emotional because… during the time that Livvy [won] her CMA Award, Nashville was still not very welcoming to outsiders, as they put it, *except* for Dolly and Loretta [Lynn], and Dolly took her to dinner [shortly afterward, as Olivia was in London when the 1974 CMA Award ceremony occurred]. Now this is almost fifty years ago, and Olivia *never* forgot that. And so, they had this conversation that was very emotional and just filled with so much love. And, you know, part of me wanted to be there to hear it, but then again part of me didn't want to be there because it was such a personal thing. But being a story of love like that, you know, *that's* something I think the world should hear, is the power that these women possessed with what they'd been through in the music business being a man's world. Hearing that conversation that day really brought to light the struggles of women, especially during that time, in the music business.

Olivia wanted her latter-day band members to play on the record. "That was fun," says drummer Mark Beckett.

That was, I think, the last time I saw her, because we did some Facetiming with everybody [at the recording session], and then she sent a really sweet email to everybody, and every now and then we'd send each other texts. I think I've still got group texts with everybody on my phone with her on them. It's just sweet to see.

One former band member whom Olivia and Bryant had not expected to be available to play on the "Jolene" duet was guitarist Andy Timmons. But as Dane Bryant says,

There were so many things that happened during the making of that [duet] that you couldn't have written it… we're starting the downbeat in Nashville… and my phone rings, and it's Andy. And I pick it up and I say, "You're not gonna believe what's about to happen." And he says, "Well, you're not gonna believe, I'm in town!"

Bryant laughs at the memory.

It was definitely divine intervention. And so I said, "Well, then you're coming to the studio, because you're going to play on 'Jolene,'" which he did later that evening [at Bryant's house, as it turned out]… and then we Facetimed Olivia, which was a huge surprise for her, and she *loved* it because she didn't think Andy would be able to play on the record.

It would be released in May 2023 on the first of two posthumous albums of Olivia's duets, most of them previously released, *Just the Two of Us: The Duets Collection (Vol. 1)*.

"That was the last recording she did," Bryant sadly notes,

because she couldn't really sing after that. That's when her health had pretty much declined, and she didn't have the bodily strength. Before she passed away, what she wanted to do was a record of just piano and vocal with me. And of course, that, you know, didn't happen. But I think this [having him produce the duet with Dolly] was just her way of saying thank you, and it changed my life.

In February 2022, the Australian magazine *Who* published an interview with Olivia with the cover headline, "The Legacy I'll Leave." "I think the joy of getting older," she said, "is you understand life's a gift. We only have the present—everything else, the past and future, we can't control. As you get older, wisdom teaches you to focus on the 'now.' I think I always tried to be in the moment because I never knew how many moments I'd have. None of us do." She also spoke to the headline with which the magazine teased the interview.

"I now realize," she said, "that if I didn't go through my own cancer journey, I might not have gone on to help create awareness about cancer, nor would I have gone on to help create my Cancer Wellness & Research Centre. No matter what successes I have had in my career, that will always be my most important legacy." Neil McMahon recalls "a story someone told me about her saying on the day the Cancer Centre opened, they were in the car with her—it might have been Michael Caprio—and she looked up and she said, 'That's going to be what I'm remembered for.'"

During the final months of her life, friends reached out to Olivia and vice versa. Greg Mathieson, who had toured with her during the mid- to late 1970s and came up with a key piano lick for "You're the One That I Want," had fallen out of touch with her. But Jay Graydon, who had played guitar on some of the same Olivia records on which Mathieson had played, told him that she was "in really bad shape," so he emailed her. "She got right back to me," Mathieson recalls, and they exchanged several emails. "She didn't, we didn't, talk about her being sick. We talked about the times, the good times we had, you know, and reminisced a couple times, and they were *nice* emails." In a Facebook post nearly one year after her passing, he wrote that someone had told him that "she spent a lot of time with her horses near the end. She loved her horses. The love you give to and get back from animals can be a great comfort to you. They love you unconditionally. I'm glad she had them at the end." She also had dogs who were her constant companions until the end, including a poodle named Jack who sat beside her while she was in a hospital bed.

Chong Lim had last worked with Olivia in 2020, but she phoned him periodically. "And I have to say, I regretfully have to tell you," he says, "that a few weeks before she passed, she rang me and left a really long message on my phone. And she said, 'Hi Chongie, it's Livvy here.' She said, 'Remember me? We used to work together.'" Lim laughs remembering this.

> She was my *boss*, and she just says, "We worked together." And it was a really long message, and I was pretty stressed working on the Commonwealth Games music. And so I thought, "I'll listen to it properly whenever, and then I'll give her a call back when I have more time and I can give her my time and listen to her properly." And the day I decided to call back… I thought, "I'll call today," and then, *flash*, on my phone was the news that she had passed away. I was devastated. And I quickly went back to my phone to check her message, but it had already been wiped out at the server, so I never heard her last message to me.

Liona Boyd had stayed in touch with Olivia regularly. "During Covid," she recalls, "she was very kind, sending me different remedies… she was very generous that way." Liona says that even though Olivia was suffering with pain, "she always was optimistic, right to the end. 'Oh, I'm going to make it. Don't worry. Don't worry about me.'" But the last time Liona phoned Olivia, days before her death, John Easterling told her that Olivia could no longer speak. "I was just devastated," Liona says sadly. Olivia's last words, spoken to Chloe, were "my sunshine."

Olivia passed away at home in Santa Ynez on August 8, 2022, at the age of seventy-three. "It wasn't just the cancer that got her," said her niece Tottie Goldsmith. "It was other complications, being in a hospital [before she returned home] and with a very susceptible immune system. She got secondary infections."

Most media reports of Olivia's passing focused on her remarkable career. "The multitalented Newton-John influenced popular culture for decades," reported *Rolling Stone* (a skeptic of her talent and relevance in her early years), "from her starring roles in *Xanadu* and *Grease* to the unofficial leader of the Eighties exercise craze with 'Physical.'" But those who helped her make music remember her legacy in broader terms. "She spent those last twenty-five years of her life tirelessly advocating for cancer awareness, specifically breast cancer awareness," says Andy Timmons, who worked with her frequently and counted her as a friend from 1999 until the end. "She just used her power for good at every turn. She really did, and that was inspiring and a joy to see. And just the genuineness of it all, you know… just the genuine desire to help. I think that's the best any human being can aspire to do, and she did it on a very high level."

ACKNOWLEDGMENTS AND A NOTE ON SOURCES

This book draws heavily upon recollections and thoughts shared with me via telephone conversations and emails by friends and associates of Olivia Newton-John's, or, in two cases, relatives of deceased friends or associates of hers. In alphabetical order, I would like to thank Lenard Allen, Mark Beckett, Peter Beckett, Steve Binder, Liona Boyd, Bob Bradshaw, Tony Brown, Dane Bryant, John Capek, John Chester, Chris Christian, Howard Cohen, Harlan Collins, Joe Creighton, Michelle Day, Jon Dee, Stephen Duros, Chris Farren, Ben Fong-Torres, Joe Giamalva, Skip Griparis, Warren Ham, John Kalodner, Patricia Kelly, Bill King, Steve Kipner, Steven Kuhn, Hallie Latos, Peter Leinheiser, Chong Lim, Rick Lotempio, Greg Mathieson, Neil McMahon, Adam Mitchell, Bill Oakes, Richard Palmese, Shanta Parasuraman, Stella Parton, Scott Paton, Neil Pharaoh, Alison Prestwood, Rick Ruskin, Martin Samuel MBE, Bill Schnee, Joe Shane, Stephen Sinclair, Tom Snow, Stephanie Spruill, Seth Swirsky, Al Teller, Andy Timmons, Dennis Tufano, Dan Wojciechowski, Dan Zuckerman, and three people who asked to remain anonymous. I am also grateful to everyone who gave me photographs and permission to publish them in this book.

In addition to what I learned from all those listed above, I also drew upon interviews with Olivia Newton-John, members of her family, and friends and associates that are available on YouTube and Dailymotion; from newspaper, trade paper (i.e., *Billboard*, for example) and magazine interviews; record, concert, and film reviews; and news reports, most of which were found on the following websites: newspapers.com, worldradiohistory.com, and the incredible archive at the fan site onlyolivia.com. Some books proved helpful, too, and the most helpful ones are listed in the select bibliography.

I also must acknowledge some others for their assistance or support, either by putting me in touch with some of the people listed above or in other ways: Eric Alper, Fortune Benatar, Wesley Hyatt, Alison Martino, Keri Leigh Merritt, Michael Price, Danielle Reiss, Tim Roxborogh, Karen Schauben, Joel Selvin, and

Taylor Patterson, the O' Trivia Newton-John trivia team, and my departed little buddy Mussa the Shih Tzu. Having adored dogs and had dozens over the course of her lifetime, Olivia Newton-John would have most likely appreciated such a reference.

Finally, thanks to everyone at Bloomsbury Publishing, especially Michael Tan and Samantha Klein.

NOTES

Chapter 2

1 In the UK, the album's title was *Olivia Newton-John*.

Chapter 5

1 Not long before her passing, Olivia sold many of the albums in her collection, with at least one album per lot signed by her, through Julien's Auctions to raise money for the Olivia Newton-John Cancer Wellness & Research Centre. One lot included all three of Andy Gibb's full studio albums, two Bee Gees albums, and the 1979 LP *The Music for UNICEF Concert*, which included one song by Olivia, one by the Bee Gees, one by Andy, and an Andy/Olivia duet. Olivia signed that album with the inscription, "Always loved my mates the BG's and brother Andy."

Chapter 8

1 Olivia told me this in an email, relayed to me via her longtime representative and friend Michael Caprio, on May 24, 2021. I had asked him if she might be willing to share a few of her memories of Andy for a biography that I was writing on him at the time, and true to her nature, she kindly and graciously agreed despite being ill.

Chapter 9

1 For an example of how record company executives could influence chart positions during this era, see Frederic Dannen, *Hit Men: Power Brokers and Fast Money Inside the Music Business* (New York: Times Books, 1990), 173–74.

2 Emerson was born on Olivia's twenty-sixth birthday.

Chapter 11

1   Incredibly, the Recording Industry Association of America's website (riaa.com), as of this writing, indicates that the platinum certification of "Physical" denoted one million singles sold and that the gold certification of "Make a Move on Me" denoted five hundred thousand copies sold. But from 1958 through 1988, the RIAA issued gold records for singles that sold one million, and from 1976, when platinum singles were introduced, through 1988, platinum records for singles that sold two million.

Chapter 12

1   In her memoir, however, which was published nearly a decade after Schmidt's book, Olivia wrote that she had been on her way for a lunch meeting with Pat Farrar, one of her best friends, and that "Pat tried to comfort me, but I was inconsolable."

Chapter 15

1   The term "dole bludgers" came into use in Australia in the mid-1970s as a snotty way to describe welfare recipients.

Chapter 17

1   Shaw was also one of Olivia's cowriters on *Back with a Heart*.

Chapter 19

1   Olivia recorded one of the Carpenters' biggest hits, "Rainy Days and Mondays," in 2004 for her album *Indigo: Women of Song*.

SELECT BIBLIOGRAPHY

Battelle, Phyllis. "Olivia: Where Can She Go from Here?" *Australian Women's Weekly*, July 30, 1980.

Bronson, Fred. *The Billboard Book of Number One Hits*. Rev. and updated 4th ed. New York: Billboard Books, 1997.

Callahan, Michael. "How *Grease* Beat the Odds and Became the Biggest Movie Musical of the 20th Century." *Vanity Fair*, January 26, 2016. https://www.vanityfair.com/hollywood/2016/01/grease-movie-musical-john-travolta-olivia-newton-john.

Christian, Chris, with Bill Ireland. *A Grandmother's Prayer: Moments in a Music Life*. Travelers Rest, SC: True Potential Inc., 2018.

Christy, George. "Olivia Newton-John (interview)." *Interview*, November 1983.

Ewbank, Tim. *Olivia: The Biography of Olivia Newton-John*. London: Piatkus Books, 2008.

Flans, Robyn. Liner notes. *Magic: The Very Best of Olivia Newton-John* CD. UTV Records, 2001.

Fong-Torres, Ben. "Olivia Battles Back." *Rolling Stone*, July 27, 1978.

Friedman, Danielle. *Let's Get Physical: How Women Discovered Exercise and Reshaped the World*. New York: G. P. Putnam's Sons, 2022.

Gilbert, Bob, and Gary Theroux. *The Top Ten, 1956–Present*. New York: Fireside/Simon and Schuster, 1982.

Halstead, Craig. *Olivia Newton-John: All the Top 40 Hits*. Rev. 3rd ed. N.p.: Craig Halstead, 2020.

Hyatt, Wesley. *The Billboard Book of Number One Adult Contemporary Hits*. New York: Billboard Books, 1999.

Kruger, Debbie. "Olivia Newton-John Interview, 30 August 1994." http://www.debbiekruger.com/writer/freelance/onj_transcript.html.

Manelis, Michele. "The Ties That Bind—The Newton-John Sisters." Mindfood, April 22, 2024. https://www.mindfood.com/article/exclusive-the-ties-that-bind-the-newton-john-sisters/.

Newton-John, Olivia. *Don't Stop Believin': A Memoir*. Paperback ed. New York: Gallery Books, 2021.

"Sarah, Sister of Olivia, Interview." *El Mundo*, August 13, 2022. https://www.onlyolivia.com/memorabilia/presscut/20s/22-08-13-es-el_mundo_madrid.html.

Savage, Heath. "My Wife's Sister Is a Celebrity. Marrying into a Famous Family Was Surprisingly Easy for Me." *Business Insider*, June 9, 2024. https://www.businessinsider.com/wife-sister-celebrity-olivia-newton-john-marriage-2024-6.

Schmidt, Randy L. *Little Girl Blue: The Life of Karen Carpenter*. Chicago, IL: Chicago Review Press, 2010.

Schulman, Michael. *Oscar Wars: A History of Hollywood in Gold, Sweat, and Tears*. New York: Harper, 2023.

Scott, Barry. *We Had Joy, We Had Fun: The "Lost" Recording Artists of the Seventies*. Boston, MA: Faber and Faber, 1994.

Selby, Daniel. *The Complete Olivia Newton-John Illustrated Discography*. Orlando, FL: BearManor Media, 2023.

Spence, Simon. *Staying Alive: The Disco Inferno of the Bee Gees*. London: Jawbone Press, 2017.

Thurm, Joel. *Sex, Drugs, and Pilot Season: Confessions of a Casting Director*. Orlando, FL: BearManor Media, 2023.

Welch, Bruce. *Rock 'n' Roll, I Gave You the Best Years of My Life: Life in the Shadows*. London: Penguin Books, 1990.

White, Timothy. "Olivia's Story: Innocence, Angst and Elbow Grease." *Crawdaddy*, July 1978.

Wikane, Christian John. "Making Her Move: Olivia Newton-John's 'Physical' Phenomenon Revisited." PopMatters, August 9, 2022. https://www.popmatters.com/olivia-newton-john-physical/2.

Wincensten, Edward. *The Olivia Newton-John Companion*. Pickens, SC: Wynn Publishing, 2002.

Gibb, Andy 77, 80, 102, 129, 145–6, 244n.;
    attends Hollywood premiere of *Grease*
    94; attends Koala Blue store openings
    166; death of 169, 224; duets with
    Olivia 98–9, 105, 108, 132; relationship
    with Victoria Principal 157; rumors
    of romance with Olivia 108; television
    appearances with Olivia 82–7, 98–9,
    105, 133, 134; US debut record of 70
Gibb, Barry 10–11, 13; duets with Olivia
    225, 235–6; songwriting of 55, 70,
    72–3, 98–9, 132, 145, 225, 235
Gibb, Robin 13, 55–6
Gill, Vince 198, 206, 217
Goldsmith, Brett 8, 228, 229
Goldsmith, Brian 8, 12, 184
Goldsmith, Fiona 8, 228
Goldsmith, Tottie 3, 190, 228, 241
Gorbachev, Mikhail 189
Gorg, Hans 8
Gormley, Peter 18, 21, 27, 30–3, 48, 129
"Grace and Gratitude," 3
Grace and Gratitude (album) 223
Grammy Awards 2, 30–2, 34–6, 44, 46–7,
    234
Graydon, Jay 66, 240
Grease (film and soundtrack album) 1,
    20, 54, 64, 97, 157–8; making of 72–6,
    147, 193; Olivia accepts starring role in
    71; Olivia's doubts about 81; reissues/
    rereleases 195–6, 202–3, 218; success of
    2, 60, 64, 87–8, 92, 94, 99–101, 103–5,
    149–50, 161, 162, 187
"Grease" (song) 72–3
"Grease Megamix, The," 195, 197
Grease 2 (film) 102, 142, 144–5, 147
Great Wall of China 225
Greenwald, Robert 102, 111
Griparis, Skip: joins Olivia's band 48; tours
    with Olivia 53–4, 59–62, 64–5, 79–80,
    95–6; visits Olivia on the set of *Xanadu*
    104, 108
Gum Leaf Mafia 57, 83, 159
Guy, Athol 15–6

"Had to Be," 192
Ham, Warren 218, 232
Harrison, George 21, 25, 26

Hartley, Mark 198, 206, 209–10, 212
"Have You Never Been Mellow," 39, 43,
    49–50, 54–6, 71, 87
"Heart Attack," 75, 143–4, 148
Hill, Faith 204, 206, 231
Hollies 45, 51
Hope, Bob 45, 152
"Hopelessly Devoted to You," 74, 80, 87,
    106; performed in concert by Elvis
    Costello 213; performed in concert
    by Olivia and Mariah Carey 207;
    recording of 76; success of 94; writing
    of 73
Hotel Sessions (album) 229
Human Nature. See Wild Life
Hungate, David 92, 105, 131
Hyatt, Wesley 21, 56

"I Can't Help It," 98
"I Honestly Love You," 43, 182, 198, 211,
    220, 231; comments by composers Jeff
    Barry and Peter Allen 38; criticized by
    Randy Newman 46–7; recording and
    release of 37, 51; remake with Babyface
    199, 201, 203–4, 205, 206; rerelease
    (1977) 78, 90; success of 39–40, 46–7,
    49–50, 54, 66, 69, 89, 103, 127
"I Need Love," 31, 181–5
"I Still Call Australia Home," 106, 156
"I Want to Be Wanted," 52, 183
"If Not for You," 21–2, 23, 26, 30
"If You Love Me (Let Me Know)," 31–2,
    35, 66, 87, 135
Indigo: Women of Song (album) 245n.
Inhofer, Gregg 34, 39, 60
It's My Party (film) 151, 193–4, 216

Jackson (dog) 51, 157, 177
Jennings, Waylon 42, 58
John, Elton 60, 72, 109, 157; charitable
    endeavors of 3; MCA Records and
    89, 172; produces and composes
    single for Olivia 177–8, 181; television
    appearances with Olivia 105, 156; Uni
    Records and 23
"Jolene," 43, 55, 211, 237–9
Journey (band) 63, 148, 150, 183
"Just a Little Too Much," 26, 30, 52